Faith Thinking

— *Faith Thinking* —

The Dynamics of Christian Theology

TREVOR HART

SPCK

First published in Great Britain 1995
Society for Promoting Christian Knowledge
Holy Trinity Church
Marylebone Road
London NW1 4DU

British Library Cataloguing-in-Publication Data
A catalogue record for this book is available from the British Library

ISBN 0–281–04870–3

Typeset by
Waveney Studios, Diss, Norfolk
and printed in Great Britain by
Redwood Books Ltd, Trowbridge, Wiltshire

Theology is faith thinking.

P. T. Forsyth

For Rachel, Jonathan and Naomi who granted me the time and the freedom to write, and disturbed me just often enough to keep me firmly rooted in reality.

— Contents —

—— Acknowledgements ——

This book began its life as undergraduate lectures in the University of Aberdeen. I am grateful to several generations of students there who tolerated earlier (and less refined) versions of different parts of it with patience, and helped me to see where it needed to be improved. I am grateful too to a selection of friends who, over the period during which the book has taken shape, have participated in the process by stimulating thought, engaging in critical discussion, correcting mistakes and misapprehensions, and generally exercising a ministry of encouragement. Particular mention must be made of Michael Partridge, who in the early stages and continually since, urged me that this was a worthwhile project to pursue, and helped me locate some sound philosophical bearings to steer by; and John Yates and Leslie McCurdy who both listened with infinite patience to drafts and redrafts of the gradually evolving text, and whose helpful comments and criticisms are reflected in the present version. It goes without saying that such weaknesses and errors as remain are indicative of the occasions when I ignored their counsel.

Thanks are due to many others without whose practical help this book could not have been written. To Andrew Walker of Gospel & Culture for inviting me to submit a proposal and duly commending it to SPCK for inclusion in this series. To Judith Longman, Brendan Walsh, Naomi Starkey and other staff with whom I have dealt at SPCK for their constant encouragement, help and support. To my colleague and Head of Department, Professor David Fergusson, for making it possible for me to take a sabbatical during which the lion's share of the work for the book was completed. To all those who kindly granted help and support in various ways in Cambridge during the autumn of 1993. To Michael and Margaret MacCormack, who kindly invited us into their home. To Tyndale House, in the sanctuary of whose library much of the research for this book was undertaken. To Cambridge University Library, the Cambridge Faculty of Divinity, and Ridley Hall, for the facilities which they each graciously made available.

Finally, thanks are due to my wife Rachel, and to my children, Jonathan and Naomi. They never complained when they found the door to my study closed, allowed me to be far too selfish with my time, disrupted their own plans to fit in with mine, and provided the security of a loving and supportive home environment which helped to keep the frustrations and difficulties of writing in their proper perspective. To them this book is gladly dedicated with my love.

Trevor Hart
Old Aberdeen

—— Introduction ——

The prime need of religion to-day is a theology. No religion can survive which does not know where it is. And current religion does not know where it is, and it hates to be made to ask. It hates theology.

Peter Taylor Forsyth

The model of theology which I shall seek to unpack and develop within the pages of this book is that referred to by the ancient description of the theological thinker as *fidelis quaerens intellectum:* a believer seeking understanding. Theology is the attempt by faith to understand itself, its object, and its place in today's world. In the words of our title it is, quite simply, faith thinking. This pursuit is an inevitable corollary of the existence of faith itself. For faith, if it is genuine faith, cannot help asking questions and seeking answers. Thus, theology is far from being a lofty academic intellectual game, the esoteric preserve of an initiated few, and essentially unrelated to the real life concerns of ordinary Christian men and women. Theology can be and is, of course, practised at highly intellectual levels, and there is a need for such professional engagement. But the activity known as 'Christian theology' is properly an inevitable consequence of life as a thinking Christian in the real world. By 'thinking' in this context I mean simply the sort of intellectual activity we engage in every day as human beings as we read newspapers, watch the TV, meet and interact with new people, new situations, and new information, and try to integrate it all into our larger picture of the world and our place within it. In this sense, while we may not all be formally trained as theologians, we are all nonetheless engaged in 'theology' to the extent that Christian faith for us forms an integral part of that picture.

In terms of the life of the community of faith, it may be argued, each level of engagement is equally vital. The church is called in every age afresh to give a coherent account of its faith, to testify to that living truth with which it has been entrusted, the gospel of Christ. Such articulation and proclamation cannot be limited to one

1

intellectual plane alone, any more than it can be restricted to any one social group or culture. Whatever our intellectual resources we are called upon to bear faithful and articulate witness to the source of our life and hope. Yet this task cannot even begin without due attention being given to the prior tasks of seeking to understand to the best of our individual ability the basic elements of the Christian story, and considering how this story might best be told afresh for our generation. For this reason alone theologizing must go on not only in the university or seminary, but in the life setting of every disciple of Christ as faith seeks to understand itself, its message and its situation in order to share what it has with its neighbour. We shall not all be great evangelists or apologists. But just as surely as there is a 'priesthood of all believers' in God's church, so too there is a theological prerogative belonging not only to an elite academic priesthood, guardians of the sanctuaries of learning, but to all God's people. For the task of responsible thinking about God, about faith, of faith seeking to understand itself and to articulate that understanding, is the essence of Christian theology. In this sense, of course, 'Every man, woman and child who thinks about God engages in theology.'[1] No one is excused! All are called to participate in the theological task as part of the community of faith and witness.

Faith musk seek to understand itself first in the sense of being aware of and confident in its own existence as a fundamental human disposition. I do not mean now specifically religious faith, whether Christian or otherwise, but rather 'faith' defined in more general terms (of which religious faith is certainly an instance): a disposition of passionate commitment to a truth which stands over against and demands an appropriate response from it, and yet a commitment the final legitimacy and veracity of which cannot be demonstrated or established beyond doubt in the situation of testimony or the confrontation with unbelief. In the current intellectual climate such a disposition may be frowned upon or treated as a second class entity. At best we shall be told that such a commitment is a matter purely of individual preference and perfectly acceptable so long as it is kept on a leash in public and not allowed to pester others with its claims. At worst we may find ourselves treated as adherents of an irrational and anachronistic superstition, a groundless opinion unsubstantiated by any firm evidence, and best abandoned in the interests of ourselves as individuals and society as a whole. The sooner we part company with our illusions

2

(no matter how ancient or dearly cherished), the sooner we can all get on with living contentedly and clear-sightedly in the real world. In such a climate, we shall suggest, faith must face up to and come to terms with itself as it is, to discover a self-confidence which enables it to live with itself, liberating it from a constant, hopeless and therefore despairing attempt to justify its existence, in the eyes of those who would challenge its very right to exist. The first three chapters of this book will seek to enable this self-adjustment to take place, considering the nature of faith as a human disposition, its role in Christian life generally and its place in relation to theological activity in particular. The result of our labours will be to suggest that the disposition of faith or belief is not quite the pariah of popular perception, but rather an integral and necessary part of all human knowing and thinking, of all truly 'rational' activity in fact.

Second, faith must always seek better to understand that in which it is faith. The fact that we believe something, or invest it with faith, in the first place implies, of course, an initial degree of understanding, however partial. After all, we could not properly be said to believe something of which we had no conception, something of which we could make no sense whatever. But very often the grasp which we do have at first is slight, and may even be virtually inarticulate. Yet the passion with which we grasp and seize it and turn it into an object of faith will not be satisfied for long with so little. Faith – when it is truly faith rather than a mere intellectual assent to some proposition or other – will always seek to enter into a fuller and deeper knowledge and understanding of that which matters most to it. And so Christian faith is driven by a desire to know more of that which is its source and *raison d'être*, to learn to speak and to think more appropriately of that reality, and of the various component parts of the knowledge of it which has been handed down through the ages by the community of faith; to consider the way in which all the things which are believed about this reality cohere with one another; and to explore the pattern of truth which pertains to it. In all this, faith is concerned with what might be called the 'internal coherence' of its own story or gospel.

This is a task within which we may, for convenience, identify two quite distinct elements: on the one hand there will be a descriptive and interpretative element in which faith seeks to set forth the sum of that which it believes in a clear and coherent manner, laying it out and seeking to make sense of it for the contemporary situation. In this there is a necessary dependence upon a received

tradition of belief and articulation of belief, a tradition which we find embodied (in the case of Christian faith) in creeds, in worship, in preaching and in many other forms of the church's life and practice. But the task of attending to the internal coherence of the Christian message goes beyond that of description, articulation and interpretation, involving an equally important normative or prescriptive task. In other words, the task of theology is not simply to ask 'What has the church said and believed, and how can we best express that so that people today will be able to understand it?'; it must also ask and answer the question 'What *should* the church say and believe today?' Consideration of the internal coherence must also entail concern for what we might call the 'external reference' of the story which the church tells, of its correspondence to some actual state of affairs in and beyond the world, its responsibility to some objective reality which stands over against itself and of which it seeks to speak. This is vital if theology is to remain essentially a quest for truth, rather than a simple bid (driven by nostalgia or a misguided sense of historical obligation) to preserve the shape and coherence of a particular theological tradition at all costs.

The sort of reflection appropriate for faith in its dialogue with the truth, that is to say, is precisely a critical reflection, and not a mere slavish reiteration of a received body of truths. This does not mean by any stretch of the imagination that we shall treat our received tradition lightly or that we shall even be able to engage in theology without beginning with and for the most part standing firmly within it. But, if our concern is genuinely to know the truth and to allow the truth to shape and mould our thinking and speaking about it, we shall maintain what one recent writer has referred to as an essentially interrogative rather than doctrinaire attitude in our theological thinking.[2] Thus we might say that faith, standing upon the shoulders of a tradition which it has inherited from the past, must nonetheless always be open to the possibility that its encounter with the truth might force it to part company with that tradition in some fundamental way. We cannot proceed on the assumption that it will, but we must always be open to the possibility that it might. At such points a tension arises between our commitment to the tradition and our sense of the need to rebel against it. For obvious reasons such a perceived need must be carefully tested and weighed; but it can never be proscribed in advance, unless we are prepared to embrace the intellectual strait-jacket of fundamentalism or dogmatism, and to banish from the outset all possibility of genuine

4

advance or discovery, or of creative genius. Once such matters are raised, of course, there must immediately follow a careful consideration of the criteria of evaluation which might be deployed in addressing them. Part of our concern in this book will be with the various 'authorities for faith' (scripture, tradition, reason, context, experience and so forth) and the ways in which they can be, have been, and are used and abused in the doing of theology.

Third, faith must seek to understand its place within its own specific historical and cultural context. Both the task of interpretation and that of critical reflection demand and lead naturally into such a quest, and to that extent the attempt to reckon with the internal coherence of the church's message cannot stand alone with this other, further task. For us this will involve asking just how far the commitments peculiar to Christian faith can be fitted together with that view of our world and the place of humans within it entertained by most of our contemporaries; the assumptions, attitudes and practices which might be referred to in a wholesale manner as the mindset of late-twentieth-century Western society. This is a vitally necessary task which must of necessity be repeated afresh on a regular basis. Yesterday's answers will not address today's questions; and while the task of theology or 'faith seeking understanding' is certainly not restricted to the answering of questions and problems thrown up by the agenda of society, nevertheless even in that more fundamental task of bearing witness, of seeking to give some meaningful account of itself and the object of its hope, faith must already take these factors into consideration – otherwise it will be forced into a ghetto of its own making, a self-imposed irrelevance and obscurantism. Precisely what it might mean for theology to be or to become 'relevant' is something which we shall be considering in later chapters. But whatever else it may or may not involve, a theology of relevance to the society within which it is forged will of necessity be one which speaks the language of that society, both literally and metaphorically, which is familiar with its concerns and its ways of thinking. Such familiarity is a prerequisite of all communication, let alone all *good* communication: we have to meet people and to address them where they are.

In reality, our situation as Christians in the world is such that for the most part we do not have to force ourselves to think about these things. It is something that we find ourselves doing as a matter of course, particularly when we encounter widely held attitudes or assumptions which appear to conflict with something basic in our Christian faith, or when our own experience of the realities of life seem to present difficulties for or to challenge one element or another of what we believe. Inasmuch as it is true that 'faith is the certainty of things not seen' and the gospel 'foolishness to the Greeks', we can reasonably expect such questions to be thrust upon us with an inevitable regularity. Nor, of course, are we dealing with a situation in which we, as Christians, are set over against the assumptions and attitudes of society or culture. That would be true if we were missionaries in some foreign land. But as Christians seeking to make sense of our faith within our own context, the truth is that we are ourselves a part of that same society and culture – products of it – and to a greater or lesser extent, therefore, its attitudes and assumptions are ingrained within us.

What we must face, then, is not merely an external dialogue with those whose views in some sense challenge our own, but an internalized dialogue within ourselves as those who in some sense belong both to the community of faith and the society which lies beyond the boundaries of that community and to which the community seeks to bear meaningful witness to the Lordship of Christ. As the American Catholic theologian David Tracy has put it, it is not so much true that the Christian is *in* the world but not *of* it as that he is *released from* the world *for* the world.[3] In terms of theology what this means is that – unless we are prepared to embrace a mentally disintegrated existence – we shall seek, in our own way and our own time and to our own level, to come to terms with the problems and the possibilities of integrating our faith in its various aspects into a wider picture of things entertained by society; thereby inhabiting a more or less integrated world, a universe rather than a multiverse. Only thus can we be faithful to the call to bear witness to the gospel in a meaningful way to those who inhabit this same world. In the process it is inevitable (since Chris-tian faith and the contemporary mind-set are certainly not identical!) that there will be an element of give and take, of rethinking and re-shaping on both sides in order to reach a satisfactory adjustment. The question of how much faith can reasonably expect to give and how much it is likely to have to take is one which we shall consider duly.

It is also bound to be the case that at any point in our lives we shall find ourselves living with many questions still unresolved, since both the faith which we share and the wider understanding of things which we inherit from our culture are forever changing and developing. This means that the task is a perpetual one. We shall refer to this task in this book as the concern of faith for the 'external coherence' of its gospel, for the integration of that gospel with the wider sweep of human understanding. Here, too, I shall suggest, the concern cannot be for coherence alone, but must embrace the question of truth as a question about the correspondence of our carefully integrated 'understanding', our ideas and our statements, with the shape of reality itself. Theology, therefore, entails the attempt to sketch an intellectual contour of reality as it appears from within the stance of a living and active faith in Christ, 'a continuing intellectual effort after honest belief capable of throwing light on existence in all its complexity'.[4] This, I shall suggest, is an activity which takes place within an existing and developing tradition of understanding, a 'community of faith and practice'. Only within such a community can serious thinking (about the gospel or anything else) take place.

In reality, these three aspects of the attempt by faith to attain to understanding are not separable, being but three elements of a common theological process. To repeat: theology, understood thus, is an activity proper to the very essence of faith, and one in which faith engages naturally and inevitably, therefore, wherever it is to be found. But what is natural and inevitable is not necessarily for that reason guaranteed to proceed in an orderly or appropriate fashion. The Church of England Doctrine Commission's report *Christian Believing* puts it neatly: 'Theology is not undesirable, it is unavoidable. What matters is that it should be good theology.'[5] It is important, therefore, that careful consideration should be given by the millions of 'lay theologians' in our churches to just how the theological task might best be engaged in.

It is with this very much in mind that this book has been written. It is addressed primarily not to the scholar or the theologically well-qualified reader, but to the person who is approaching the question of how to do theology for the first time. For this reason it will be shorn of much of the technical language and jargon of theological writing, and will attempt to unpack and explain it where its use becomes unavoidable for one reason or another. It will seek to tackle some of the central questions raised by the doing of theology, not in an attempt to provide prescriptive answers leading to guaranteed success (as if that were possible!) but rather to see how in actual fact these various questions have been and are answered by faith in action in the world. What we shall try to do, in other words, is to describe the ways in which theology is done, and to seek among them some lessons to guide the reader in his or her own ventures into theological territory. Along the way (to attract back those who have read other introductions to theological method, and are just about to place this one back on the shelf!) I hope that what will begin to emerge is a model for the doing of theology which has some new and creative aspects to it, and which may bring something fresh and illuminating to the approach to some old and tired problems.

'Asking questions is part of what it means to be human ... asking questions in the light of the grace of God in Jesus Christ is part of what it means to be Christian.'[6] Thus we might say that every Christian has a theological calling and a theological responsibility under God, a calling and a responsibility to think about the gospel of Jesus Christ and to reflect on its internal and external coherence. My hope is that this book will serve in part as a guide to those who wish to take their responsibility to respond to this common calling seriously, which will help them to avoid some of the many pitfalls and to identify some of the clearer and more fruitful paths, and which will help to engender a renewed confidence in Christian faith as a respectable standpoint from which to view and to participate in life in the modern world.

NOTES
1 Church of England Doctrine Commission, *Christian Believing* (SPCK 1976), p. 4.
2 Migliore, D., *Faith Seeking Understanding* (Paternoster Press 1972), p. 1.
3 Tracy, D., *The Analogical Imagination* (SCM Press 1981), p. 48.
4 *Christian Believing*, p. 4.
5 *Christian Believing*, p. 4.
6 Migliore, *Faith Seeking Understanding*, p. 17.

—— Part One ——

The Rehabilitation
of Faith

— 1 —

Faith Seeking Respectability

'I ca'n't believe that,' said Alice.
'Ca'n't you?' the Queen said in a pitying tone. 'Try again: draw a long breath and shut your eyes.'
Alice laughed. 'There's no use trying,' she said. 'One ca'n't believe impossible things.'
'I dare say you haven't had much practice,' said the Queen. 'When I was your age, I always did it for half an hour a day. Why, sometimes I've believed as many as six impossible things before breakfast.'

Lewis Carroll

Theology is an inevitable activity of faith. Wherever people are to be found who believe in Jesus Christ and who seek to live as his disciples, that is to say, there will be Christian theology of some sort going on at some level. Whether it will be done well or badly is, of course, another matter. Good theology, I have suggested, is the disciplined and critical reflection of the community of faith upon the gospel entrusted to it. It is reflection carried out within the community of faith, from the standpoint afforded by faith, and (though not exclusively certainly primarily) for the sake of the community of faith. Christian theology, then, is a pursuit of the church. It is the attempt on the part of those who belong to the church of Christ to explore and to comprehend more fully the shape and structure of the truth which they are called upon to profess and to live out in all its varied aspects.

This is a controversial way of thinking about theology. To the theologically uninitiated it might seem to be a relatively tame and even straightforwardly obvious definition; but in the current intellectual climate it is a radical and even scandalous way of thinking. Objections will be raised and questions asked of us the moment that we speak of theology in this way, and we must anticipate and address them at this stage.

Faith's Crisis of Respectability

The likely focus of such objections will be the explicit linking of theology to faith. No one could reasonably deny, of course, that theology is intertwined with faith in one way or another. At one level it is clearly parasitic upon faith. Without faith it would not and could not exist, since it is with faith's concerns that it has directly to do. It is perfectly possible to define this relationship in such a way that faith remains firmly on one side of it and theology on the other. Theology describes and explores the concerns of faith, we might say, while faith for its part provides theology with its legitimate object of study. Such an account of things is unlikely to provoke indignation from any quarter.

But the moment that faith is introduced to the other side of this equation, and theology described as an *activity* of faith rather than merely the scientific *study* of faith, objections are likely to fly thick and fast from quarters within the community of faith as well as outside it. For faith, in our society, faces a crisis of identity and respectability. There is a widespread assumption that personal beliefs or commitments are best set aside when we turn to engage in serious intellectual activity lest they exercise an unhelpful influence over what we do, or blind us to certain possibilities and realities. Faith, then, is generally perceived as a potential hindrance rather than a help in the search for knowledge and understanding, a likely obstacle to the honest asking of questions and the serious facing of doubts. The hallmarks of intellectual respectability and credibility are identified in an unambiguous appeal to reason and such empirically establishable evidence as is available. To trespass beyond these agreed sources, and to appeal to things which are simply 'believed' rather than known to be the case is to risk dragging the whole enterprise into disrepute and undermining the integrity and value of any results obtained.

The Privatization of Commitment

This account of things, which is widely subscribed to within our culture, can be traced back some three and a half centuries to the origins of the so-called European Enlightenment, an episode in Western intellectual history to which we shall turn in the next chapter. One particular manifestation of it is the divide between what have come to be termed the public and private spheres.[1]

The language of public and private is more familiar, of course, from its use in capitalist economics where it refers to that which is owned by the state (or the public as citizens of it) on the one hand, and that which is owned by individuals expending their own private incomes on the other. The metaphorical extension of the terms to apply to the ownership of truths, ideas and beliefs is a helpful and instructive one. Here the 'public' sector is the realm of universally 'owned' or agreed knowledge; the sort of knowledge which is available to everyone by virtue of their nature as intelligent persons; knowledge which is, we might say, common property, jointly owned by all citizens of the human race. If something is 'public truth' then it must be something which *everyone can know to be true*, a truth available to observation or self-evident to human reason, and therefore universally binding.

On the other hand, to the private realm belong all statements or propositions which, for one reason or another, do not lend themselves in this way to public ownership or scrutiny. The private sphere is the sphere of values, matters of opinion and beliefs; anything, in fact, the truth or falsity of which cannot in principle be demonstrated on publicly agreed terms, and which cannot, therefore, be granted any universal warrant. It is here that those things which we may choose to believe as private individuals, but for the truth of which we cannot provide any objective or publicly convincing proof or demonstration, properly belong. Such things may be the object of our personal faith commitments, but they cannot be carried into the public realm without the passport of their justification by reason. They are the things of which we habitually say 'That's your opinion and you're quite entitled to hold it; but unless and until you can prove it to be true I shall feel quite free to dissent from it.' Such things, it is contended, do not properly count as knowledge.

Christian faith is generally considered in our society to belong to this latter category. Together with many other areas of human belief it has long since been privatized, and is habitually viewed as something to be kept safely within the confines of our private lives. It has no legitimate place in the public discourse of the workplace or the market-place, and those who insist on introducing it there can expect to be met either with bemused embarrassment, justifiable indifference, or even antagonism from those who feel that their own privacy has in some way been encroached upon. To speak of such things in public simply is not done!

13

Theology as Public Inquiry

This compartmentalization of our intellectual lives is one which many theologians have collaborated with, fearful, perhaps, of the consequences of doing otherwise. Theology, they would insist, is an intellectual pursuit and must therefore be practised on a properly academic and scientific basis. Thus, while faith may furnish the motive for engaging in theology, faith itself must remain on the sidelines while the game is played according to 'public' rules, allowing reason to pursue its course unhindered. This insistence upon theology being pursued as a sort of external inquiry into faith, prosecuted by reason, it is held, can only be for faith's own ultimate good. Such an inquiry, in which the terms of reference are laid down not by parties with a vested interest in seeing a particular outcome reached but by universally accept canons of truth and reasonability, and in which there is an honest 'no holds barred' exposure of Christian faith to the rigours of reason and critical reflection, can only strengthen and not weaken faith. A Christianity thus tried and tested, it might be supposed, would be more likely to commend itself to intelligent people in the modern world.

The Dangers of Theological Freemasonry

If, on the other hand, it is insisted that Christian faith is just as vital a component in the theologian's essential tool kit as reason, the possession of certain historical, linguistic and analytical skills and so forth, then, it will be maintained, the integrity and the public credibility of the discipline is called into question. Theology which cannot be done by someone who lacks faith, which is, as it were, a closed shop, an activity for paid-up Christian believers only, cannot count as a properly scientific pursuit. It transgresses the accepted canons of publicness which would admit it to the academy. It courts disdain and even rejection from those who embrace these intellectual standards, and risks isolating itself altogether from serious debate and dialogue within the wider human community. More seriously, it risks failure to attain its own stated objectives. An intellectual inquiry which, because it begins with unproved but non-negotiable beliefs and commitments, excludes from the outset certain avenues of questioning, or refuses to admit the legitimacy of particular conclusions being reached, is not so much a genuine inquiry as a cover-up, a circular process the outcome of which is in effect a foregone conclusion. To insist that theology is an explicit activity of faith or commitment in this sense, therefore, is to leave faith without defence from the charge that it is engaged in believing 'six impossible things before breakfast'. But it is precisely the task of theology to be able to give reasons for those things which faith believes, not simply to draw a long breath and shut its eyes!

Thus, for example, Brian Hebblethwaite argues: 'Neither conversion nor faith is a necessary condition of theological thinking.' To suggest otherwise, he argues, 'lifts theology out of the sphere of rational discussion and leads to the absurd claim that theological rationality has its own private logic'.[2] Hebblethwaite's complaint, then, is that to demand the vantage point of faith as a necessary condition for the pursuit of theology, and to argue that anyone who does not share that vantage point cannot appreciate the logic of theology or engage in meaningful theological discussion, is to tear theology away from the context of proper rational dialogue in the public forum. Theologians, he maintains, whatever their personal commitments may be, cannot *as theologians* live and operate in a private world. The claim that it is necessary to do so constitutes a form of obscurantism which can only result in theology finally being banished to an intellectual ghetto of its own devising.

If the gospel is truly a universal gospel, if it is public truth in the sense that its truth transcends cultural and historical boundaries, then surely, Hebblethwaite suggests, that truth must be presentable in ways which will appeal to the faculty of reason which all humans share in common? It cannot be treated as if it were some secret gnosis restricted to the enlightened few. Theological freemasonry can be pursued only at the expense of intellectual credibility and apologetic purchase in the minds and consciences of those outside the church and its sphere of faith.

The Demand for a Level Playing-Field

What this means in practice, according to Hebblethwaite, is that academic theology must be practised as an open-minded dialogue between belief and unbelief, a consideration conducted on rational grounds of the questions concerning the ultimate meaning and purpose of human existence, and of the answers given to those questions within the Christian tradition. On the part of the believing theologian this will entail a self-critical detachment from the framework of faith, and on the part of the unbelieving, a willingness to enter into and to explore the hypothesis of God's existence and nature as described by Christian theology. Thus, 'The fundamental hypothesis to be tested in theology by both believer and unbeliever in dialogue is whether critical investigation of the alleged media of divine-human encounter yields an objective and plausible view of God and the world.'[3] For the purposes of such a discussion, neither faith nor unbelief furnishes any particular advantage or disadvantage. The methods employed will be those which are 'the common property of philosophers, historians and students of ancient texts as well as theologians'.[4] On such terms, and on such terms alone, theology may lay claim to proper academic integrity. But theology of this sort is strictly an activity of reason, and does not bring faith directly to bear on its procedures.

Behind this concern lies a deep conviction that the Christian story is one which can, at least in substantial and significant part, be demonstrated by such a method to be rationally and morally compelling, to be 'true' in the sense of conforming in some identifiable manner to the nature of reality. There is, in other words, an apologetic as well as a strictly academic drive behind Hebblethwaite's refusal to accept faith as a prerequisite for the theological task. The rational and moral truth of the claims of Christian faith must be recognizable and demonstrable apart from that faith itself; otherwise no one who did not already possess faith would ever be able to acquire it, being quite incapable of seeing, recognizing or grasping that truth for themselves. For Hebblethwaite, then, it is precisely a conviction of the truth of Christianity which leads to a steadfast denial of the need for faith as a condition of or an indispensable tool in the pursuit of theology.

On the Arrogance of Absolutism

For others in our society the bringing of explicit faith commitments into the public domain is inappropriate precisely because the truth of the Christian story *is not and could never be* demonstrable. For those of the sort of radical pluralist sympathies which are increasingly fashionable in many intellectual circles today truth is never something absolute or universal, but always relative to particular contexts – cultural, historical, linguistic, religious or whatever. What constitutes truth in one time and place and for one community will not, therefore, necessarily be 'true' for others. Thus there can be no demonstrably true perspectives on life and its meaning. There can only be a diversity of frameworks, each possessed of its own views about what is and is not 'rational', a legitimate diversity in which, once we have recognized it, we should rejoice as an enriching feature of human existence, engendering those attitudes of humility, tolerance and mutual respect which so ennoble human personhood and community. As individuals we shall inevitably belong to one community and indwell one particular perspective from within which we will view and make sense of our world. But we must learn that we cannot reasonably expect others to see things in the same way as ourselves, or to share the canons of truth and reason which we have inherited. And there are no legitimate grounds for seeking to persuade or convince them of the superiority of our view over theirs. Such persuasion amounts in practice to rejection of the equal validity of their outlook, an intolerance which modern society must reject in its bid for the peaceful and contented coexistence of differing convictions. The context and tradition from which others come may have granted them a different perspective on things, but, since no absolute truths may be identified, we must endorse that perspective as equally as valid as, and as complementary to, our own. There is no conveniently neutral 'no man's land' to which an intellectual engagement or dispute may be carried in order to provide an objective and authoritative adjudication.

In such public contexts as the academy, therefore, where members of numerous different human communities gather in pursuit of knowledge, the only appropriate mode of activity will be one which treats each tradition or framework as equally worthy of consideration, which is prepared to adopt or to enter sympathetically into each as a distinct place from which to engage in the quest for an underlying and ultimate truth and meaning which, if it exists, lies as yet wholly beyond our grasp. What we must never do here is to affirm any one framework as providing a better standpoint than any other. Here again, academic integrity is deemed to consist in a 'hands off' noncommittal approach, the 'phenomenological' description of different viewpoints not from some detached vantage point, but from within and on their own terms. For the pluralist there can be no absolute truth; or rather, we cannot know that there is any if there is. The question to be asked of a religious tradition (for example), therefore, is not 'Is it true?' (the agnostic answer to that question is a foregone conclusion) but 'Does it provide a helpful place to stand in our search for spiritual meaning and fulfilment?'

Christian faith, I would suggest, implies an ultimate commitment to truth at some level. Its characteristic form is not that of an endless quest in which it is better to travel than to arrive, but rather of witness, witness which has in the past cost many a great deal. But in the pluralist ethos while such commitments may be held by individuals in private, they cannot be tolerated in public. If people wish to engage privately in tribalism or fundamentalism (as all claims to ultimate truth come to be branded) then that is a matter for their own resolution; but they cannot as self-respecting public citizens allow such convictions to interfere with or intrude into their intellectual intercourse or professional methodologies. On this view it is fine, for example, to seek truth from within the perspective of Christian faith, just so long as we treat this as only one possible route among many, and never claim actually to have found what we are supposedly seeking there. The academic who manifests most integrity, therefore, is the one who is able to step out of his own faith commitments at will and exchange them for others in order to engage in a genuinely open-minded and tolerant quest for a truth which can never be had.

Rejecting Intellectual Apartheid

In our society, then, pressure is brought to bear on us to live in various ways as citizens of two quite different worlds. We are granted a dual passport, as it were, allowing us to pass freely from the world of our private commitments into the world of public intercourse and back again with no questions asked. The only demand which is made upon us is that we should at all times remember in which world we are, for the rules by which conduct is governed in each are quite distinct. We must not forget that the currency which buys so much in the one is not recognized as legal tender in the other, and must be exchanged at the border at an extremely unfavourable rate.

My contention in the coming chapters will be that this carving-up of life into two distinct intellectual territories is both dangerous and unnecessary. It is dangerous, for Christians at least, because it engenders a mind-set which compartmentalizes our commitments and thereby encourages a Christianity which is hung up in the wardrobe with our Sunday best, or left on the bedside table together with our Bible, rather than being carried with us into the office, the factory or wherever, as salt and light for a society in need of purification and illumination. Theologically it is quite unacceptable, for it constitutes a denial of the truth that Christ is Lord of every aspect of human existence, and not just those parts which society deems as belonging to our private worlds.

The very nature of the Christian gospel, the confession of Christ as Lord, would seem to contradict this apportioning of territories. Christianity is not a faith susceptible to being turned on and off like a tap. Christ's Lordship is not true for some people but not for others; or a truth confessed in some sectors of our lives but not recognized in others. The message which Christians profess, which is the basis of their transformed lives, lays claim to the status precisely of 'public truth', that is to say something which is equally true in all times and all places, and for all people.[5] To keep quiet about it, or to set aside one's commitment to it in public contexts, therefore, would seem to be quite wrong, for precisely what we are called upon to do is to share it, to lay it before others for their consideration, and to allow it to shape and mould our thinking and our action in every sphere of life. Exactly what this means in practice is a question to which we must return later; but let us note already that to endorse or accept or agree to be bound by the effective partition of human life into homelands based on the exercise of faith or commitment on the one hand, and such allegedly universal dispositions as 'reason' or 'experience' on the other, is to put at risk all that is involved in living a life of discipleship under Christ.

Admiring the King's New Clothes

But not only is this dualistic outlook on life dangerous, it is also quite erroneous, and therefore there is no need to saddle ourselves with it. It rests on a fundamentally flawed but common misunderstanding of the nature and relationship between faith and 'reason'. Faith is perceived as a disposition utterly distinct from reason, and, as we have seen throughout this chapter, in some sense a less reliable or worthy or justifiable disposition. Whenever the two are set alongside or against one another (as they so often are in popular understanding) it is reason which must prevail. Faith can do so only at the cost of a *sacrificium intellectus*, for, in the words of Alice, 'one ca'n't believe impossible things', and reason, it is commonly supposed, is our only reliable index of the possible. That Christianity is indeed engaged in believing 'six impossible things before breakfast' is a common enough charge in our day. The demand to bring the gospel into line with 'what any reasonable person could believe nowadays' is often heard, both from without and within our churches. The quest for a 'reasonable Christianity' is evident in many places and takes many forms. But the foundations on which the quest of what we might legitimately call 'faith seeking respectability' is so often built are rotten and need to be replaced. The wedge driven between faith and reason as human dispositions and the consequent elevation of reason over faith is, we shall contend, dangerously misleading, both for those who wish to commend and justify faith, and to secure for it some measure of respect, and those who would eschew it altogether. The concerns of heart and mind are far more closely intertwined than either faith's defenders or its strongest critics have generally been prepared to recognize.

In this book I shall present theology as an explicit and un-ashamed activity of faith. The word faith in this context can mean two quite distinct things, both of which are important for our purposes. First, it refers to a fundamental disposition of the agent; a disposition of commitment and trust, a willingness to accept and to build upon unproved assumptions and beliefs as an entirely suitable platform for the execution of the theological task. Second, the word faith may refer to the particular sets of beliefs and assumptions which characterize Christianity as a tradition of thought and action. Theology, I shall argue, is *always* an activity of faith in the first of these two senses, notwithstanding efforts to purge it. When it is properly Christian theology, I shall suggest, it will also be an activity of faith in the second sense.

Clearly this is a provocative line to take. As someone teaching theology in a university environment I certainly have no desire to be branded an obscurantist, or accused of retreating from the sphere of rational discussion. Nor do I wish to appear tribalistic or intolerant. There are genuine errors corresponding to these charges. But I utterly reject the claim that to construe theology (or any other intellectual project) as an explicit activity of faith is already to have committed them. On the contrary, my purpose in the first few chapters of this book will be to pose some difficult questions for those who, in a bid for intellectual respectability, play the modern or post-modern game and misguidedly seek to fashion a theology without commitments. Faith, I shall argue, has an irritating habit of surfacing in the most unexpected and unwelcome places, and the bid to be rid of its influence altogether is a lost cause. Those who think that they have succeeded in doing so are in reality more vulnerable than ever to its moulding and direction. Far from mastering it they become its unwitting slaves.

In reality there can be no confining of faith to a ghetto, or any neat dividing line drawn between its exercise and that of human 'reason'. Rather, I will argue, faith is an unavoidable and necessary component of every act of human knowing. Far being being a poor cousin or a shabby alternative to reason, therefore, faith actually furnishes the conditions under which reason must operate, and without which it can achieve nothing. Thus a realm in which reason is exalted is also, in truth, inevitably a realm in which faith is alive and active. Likewise, where faith acts, it does so precisely together with and not apart from an activity of reason. Faith and reason, that is to say, are in actuality inseparable and interdependent. The only question is whether or not this will be recognized. Those who, for whatever purpose, would drive a wedge between the two are perpetrating or labouring under an illusion which persists in our society. But we do that society no favours by conforming, and pretending to admire the king's new clothes.

To insist that theology can and must operate from within a framework of commitment, on the basis of faith, therefore, is in no way to indulge in special pleading, or to banish oneself willingly to an intellectual ghetto. *All* intellectual activity takes place within one framework of commitment or another. The fact that this is so often denied does not make it untrue. But failure to recognize it and to make suitable allowance for it can and does lead to gross self-deception and the making of ridiculous and arrogant claims concerning the status of one's knowledge. The question with which we close this chapter but take up in the course of the rest of the book is this: if faith and critical enquiry are not incompatible, belonging to separate compartments of our lives, but in some sense demand one another, then in what sort of critical reflection is it appropriate for Christian faith to engage in the theological task, and what might that engagement look like?

In the next two chapters we shall be concerned to substantiate this claim that faith, far from being inimical or a hindrance to the effective use of reason, is in fact an indispensable condition of it. We turn first to consider the circumstances in which the modern polarization of faith and reason, and the disparagement of faith as a disposition falling short of real knowledge, emerged.

NOTES
1 See, e.g., Newbigin, L., *Truth to Tell: The Gospel as Public Truth* (SPCK 1991).
2 Hebblethwaite, B., *The Problems of Theology* (Cambridge University Press 1980), p. 20.
3 Hebblethwaite, *The Problems of Theology*, p. 17.
4 Hebblethwaite, *The Problems of Theology*, p. 18.
5 See on this theme Newbigin, *Truth to Tell*.

— 2 —

Faith and the Search
for Certainty

Faith, I have suggested, is, in the modern age, facing a crisis of respectability. How, then, did this crisis come about? Its emergence, I shall suggest in this chapter, was tied ineluctably to another: namely a crisis of confidence in the reliability of human knowledge and a concomitant quest for certainty which together characterize the intellectual mood of modernity.

The quest for certain and reliable knowledge is not a peculiarly modern one. It may be said to characterize the human quest for meaning through the centuries. We search for something lasting and immovable which cannot be shaken by the apparent contingencies and unpredictabilities of life. We crave something firm to which we might cling in the midst of apparent meaninglessness, upon or around which we might build, however modestly, a system of values, and from which we might take bearings in charting a course through life's choppy and often treacherous waters. Somehow humans seem always to have felt the need for some such basis for living and, indeed, for dying. Scepticism (the view that we can ultimately know nothing reliable) leaves us either embracing meaninglessness or else engaged in the dubious project of constructing a meaning of our own design. It is one of the great ironies of the modern condition that the course of its quest for certainty has led it to the point where its fate appears to be certain shipwreck on this Scylla or Charybdis. It is with this fateful quest that we shall be concerned in this chapter.

The Loss of the Common Sense Universe

A TV advertisement for a well-known brand of German beer begins with a view of a man shaving in front of a bathroom mirror. At least, that is what appears to be the case. The impact of the advert lies in the mental adjustment we are forced to make as the man inserts his hand into the mirror, his reflection distorting horribly as the surface appears to melt before our eyes, breaking in liquid fashion into myriad ripples and waves. The sequence continues, and our offended sensibilities are soothed as the camera zooms out to reveal the wider perspective on things. It becomes clear at once that the 'mirror' in question was in fact all along a perfectly still pool of water, over which the man was stooped, and into which he plunged his hand to grasp a can of refreshingly cold beer. The thought with which the advert leaves us is that things are not always what they seem to be at first sight. Even the most straightforward of appearances can be highly deceptive. We should beware of trusting too quickly what we see or hear, and be prepared to question, to enquire further, to seek other perspectives, to ensure that we obtain a view of things as they really are.

The advert is entertaining, and even powerful during a first viewing of it. But the likely truth is that most of us will set its philosophical point (perhaps together with its commercial one!) lightly aside and return to an approach to life in which, while we might entertain a 'healthy' degree of scepticism about many things, we generally feel pretty confident about things which we can see or hear or touch for ourselves. We feel at home in the physical world, and consider nothing so certain as the reality of the chair in which we are sitting or the cup of coffee we drink as we sit and gaze at our TV sets. But this reflects the fact that most of us are singularly unphilosophical creatures; for the most profound and searching questions raised by philosophers in modern times have served, like our advert, precisely to call such comfortable certainties into account, and to suggest that the world as we experience it may be significantly different to what (if anything) is really 'out there' beyond our minds. The attitudes and assumptions which such philosophical debates have fed into society are ones which, however philosophically philistine we may think ourselves, will have had a profound impact on us.

Hannah Arendt has suggested that this pecularily modern crisis of confidence in knowing can be traced back to a series of technological developments in the early seventeenth century, developments which quite literally furnished us with a new way of looking at things, and thereby revolutionized our ways of thinking about the cosmos and our engagement with it. The hand of science plunged, as it were, into the surface of the mirror of the universe, and forced upon people a profound and painful mental adjustment. Hand in hand with this fundamental change in perspective went a recognition that what had hitherto seemed obvious to everyone was not in fact how things were in reality. The effect was to shake to its very foundations that basic trust in sensory perception which most had previously naively enjoyed. Just what was it, then, that prompted this anxiety attack?

The Final Setting of the Sun

One of the most dramatic events in this period was the development of a new scientific instrument, the telescope, by the Italian mathematician and physicist Galileo (1564–1642). This invention opened up a vast new field of observation and discovery, which had lain hitherto altogether beyond the effective range of human vision. Now for the first time human beings could penetrate into outer space and see for themselves marvels previously hidden to the naked eye. As they did so it rapidly became apparent that things were not as they had once seemed. It was not simply that astral phenomena previously hidden now came into view, and the universe was discovered to be far more vast and complex than anyone, even with the sharpest eye and on the brightest and clearest night, had ever dreamed, although that was remarkable enough. But by far the most significant aspect of this entire episode was Galileo's demonstration, using his new instruments, of the fact that, contrary to all appearance and the dictates of common sense, the star which we call our Sun did not 'rise' in the morning and 'set' in the evening. It was not, that is to say, circling around us, but rather we around it. This perspective is so familiar to every schoolchild today, mapped, as it is, on so many colourful wall charts or book plates of the solar system, that we find it hard to imagine the intellectual trauma which this demonstration must have provoked in its day. For those who took the trouble to explore and verify his experimental claims, Galileo had turned the universe upside down and inside out. The mirror in front of them turned to water before their very eyes!

Two major adjustments were now forced upon people's thinking about themselves, their world and their knowledge. The first was stupendous enough. Since time immemorial humans had assumed that their world lay literally at the centre of reality and that all else revolved around it, both in cosmological terms, and also in terms of the status and significance of human existence. The evidence of the senses suggested an earth immeasurably large and set at rest, providing a platform for human existence, while the altogether less substantial Sun and Moon took it in turns to appear and to provide light and heat required by that existence. This evidence was corroborated in the story told by the Christian tradition according to which humanity and its history lay at the centre of God's creation and purposes. In both senses, therefore, human beings thought of themselves as lying at the centre of God's universe. But now, with this devastating discovery, the globe, and together with it human life, was displaced from this exalted position, cast from the centre of things to a lonely orbit around a solitary star, one of a countless number of similar satellites circling many millions of similar stars, and all set in a vast and for the most part quite empty darkness to which no end could be imagined. The implications of all this were bewildering, and sufficient in themselves to induce a temporary loss of existential balance among those of a more reflective disposition. As one commentator has put it: 'Such a change does not necessarily involve the dethronement of man from his proud position as the summit of creation, but it certainly suggests doubts of the validity of that belief.'[1]

But the second mental adjustment was even more far-reaching in its possible ramifications. What Galileo had done was to demonstrate that sense experience was capable of fraud on a grand scale. The suggestion that the Earth revolved around the Sun rather than vice versa had actually already been made some hundred years earlier, without recourse to the sort of experimental verification which Galileo's telescope provided, by the Polish astronomer Copernicus (1473–1543). He advocated a heliocentric rather than a geocentric model of the universe on the grounds of mathematical simplicity. But his theory, together with its uncomfortable implications for human self-understanding, was easily and willingly dismissed as mere hypothesis. Neither the scientific nor the ecclesiastical community of the day was willing to see humans wrenched from their long held position centre stage, and as yet they had the clear evidence of 'common sense' firmly on their side.

With the advent of the new technology, however, all this changed. What Galileo showed was that Copernicus's intellectually satisfying account of the solar system was capable of experimental verification. He 'established a demonstrable fact where before him there were inspired speculations'.[2] By extending the range of human vision and thereby rendering the distant realities of the universe open to human knowing 'with all the certainty of sense perception'[3] he forced people to reckon with its truth and all its discomforting ramifications. That the world was still not ready for

this painful transition in perspective is illustrated on the one hand
by the attitude of the Roman Church to his discoveries, and on the
other by the reported behaviour of the professor of philosophy at
Padua, who, when invited to do so, refused absolutely to look
through Galileo's telescope and see for himself the evidence which
made the transition needful![4]

Of Atoms and the Void

It was not only at the level of the macroscopic but also the microscopic that technology made new advances in knowledge possible
during the seventeenth century. Here again optical instruments
were developed which extended the range of human vision to see
things which had never been seen before. The resultant analyses of
matter in terms of atoms and molecules posed just as many deep
and serious questions concerning the nature of our everyday
knowledge of the physical world as Galileo's discovery that the surface of the Moon was not smooth and polished, and that Jupiter
had a mini solar system of moons orbiting around it. Galileo himself was a keen exponent of the atomic theory of matter, and drew
out some of its more challenging implications. To the naked eye,
and the touch of the hand, the objects of our daily experience
appear to us to possess certain qualities. The desk at which I am
sitting as I write is hard to the touch, brown in colour, and has a
smooth surface. A cricket ball which sits upon the desk is round,
red and has the rough surface which results from having made fre-
quent contact with a bat. But what the microscopic perspective
reveals is altogether different. In an analysis informed by the magnification of powerful lenses, the objects before me would prove
to consist of complex arrangements of atoms devoid of any of the
qualities which I have listed. Whence, then do these apparent
aspects derive? Galileo was quite clear. The basic constituents of
matter are themselves possessed of no colour, sound, taste, or
shape whatever. These, he writes, are supplied by our five senses,
and thus derive within us, rather than being 'out there' in the world
beyond our consciousness. 'Out there' there is only 'atoms and the
void' as the Greek philosopher Democritus had speculated many
centuries earlier. The colours, tastes, textures, shapes and other
qualities which characterize the world of our experience are to be
credited, therefore, not to 'reality itself,' but to our minds which
supply these and make the world a more attractive place than it
actually is. Again, then, the reliability of what sensory perception

ordinarily renders to us as knowledge of the real word was called radically into question. Between the physical world of our daily acquaintance and the colourless, formless, tasteless, noiseless substance which, it was now held, constitutes physical reality, an ever-widening gap had begun to yawn.

There is profound irony here. For what these respective technological developments had effectively done was to offer humans an extension of their powers of sensory perception which served ultimately to undermine confidence in the story which those same powers ordinarily told about the world. Sense experience was pitted against sense experience in a match which served to tarnish its reputation. The fact that the senses could be deceived, that optical illusions were possible, was nothing new of course. Generations of conjurers and magicians had thrived on this knowledge. But there is a significant difference between the impact of, let us say, a rabbit being produced from a hat or a lady sawn in half, and the demonstration (with the tap of a scientist's wand) that the world as we have known and loved it from childhood is in truth bereft of real existence, a carefully manufactured cosmetic veneer to cover a chaos of particles in space. Those who sought to integrate the new discoveries into their philosophical reflection, therefore, were faced with an awkward question. How was it possible, any longer, to be sure of *anything* when this most basic and all embracing and apparently obvious facet of life, the familiar world round about us, and the Sun, Moon and stars in their heaven, had been shown to be the subject of a grand illusion perpetrated by our senses?

Thus it was that the consequences of this epoch-making advance in human knowledge were essentially bitter-sweet. The triumph of science in probing out into the recesses of space, and down into the invisible molecular substructure of the world, thereby pushing the horizons of human understanding ever further back, was greeted in other more philosophical quarters not with exultation but with a measure of reflective despair. For while the territory of human knowledge may have been expanded, it was recognized by some that in the process the very integrity of human knowledge itself had been called into question. The sense of betrayal felt towards sense experience was accompanied by a mood of 'once bitten twice shy'. The reaction which ensued, therefore, was one of profound philosophical scepticism accompanied by a desperate search for a type of knowledge which would be beyond all suspicion, and which might prove a certain and enduring route to the truth.

Doubt as the Only Basis of Certainty

Chief among those who, paradoxically, both fostered this strategic lack of trust and sought to deliver humans from the anxiety and unease which accompanied it was the French mathematician and philosopher René Descartes (1596–1650). Himself an enthusiastic convert to the Copernican hypothesis, Descartes was quick to recognize its more unfortunate implications for an understanding of the nature and status of human knowledge of the world. On pondering the matter he came to the view that ever since youth he had, like most of his fellows, accepted a great many things as true which he did not know for sure to be true, but regarding which he had relied instead for his information on the testimony or authority of others. But, quite clearly, it was possible to be deceived by adopting in an uncritical manner the perspective of things offered by others. Even our own senses (those apparently most reliable and least dubious of all authorities) could no longer be trusted absolutely. When tested by the methods of modern science they had been exposed as capable of deceit on a grand scale. But if the senses could deceive in this way and on such a large scale on one occasion, Descartes reckoned, then they must henceforth always be treated with suspicion, as unreliable guides prone to furnish a skewed or distorted picture of the way things actually are.

Unwilling either to exist in a state of mental uncertainty or to rely upon untrustworthy sources of information, Descartes determined to find a route to a knowledge which was absolutely certain and which could be trusted in every situation. What was needed, he urged, was some way of bypassing the fault, of accessing the world directly as it really was, and hence providing criteria whereby every perspective and point of view might be tested and their potentially prejudicial or distorting effects neutralized.

Establishing a Faith-Free Zone

The route via which Descartes sought to attain such knowledge was his so-called 'method of doubt'. This might reasonably be construed as an attempt to render human knowledge a 'faith-free zone'. Faith, as essentially an attitude of trust in some authoritative source, had now been proven liable to result in deception by untrustworthy guides. It was precisely by trusting the evidence of their senses, rather than testing that evidence, that humans had laboured so long under the illusion of a geocentric universe. But an essentially similar process might readily occur whenever men and women accepted without questioning the account of things offered by others. In the brave new world such uncritical trust must therefore be acknowledged to be naive, and to amount to a refusal to grapple seriously with reality for oneself or to take responsibility for one's own knowledge. Thus, one immediate consequence of Descartes' philosophy was the banishment of faith from the sphere of knowledge. Faith came to be viewed, as the English philosopher John Locke (1632–1704) later expressed it, as 'a persuasion which falls short of knowledge', a view which affords it an altogether subordinate and provisional status. Faith, then, must give way to knowledge, for that which is the object of mere faith or trust must also by definition be capable of being doubted, and thereby contributing further to the general malaise.

Descartes determined that he for one would not be found wanting in this respect, and would therefore set aside all his previously held beliefs and commitments and begin from scratch the task of building up his knowledge. This clearing of the ground he hoped would uncover the things which were truly worthy of human credence, and which might legitimately serve as the foundations of a reliable knowledge of the truth. His method was radical indeed. To achieve his ends he committed himself systematically to doubt any proposition which could be doubted, and to accept only those which could not be, which manifested the quality of self-evident certainty or necessity. On such a foundation alone, he insisted, could knowledge henceforth be based. Nothing which did not present itself for consideration, or could not be demonstrated, on this absolutely certain basis was worthy of the appellation 'knowledge', but must remain the object of mere faith or superstition.

Here we touch upon what is arguably the most significant factor in Descartes' project, and that which has bequeathed the most problematic inheritance for modernity. Descartes, as we have noted, was a mathematician, and brought with him to philosophy a mathematician's penchant for necessary, and hence absolutely reliable, truth. A truth which is 'necessary' is precisely one which must be the case, which cannot logically be otherwise, and which must perforce be true in all circumstances and at all times. Thus it is by definition a universal truth, entirely free from the vagaries or fluctuations of changing perspective, or the distortions of prejudice. 'Those,' he wrote, 'who are seeking the strict way of truth should not trouble themselves about any object concerning which they cannot have *a certainty equal to arithmetical or geometrical demonstration.*'[5] Descartes, that is to say, wanted all his knowledge to be possessed of the same degree of certainty as is to be found in the propositions that a triangle will always have three angles which add up precisely to 180 degrees, or that the square root of 25 is 5. No proposition which could not be demonstrated with this degree of assurance was worthy of human credence or could suffice as an object of knowledge.

With this single stroke Descartes had driven a wedge between the categories of faith on the one hand and knowledge on the other, and had set the entrance requirements to the latter category very high indeed. His call was to leave behind the way of mere faith and to graduate into the way of certainty, and thereby at once to fulfil one's responsibility and to grasp one's birthright as a rational human being. As he presented the challenge it was an impossibly tall order, and one which was to prove altogether too demanding for the generation which embraced it as an ideal.

Inoculating Against Despair

Descartes himself, however, was optimistic about the possibility of meeting this demand. All untested perspectives or points of view, he argued, could exercise a damaging bias on human knowledge and result in error. The evidence which they offered must therefore be set temporarily aside until it could be either verified or falsified by some reliable criterion. What was required was a wholly objective standpoint from which to view things as they really were, a privileged glimpse of reality unhindered by the deceptions of a perspective, a direct and immediate engagement with the world itself, a 'spectators' gallery'[6] from which to observe the universe, a 'God's-eye' view of things. If we are presented with what purports to be a series of photographic images of the same place, all of which differ from one another significantly, then in order to decide which images are the most reliable representations of the place itself our best bet will not be to view yet more photographs of it, but to set the photographic evidence aside and go to see the place for ourselves. What Descartes desired, in effect, was something similar; namely, the ability step out from behind the screen of his senses, to peer behind that screen and to see for himself just what lay behind it. Only then could he confidently adjudge the truth of what appeared on the screen, and make the necessary adjustments. He would then no longer be forced to trust, and no longer be deceived. He would be able to say that he truly knew.

This bid to step outside one's perspective-bound relationship to the world in order to see it objectively is as old as philosophy itself. Descartes believed that the possibility of doing so lay close at hand. The human mind, he claimed, once liberated by the principle of doubt from every prejudice or unwarranted conviction, had within it the resources to discover truths which were absolutely certain, and which might consequently serve as a reliable basis for adjudging and shaping the rest of our knowledge. There is, in other words, a firm bedrock of self-evident and necessary truths which the human mind knows absolutely and without need of any further justification. These are capable, if allowed to do so, of operating as a sure and objective foundation for the construction of knowledge based on information received from other sources. The mind, once the ground had been cleared for it by the rigorous doubting of all dubious testimony, could in effect peer around the edge of the screen and tell us how the world must be, and this knowledge would either confirm or deny the testimony of our senses or of other possible sources of information concerning its appearance. Here was a source of truth which could not possibly be doubted, and which might, therefore, serve as a criterion for the evaluation of all alleged knowledge.

By this rigorous application of the principle of doubt, then, Descartes' intention was certainly not to leave humans in a state of doubt, but rather to succeed in relieving them from it. Rather like an injection for a disease, he considered it necessary to use the virus against itself, to enable the system to find some immunity from it. He used doubt as a tool in an attempt to discover things which it was not possible to doubt, and which could therefore be the focus of a renewed confidence in the project of knowledge. Galileo, by confirming Copernicus's hypothesis, had displaced humans from the centre of the universe and thrown them into a crisis of confidence. Descartes' solution was effectively to put them back at the centre of things, if not cosmologically, then at least in terms of their power to step beyond the limits of their terrestrial vantage point and capture the universe by the power of reason.

Fleeing the Evil Demon

Our account of Descartes would be incomplete without mention of the fact that at his most ruthlessly consistent he was forced to admit the dubiety even of those 'self-evident' truths of reason upon which his reconstruction of knowledge ultimately depended. After all, he mused, it is *possible* that these have been put in our minds by some malignant spiritual influence and are, together with the whole of our experience of the world, part of a massive illusion, a trick of cosmic proportions played upon us by an evil demon. Descartes did not, we should hasten to add, believe that this was actually so. But the criteria which he himself had set up for all true knowledge backfired on him at this point, for he could not demonstrate to himself *with absolute certainty* that it was not so. It was here that he found himself driven to regroup around the one single truth which could not be doubted even on this worst possible scenario: namely the truth of his own existence as a thinking subject. The words 'I think, therefore I am' must rank among the most famous in the history of thought, and it is here that they have their origin. Even, Descartes reasoned, if the whole of my experience and the ideas which fill my mind are a grand deception, nonetheless one thing cannot be doubted: the fact that 'I' exist in order to be thus deceived. So long as I can question and doubt my knowledge and my experience, therefore, I can be sure of my own existence as a mind. As Descartes was the first to admit, this was at first sight a pretty poor return on his initial investment. It was, nonetheless, he believed, the immovable foothold which he required in order to gain a purchase sufficient to construct a workable and reliable knowledge of reality. Upon this slender but rock solid basis he proceeded at once to fashion two rational proofs for the existence of a benevolent deity; a move which, he insisted, at once dispelled the diabolic nightmare, and served to underwrite the veracity of the truths of reason given in the human mind.

Descartes was thus able to proceed in the project of knowing the world with confidence, having doubted all that was susceptible to doubt, and having identified in the process (he believed) a slight but nonetheless sufficient foundation upon which to build an indubitable account of the nature of things, a project in which he now enthusiastically immersed himself. As numerous commentators have observed, however, his success was obtained only at a very high price. He had on the one hand conceded the fundamental dubiety of sense experience as a guide to reality, and banished faith as a disposition worthy of the responsible knower; and on the other hand, by adopting his own beloved mathematics as a paradigm, he had established standards for knowledge which the market ultimately proved incapable of sustaining. For those who, for one reason or another, could not accompany him on his particular route to the reconstruction of knowledge, what Descartes left behind him was a veritable Slough of Despond in which no absolutely firm footholds were to be found, and where the only alternative seemed to be a refusal to commit oneself to any one spot for very long for fear of sinking without trace. It was not long, therefore, before his influential quest for absolute certainty begat its opposite: the despairing conclusion that there was none to be had, and the shutting up of humanity within the prison of its own experience. As we shall see, the spectre of Descartes' evil demon, once summoned forth, was not exorcized quite so readily as he himself had intended.

From the Spectators' Gallery to the Hall of Mirrors

Galileo, as we have seen, was among those whose scientific hypotheses and discoveries served to open up a gap between the world as we perceive it ordinarily and 'as it really is' when things are viewed with the assistance of such scientific instruments as the microscope and the telescope. To cite the words of Democritus once again, 'by convention coloured, by convention sweet, by convention bitter, *in reality* only atoms and the void'. Thus far we have allowed such phrases as 'in reality' and 'the world as it really is' to stand unchallenged. But the time has now come to call their bluff. On what grounds, we might legitimately ask, are we to accord such privileged status to the perspective granted us by the powers of magnification? Here, indeed, are two very different accounts of the world: the one granted us ordinarily by our five senses, and the other by a technology which allows us to see things from a different perspective altogether. But on what basis do we ascribe the status of 'the ways things really are' to the one view, and concede the inaccuracy or relative deception attaching to the other? Why is the view which the electron microscope provides of things to be thought of as the more authentic view (as if reality were only to be had by breaking things down into the smallest possible bits), and the view which the ordinary operation of our eyes and fingers and so forth gives (with its colour and texture and taste and sound and smell) a deception? Or why should the view of the Sun in its relationship to the Earth granted from the Earth's own surface be considered 'misleading,' while the view of that relationship as imagined from the Sun itself is accepted as the correct account of things? If it be argued that our senses are prone to deceive us, then we must remind ourselves that neither the microscope nor the telescope grants us the possibility of avoiding this risk. We still have to look through them. What we are given in each case is an alternative set of sensory data to that which we ordinarily receive. Things look different. We are allowed to see them from a new perspective. But why should we insist that this new perspective grants us access to reality as it really is, while the more familiar outlook distorts or conceals that reality to some extent? The answer is not at all obvious.

It Depends on Your Point of View

It may help us to grasp this point if we choose rather more mundane illustrations of it.[7] We are all well aware of the fact, for example, that size is a quality which appears to change as we alter our perspective. According to authoritative guide books, the magnificent tower of Durham Cathedral stands some 218 feet high. Yet approaching the city from the south and catching an initial glimpse of the building on the horizon it really seems much smaller than this; so small, in fact, that if you hold your hand up in front of your face the distant tower appears only half the size of your index finger! Even from closer in the tower appears bigger, but not the full 218 feet specified by the guide book. In fact, the truth is that the tower appears to have many different heights, depending on where you stand as you view it. Of course, it will be responded, this is simply a trick of perspective with which we are all quite familiar. But there we go again making the gratuitous assumption that there is some sort of ready distinction to be drawn between these various 'perspectival' views and heights, and the 'actual' or 'true' or 'genuine' height of the tower. This, we probably assume, is to be had by one brandishing appropriate measuring apparatus directly alongside the tower itself, by running a very long tape measure, perhaps, from top to bottom of it. But is this not also just one more 'perspective', another 'point of view'? Of course it is. It happens to be the perspective which (of the many available to us) for practical purposes most of us would recognize as granting a true or accurate account of the height of the tower. But we must also recognize that there is no absolute necessity about this. So long as we are all agreed upon which perspective should be granted this privileged status, we shall be able to agree on the tower's true dimensions. But such agreement might be held to be a matter of scientific (and hence culturally relative) convention, and the conclusion reached, therefore, that there is no absolute 'true height' but only a variety of perspectives from among which one may by choice be selected as granting the 'agreed true height'.

A similar phenomenon may be observed in the case of shape. If we consider, for example, a one pound coin then most of us would be agreed that its shape is circular. But is it? Again, the strict answer seems to be that it rather depends which angle we look at it from. From two particular angles, that directly and vertically above and below the coin's two sides, its shape does indeed conform to the geometrical expectations we have of circles. We do not have to alter our point of view very far, however, before this changes, and what we see is not a circle at all but an ellipse. In actual fact almost every time that we view the coin in the course of our ordinary dealings with it, it appears to us to be some other shape than circular. Why, then, do we insist that it is circular? Again, we might say that most of the time we are subject to the optical illusions created by perspective. But again, what we mean when we say this is that the coin has a different shape when viewed from a perspective other than that which we have singled out (not one which most of us ordinarily occupy particularly often) and which we treat as in some way special.

Where this leads us, then, is to the suggestion that in the strictest sense these qualities which we perceive in objects in the world vary depending on the perspective which we adopt. They are, that is to say, relative to ourselves as those who perceive them, to our 'point of view'. The recognition that this is so led some philosophers in the decades after Descartes to account for it by insisting that such qualities (size, shape, texture, smell, sound and so on) were not really 'out there' in the external world at all, but rather were in the mind of the individual knower. What we 'know', in other words, are images or sensations produced in our minds, rather than the actual things themselves 'out there' which (it might be supposed) cause these sensations. If we look at something from one angle or position, the picture that we get of it, what we 'see' as we would say, can be markedly different from the view afforded by another (even if we are looking at the very same aspect of the object). What we 'see' has changed. But we would nor ordinarily suppose that the thing itself has changed; so we must admit immediately that what we 'see' is not simply identical with 'the thing itself as it really is' This, John Locke argued, is because what we 'see' is not the thing itself but rather a representation or appearance of the thing which our brain produces when certain stimuli are supplied by our sensory organs. Such representations will vary according to our closeness to the object, the angle from which we view it and so on, while the thing itself remains unchanged. A similar situation pertains with regard to our other senses. The proximity of flame to our skin produces in our minds the idea of heat, which may be accompanied by an idea of bright yellow or orange transmitted by our eyes, and perhaps an idea of the crackling sound of a fire burning supplied by our ears, and the idea of the smell of smoke by our nose. This is certainly not the way in which most of us think about our daily experience of the world, and at first sight it may appear to us to be an unnecessarily complicated account. But a few moments' reflection shows us that it is granted a certain amount of support by physiological descriptions of how our eyes, ears and so on actually work.

Reality ... Virtually

When we say that we 'see' something, physiologists tell us, what we are actually referring to is a complex process in which light waves travel from an object to our two eyes, casting two slightly different images onto our two retinas, from whence information is borne by the optic nerves to our brain where the two bits of data are unscrambled and coordinated, and a single image (identical with neither of the two) of the object results. This process takes time. In the ordinary run of things the time involved is a mere fraction of a second, but time has nonetheless elapsed between the departure of the light waves from the object and the perception of that object by our brain. Theoretically speaking, in the meantime the object itself may have ceased to exist. This may sound ridiculous, and indeed it probably is where most of our visual experience is concerned. But when we see a distant star scientists tell us that the light waves which stimulate our organs of sight may have taken millions of years to reach our planet, and that the star from which they once departed has very likely burned out long since. In this case, then, what we are seeing can hardly be the star itself, although we happily speak as though it were. The difference here is one of degree alone, and the same qualification must be applied to our 'seeing' of all the things around us. Similar accounts could be developed with regard to the other senses. Touch, for example, where, physicists tell us, what I feel as I press the keys of my word processor with my fingertips is not those keys themselves as I might ordinarily suppose. Strictly speaking my fingers never make direct contact with those keys. Rather, what I 'feel' is the result of a series of electrical repulsions between the atoms which are my finger and the atoms which are the keyboard. These are conveyed to my brain by the nerves in my hand and arm, and my 'feeling' of the keys is the result. But in actual fact the same 'feeling' can be produced in the absence of any object, so long as the relevant nerves are stimulated in the proper way.

Given that this is so, where does it leave us? If we are to believe Locke's account, it leaves us having to admit that our sensory engagement with the world is at best indirect. There are, as it were, three factors involved: our minds, the world 'out there', and in between the two the mediating 'representations' or 'ideas' supplied by our sensations. For Locke, what the mind knows is the ideas, these having been created or caused or stimulated by objects in the real world. But, once a gap has been opened up in this way between the content of our knowledge and the world 'out there', the question very soon arises as to the precise relationship between the two, and the reliability or truth, therefore, of what we know. After all, on Locke's account of the matter, we never know the 'real world' itself; we simply infer its existence from the contents of our experience. Furthermore, Locke himself (following Galileo at this point) argued that many of the qualities which we perceive in objects are not really out there in the external world at all, but are supplied by our minds as part of the process of knowing. The following quotation from Whitehead draws out the uncomfortable conclusions of such a view:

> Thus the bodies are perceived as with qualities which in fact are purely the offspring of the mind. Thus nature gets credit which should in truth be reserved for ourselves: the rose for its scent: the nightingale for his song: and the sun for his radiance. The poets are entirely mistaken. They should address their lyrics to themselves, and should turn them into odes of self-congratulation on the excellency of the human mind. Nature is a dull affair, soundless, scentless, colourless; merely the hurrying of material, endlessly, meaninglessly.[8]

Trapped Within our own Subjectivity?

But more radical conclusions still were to follow. The Scots philosopher David Hume (1711–1776) took up Locke's account of the nature of human knowledge and pushed it rigorously through to its natural conclusion. If, he mused, we only ever have an indirect knowledge of the external world, so that what we actually *know* is not that world itself but rather the representations of it which arise in our mind, then it follows that we can never be certain that these representations are reliable, or render an accurate account of the world 'out there'. For all we know the world might be utterly different from what our senses tell us, and we should never know, because we have no way of comparing our ideas with the things of which they are representations. We cannot check the copy against the original. We are, as it were, trapped behind our ideas, which serve to conceal the external world from us just as surely as they might be reckoned to reveal it to us. It was at this point, as we have seen, that Descartes attempted to save the day by appealing to certain foundational rational truths which serve to enable us to sneak a glance at 'the real world' by telling us how it must necessarily be, a mental spectators' gallery from which to obtain a privileged view. But Locke and Hume rejected this account of things. As far as they were concerned human knowledge had only one source, namely, that which sense experience supplies to the mind. There were no universal and eternal truths of reason to fall back upon. The consequences of this stringent empiricism were far-reaching, for what Hume was forced to concede was that, since the mind of the knower could never penetrate beyond the ideas or representations of reality granted by the senses, and since there was no basis for speaking of genuine knowledge of anything which was not granted in experience, in the strictest sense there could be no knowledge of the world 'out there' at all. Indeed, there was no real warrant, no need, to posit the existence of such a world. All that the mind knows, in other words, is its own contents, the ideas rendered by the senses. Beyond this veil it cannot trespass.

But if there is no 'external world', or, more properly, if we can never know that there is such a world or what it is like, then, of course, the question of truth becomes highly problematic. There are many ways of defining 'truth', but one with a highly respectable pedigree views it as entailing a correspondence between what humans think or say about the world on the one hand, and the way the world actually is on the other. A true thought or statement, in other words, is one which corresponds in some sense with the way things really are. But if we can never have access to 'the way the world actually is', if, perhaps, there is no such thing as the 'real world', then there can be absolutely no verifying of the truth or falsity of our thoughts or perceptions, for there is nothing with which to compare them. We are effectively incarcerated within our experience which, for all we know, may be all there is. We are left with the lurking fear that 'reality as we know it' or as it appears to us may be no more than a breathtaking virtual reality game fashioned by the computer of our minds. We are like someone confined in a hall of mirrors where, no matter where we stand or where we look, all that we see is one reflection or another of the contents of our own minds. The world itself has disappeared from view, and all that we are left with is a series of more or less distorted images of our own making. In such a circumstance truth cannot but become a matter of 'the way things appear to me'. Every perspective must be acknowledged as just as true as any other, for there is no accessible source of comparison against which any particular point of view can be tested. Truth must consequently be redefined in terms of the coherence of the accounts which the mind renders to us, rather than appealing to some alleged correspondence of those accounts with the world lying (hidden) beyond them.

The Mind as the Maker

One more player on the philosophical stage must be considered in setting the stage for the peculiarly modern crisis of knowledge. It was the genius of Prussian-born Immanuel Kant (1724–1804) to take up and fuse together the several insights of the rationalism of Descartes and the empiricism of Hume in an attempt to avoid the major weaknesses in each. He strove to furnish an account of human knowledge which would provide a basis for confident dealings with the world, while yet recognizing the genuine limits of the powers of human reason. The story which he tells has exercised a profound influence over the modern age, so that even those who have never heard of him, let alone read any of his works, can reasonably be said to have had their understanding of things affected by Kant.

Unlike Hume, Kant subscribed to Descartes' view that the human mind brings to the process of knowing a set of basic truths which it knows innately, which are part of its own structure and make-up. Descartes, as we have seen, saw this as a safeguard against the possible deceptions to which sense experience might subject us.

But Kant believed that there was already a fairly good correspondence between the principles of reason and our sensory experience of the world. The world of our experience is, in other words, pretty much as our mind tells us in advance it ought to be. The senses are a rather more reliable guide to the nature of things than Descartes' extreme scepticism had allowed. There are occasions, certainly, when first appearances need to be corrected and tested by the dictates of reason, but these form the exception rather than the rule.

Thus the scientist, for example, whose profession involves both the framing of rational hypotheses and their subsequent verification under experimental conditions, finds more often than not that the behaviour of things in the world conforms rather well to the general 'laws' which she has formulated in advance by thinking things through. But this predictive power of science raises a question which, due to our familiarity with and acceptance of science as a reliable guide to the world, it would be very easy for us to overlook. Just why should it be the case that there is this close correspondence between reason and experience? Why should our minds be capable of rendering up to us in advance of our actual experience of the world a picture of how the world actually is? Was Copernicus's daring hypothesis simply a remarkable piece of imaginative coincidence, or a genuine insight into the inherent rationality of the universe, granted to him in advance of any possible sensory verification, by his mind? Kant accepted that it was the latter, and was thus faced with the question which we have articulated. One possible answer, perhaps, might be that God, the creator and fashioner of all things, the source of the Logos or reason of all things, had granted human minds, themselves created in his image, a degree of access to the blueprint of his grand design. Some such version of things was inherent in certain strands of rationalism, and was attractive to many as a resolution of the riddle. It was not, however, the answer which Kant gave.

Sense Experience is Edited Rather Than Raw

Kant's answer to the problem took its point of departure in a denial of the terms in which it was ordinarily cast. We do not deal, he argued, with the evidence of our senses on the one hand, and that of our reason on the other, as Descartes had suggested. Sense experience is not to be considered an independent source of information about the world at all, but is rather a composite product in

41

which that which enters the mind from beyond it is, in the process, sorted and shaped, has form imposed upon it, and is modelled by the mind in accordance with the principles or categories of reason. He concluded that sense experience conforms to the principles of reason precisely because reason itself has already operated upon it and stamped it with its own rational form! In becoming our experience it has undergone a treatment in which our mind 'acts as a lawgiver to nature, prescribing to the world we know the forms and conditions under which it shall appear to us'.[9]

Here, then, we have a model of human knowledge in which the active role of the human mind is stressed to the utmost. The order and beauty which we perceive in the world are not the fruits of God's good creation; they are in fact the product of our own minds, which impose structure on the universe rather than discovering it there. What the mind knows, therefore, is not the world itself, but the product of a transaction between reality and the mind, a heavily processed version of the world out there, rather than the raw reality itself. Here Kant agrees with Hume, and is utterly sceptical about our capacity to know the world 'as it is in itself'. Indeed his philosophy insists that we do not do so, since what we know is a massively edited version of reality.

Kant's intention, however, was, like Descartes' before him, precisely to rescue humans from the sort of philosophical scepticism engendered by Hume and others, and to grant them a view of things not subject to the fluctuations of changing points of view. At one level his philosophy denied humans access to any privileged view of 'things as they are in themselves', locking them firmly into the perspective granted by their minds. At the same time, however, he insisted that all human minds were structured in the same way and employed the same conceptual apparatus; therefore the view of things which they granted was one which could be treated effectively as a universal and objective standpoint. Given, that is to say, that what I experience of the world is not identical with the world itself but rather a product of my mind acting upon the world, what I can nonetheless be sure of is that all other peoples' minds will be acting upon the world in precisely the same way, applying to it the very same principles of reason, and that the world in which we live, the view of things which we indwell, will therefore be the very same one. Even if I am, in effect, participating in a vast virtual reality package, then, just so long as everyone else is participating in the same game and playing by the precise same rules, the notion of truth and falsity can be reintroduced with impunity. Truth is more than a matter of 'the way things seem from where I stand'. For in practice where I stand – the world as I see it – is also where everyone else stands, even if it is not strictly 'the world as it is in itself', whatever that might be. Thus we can agree about the 'facts' of the matter – which is to say, the way in which all our minds present a certain aspect of the world to us. The universal categories of human reason, therefore, function to provide and underwrite an agreed perspective from which questions of truth and falsity may be posed and answered, and claims to truth proved and disproved.

Kant placed one serious limitation upon all this, and it was one which has seeped to the very roots of our society's consciousness, and which has particularly damaging implications for theology. Reason, he informed us, is capable of rendering certain factual knowledge of this sort, but only within specific boundaries, namely, those laid down by the limits of our sense experience. Nothing which is not given to us in a sensory manner, therefore, can be granted the imprimatur of our reason, or deemed factual, or a part of our knowledge as such. We can never be sure of it or demonstrate it, and therefore it must be classified altogether differently as part of that realm where 'faith' is operative. Kant did not intend this as a criticism. He simply viewed certain sorts of human engagement with reality as of a different sort, and as falling outside the remit of human reason. Religious faith was precisely such a category. Engagement with God, he insisted, was not of such a sort as to be susceptible either to proof or disproof by reason. It had nothing to do with 'factual' claims, but rather was of a more direct, intuitive and moral variety. It was a relationship with an absolute moral reality, and not an indirect mental encounter with the physical world. In this 'making room for faith' as he himself put it, however, Kant effectively removed theology from the sphere in which rational discourse and argument is deemed appropriate. The fruit of this in the modern age has been the bifurcation in human understanding between what is deemed to be real knowledge (the testable 'facts' of our experience and truths of reason) on the one hand, and that which is a matter of mere belief or faith on the other.

Are We All of Like Mind?

Kant's philosophy succeeded for a time in banishing the spectre of relativism and anxiety concerning the status of human knowledge of the world. Humans need no longer quest, as Descartes had done, for a 'God's-eye view' of things. After all, the world in which we 'live' is constructed not by God as such, but by the human mind. Thus the perspective provided by our minds is every bit as good as a God's-eye view. It is precisely a view through the eyes of the maker! Kant, as we have said, believed that this perspective was necessarily identical in every case, that the innate concepts which each mind would bring to bear on things provided a universal constant, thereby furnishing us with a firm basis for making and testing truth claims.

It was not long, however, before this inherently untestable assumption was called into question, and the demon doubt let loose to plague us once more. Perhaps, it was suggested, the world constructed by human minds is not the same in every case; perhaps the concepts or rational tools which it employs in its creative task are not universal but rather vary from time to time, place to place, culture to culture; so that in a very real sense we live in very different worlds depending on our particular historical and cultural location. Maybe the way in which we understand and see the world is not a universal 'given', as Kant supposed, but is determined by the particular story which our culture tells concerning the world and its structure and direction. The most obvious and straightforward means of refuting this suggestion would, of course, be to appeal to 'the way things really are', a direct demonstration of the truth. But this is precisely what Kant's whole philosophy denies us.

The two centuries since Kant have witnessed huge strides forward in our knowledge of human existence past and present. What we have learned does little to bolster his optimistic universalism. Very often it is the fundamental differences between what various human groups treat as reasonable belief or acceptable behaviour which strike us most forcefully. The attempt by philosophers, moralists, historians and anthropologists alike to identify principles of reason and ethics undeniable by any rational person has failed to produce agreed results. Instead what emerges is a virtual Babel of diverse and confusing signals concerning the true and the good. Thus it is that in the modern age we frequently find it suggested that the ideal of a universal, testable, and therefore certain knowledge is little more than a will-o'-the-wisp, and to pursue it is simply a waste of time. More radical still is the despairing claim that there is no truth. In the words of the influential German philosopher Frederick Nietzsche, 'truth is fiction', and our world and its standards are precisely what we make them, their meaning a value with which we invest them, and so on. Each human community tells its own story, invents its own version of the world for itself to live in. Rationality and morality are historically and socially context-bound, precisely because each community fashions and develops its own, just as it fashions and develops its own language. Indeed, according to the more radical representatives of so-called postmodern thought, not only are these various world views not the same, they are utterly incompatible. As Brian Hebblethwaite puts it, 'The world as it is in itself has disappeared behind a whole set of different culturally determined screens'.[10] In such an environment the rational means for adjudicating between competing outlooks is missing, and the potential for conflict and tribal self-assertion fills the vacuum.

And so we arrive back from our survey of the philosophical developments in what has become known as the Age of Enlightenment to consider the present day with its various attitudes and assumptions about life. In what is admittedly an eclectic and sweeping summation, we may identify once again two main strands in the mind-set of modernity, both of which manifestly emerge from this complex philosophical flux. Each presents in its own way a significant challenge to faith as an intellectually respectable disposition in our society, and to theology as a discipline pursued openly on the basis of the same.

On the one hand we find those who would demand of us that before we invest ourselves in any claim to truth, or before we can reasonably expect them to do so, we should be able to provide the factual or logical evidence which will render such 'belief' reasonable. There is, in many quarters, a profound Cartesian scepticism abroad that refuses to place its foot on any surface which will not bear the weight of resolute certainty. We want to be able to put our hand into the broken side of reality before we will say 'I believe'. We want 'the facts' clearly presented, and strive to clear away the accumulated detritus of interpretations, personal judgements and perspectives, to dissolve with the acids of doubt all untestable beliefs and assumptions. We must attain to an objective viewpoint, and see things 'as they really are' for ourselves before we will commit ourselves. We are eager to meet the expectations of the Enlightenment, and to take responsibility for our knowledge, not taking anyone else's word for it, but testing all things in person. This view we may refer to as *objectivism*.

Then, on the other hand, there are those who, having become utterly disillusioned with the quest for certainty, and viewing it as a failed attempt, have instead embraced *relativism* as their absolute. For these there is no truth except that which each community (or in extreme cases each person) creates for itself. There are no 'facts' which are not already polluted by interpretation, discredited as the products of a trade-off between mind and world. There are no universal truths of reason to compensate for this. There are only perspectives, yours and mine and the next person's, and who knows which, if any, is better than the others? The only thing which is certain is that nothing is certain!

For neither of these outlooks, we should remind ourselves, is the profession 'I believe x to be true' tolerable. For the one it fails to meet the basic criteria for acceptance by intelligent human beings; for the other it constitutes a piece of dogmatic arrogance, an attempt to foist one's own chosen outlook upon an unsuspecting world, to absolutize or universalize what is and can only ever be one perspective on things. Both outlooks, ironically, constitute the very opposite of what they claim for themselves. Both, that is to say, represent in practice an abdication of personal responsibility for knowledge. The one simply shrugs its shoulders and says, 'Don't blame me. It's obvious – just consider the facts of the case for yourself.' The other, throwing its hands in the air, entreats: 'How should I know? Truth is what you make it, so just do your own thing!'

There is a third way, however, a way which truly involves us in taking responsibility for our knowledge. As well as being a more satisfactory model for human knowing, this alternative way of knowing provides an intellectual atmosphere in which Christian theology as 'faith seeking understanding' may take its place and where faith in Christ may hold its head high as a respectable standpoint from within which to view and to participate in life in the world today. It is to this third way, steering between the equally unpalatable and impossible options of objectivism and relativism, absolute certainty and despairing scepticism, that we turn in our next chapter.

NOTES

1 Dampier, W., *A History of Science and its Relations with Philosophy and Religion* (Cambridge University Press 1946), p. 123.

2 Arendt, H., *The Human Condition* (Chicago University Press 1958), p. 260.

3 Galileo, *Sidereus Nuncius* (1610), cited from Alexandre Koyré, *From the Closed World to the Infinite Universe* (1957), p. 89 in Arendt, *The Human Condition*, p. 260.

4 Galileo took his discoveries to the papal court in Rome and in 1616, after a clash with the essentially conservative authorities there, he was formally silenced and detained, and the Copernican view pronounced 'false and opposed to Holy Scripture'. Not until 1822, some two centuries later, was the Sun finally granted freedom by the Pope to take up its legitimate place at the centre of the solar system! (See Dampier, *A History of Science*, p. 124.)

5 From *Rules for the Direction of the Understanding*, cited in 'Descartes', *Dictionary of Philosophy* (Pan Books 1979), p. 89.

6 I am indebted to Bishop Lesslie Newbigin for this metaphor.

7 With apologies to C. E. M. Joad for having borrowed and adapted his very helpful account of this matter. See Joad, C. E. M., *Guide to Philosophy* (Victor Gollancz 1936), pp. 26–30.

8 From Whitehead, A. N., *Science and the Modern World*, cited in Joad, *Guide to Philosophy*, p. 40.

9 Joad, *Guide to Philosophy*, p. 368.

10 Hebblethwaite, B., *The Problems of Theology* (Cambridge University Press 1980), p. 75.

— 3 —

Admiring the View from Nowhere

Give me the facts, Ma'am, just the facts!
Joe Friday in Dragnet

Facts, like telescopes and wigs for gentlemen, were a seventeenth century invention.
Alasdair MacIntyre

In this chapter I shall draw in particular on the philosophy of Michael Polanyi and Alasdair MacIntyre, both of whom have sought to steer a course between the Scylla of objectivism and the Charybdis of relativist pluralism in their attempts to give an account of the nature of human rational activity. Both, in their distinct ways, have submitted the Enlightenment quest for an absolute objectivity to a rigorous examination, finally abandoning it as inherently futile. It is the quest for a 'view from nowhere' as the American philosopher Thomas Nagel has called it. Yet both Polanyi and MacIntyre remain fundamentally committed to the notion of truth, and to human knowledge as the search for it. Each refuses to concede the relativist claim that the only alternative to absolute certainty is the absolutizing of uncertainty. Neither is content to acquiesce in the redefinition of truth as a relative quantity definable in terms of coherence within a particular system of beliefs, rather than correspondence in some sense with reality.

What is fascinating (and what makes their respective treatments potentially fruitful for Christian theology) is that in their accounts of the nature of human rational activity as a meaningful engagement with reality, each finds himself driven to introduce and to employ in central roles categories which have long since been discredited and thrust aside in the mainstream of modern discussion, and effectively banished from the sphere of public truth. Thus MacIntyre's account centres around the notion of critical rational activity as something which takes place within the life and development of an authoritative tradition, while Polanyi focuses rather upon the categories of personal commitment and belief as integral to all truly rational and 'objective' knowledge. Both men borrow these categories quite explicitly from their use within the Christian theological tradition and employ them to furnish a way out of the dead end into which they see modern philosophical discussion as having got itself. Thus in drawing upon their thought we are not engaged in any simple borrowing of materials from philosophy in order to construct or bolster a model of Christian theology. This is not a case of philosophy calling the tune and theology dancing. Rather, we are reclaiming insights and emphases once borrowed from Christian theology, but which, in the climate of modernity, theologians themselves have too often been afraid to own. For their safekeeping, development and eventual return therefore, we must acknowledge our indebtedness to philosophy.

We might sum up the central aspiration of the European Enlightenment as an attempt to provide all humans with a clear set of standards and methods for determining what, in a given situation, might merit rational or moral justification. What, in other words, is it 'reasonable' to believe or to do? Which course of action would a reasonable person embark upon in this circumstance, or to which set of beliefs might they commit themselves? Armed with such principles, it seemed, men and women would be able to take responsibility for their own actions and beliefs, guided by the inerrant light of that which any reasonable person could accept or tolerate. The process whereby these universal principles of reason or justice were to be arrived at involved a conscious effort to transcend or to strip away the things which differentiated one physical, historical, cultural or social context and outlook from another. Layers of the onion of personal particularity were gradually to be peeled away until the universal, absolutely certain heart of human rationality and morality was laid bare. As we have already indicated, however, it proved in practice incredibly difficult to secure lasting agreement about just what was left once this process had been completed. When exactly should the peeling cease? And what did what was left actually look like? The disagreements which raged back and forth on this matter have led many to conclude that the quest was a worthless one, that there is no universal core of shared human rationality and morality; that when the last layer of the onion is peeled away what is discovered is the disturbing truth that there is nothing left.

Passion and Scientific Procedure

Nonetheless, the ideal of a knowledge untainted by the vagaries of specific historical and cultural location, unpolluted by the potentially distorting effects of any particular human perspective, prejudice, or framework of interpretation remains alive and well in our society. It is preserved above all in the popular conception of the methods of the natural sciences, methods which are in turn exalted as role models for a responsible approach to knowing in our society. As Polanyi (himself a scientist) observes, the picture of scientific activity painted by the popular myth-makers of our day is of an essentially dispassionate approach to reality. White-coated men and women engage patiently in a process in which the workings of the natural world are observed, and data gathered and catalogued in an impartial manner. Experiments are carried out and facts garnered under carefully controlled conditions from which all potentially distorting factors are excluded. Then 'laws' and theories are formulated which amount in practice to little more than 'a mere economical description of facts'.[1] These descriptions serve on the one hand as a convenient record of the substance of past experience, and on the other to enable us to compute the likely future course of events.

Here, then, it seems, is an approach to knowing in which there is no room for distortion, no room for deception, for the misappropriation or misrepresentation of facts through the distortions of personal prejudice or privately held convictions. In the strict sense, the scientist can take little personal responsibility for the results. She simply observes, reports what she sees in an objective way, and then weaves the pieces together into a descriptive narrative about the sort of place the world in which we live is, and the sorts of things which routinely happen in it. The story she tells is one which can be tested and verified by agreed methods. Here, surely, is objectivity of the sort which the Enlightenment craved?

This conception of objective knowing owes much to the Kantian tradition. It views 'facts' as things which are simply given to the knower as part of a universally accessible human experience. The facts of the case simply are what they are, whoever we are and whatever our outlook or background or other beliefs may happen to be. Facts are there to be collected, collated, and then made sense of. The latter procedure (what we would call interpretation) invites a degree of variation and possible conflict of results, since it introduces the factor of human subjectivity; but so far as our dealings with the facts themselves are concerned we can be content that there is a basic objectivity involved. Facts are facts, the same for you and me and the next person, the guaranteed pre-reflective, pre-interpretative, pure data afforded us by experience. To the extent that we can base our rational activity on these universally recognizable units of experience, therefore, and purge our procedures to the greatest possible degree of the pollutants of perspective, prejudice, passion and unproved assumptions, we shall attain to that objectivity in knowledge which alone furnishes the road to light and truth. It is the scientist, together, perhaps, with a handful of others such as the historian and the detective ('Give me the facts, Ma'am, just the facts') who in our society are perceived as coming closest in their everyday activities to this ideal of an impersonal, detached and truly objective knowledge.

Knowing as a Skill

Polanyi is unrelenting in his attack on this myth of scientific objectivity. Neither the scientist in the laboratory nor anyone else, he insists, is ever in the position of being merely a neutral and passive receptor of guaranteed pure data of the sort which this picture suggests. Reality is not handed to us on a plate in this way, as if our only responsibility in the act of knowing were to preserve it unspoiled. On the contrary, every act of knowing, in science or elsewhere, is an *action* which requires skill. In order to do it properly we have to use various physical, conceptual and linguistic 'tools', we are frequently required to make fine judgements, and to commit ourselves to procedures, suppositions and results. As an activity of this sort, knowing is a process the outcome of which cannot be guaranteed. Its success depends on the knower's own contribution to a considerable extent. There is always the risk of failure, and the results are never of a sort sufficient to generate absolute certainty. There is a built-in contingency related directly to the 'personal coefficient' as Polanyi calls it.

The Scientist as Visionary

Where the activity of the scientist is concerned, we may identify several levels at which this personal coefficient is evident. An essential part of the formulation of scientific theories is the ability to discern or intuit the existence of patterns of order, or intrinsic rationality, in nature; an intuition which subsequently forms the basis of experiments and tests designed to verify its tentative claims. In this sense scientific theories provide a starting point for fresh scientific activity, and not just a conclusion or description of past experience. But, try as we might, this ability to recognize pattern or form cannot be construed as an essentially impersonal or passionless objective procedure. Polanyi describes it thus:

> The discovery of objective truth in science consists in the apprehension of a rationality which commands our respect and arouses our contemplative admiration; ... such discovery, while using the experience of our senses as clues, transcends this experience by embracing the vision of a reality beyond the impressions of our senses, a vision which speaks for itself in guiding us to an ever deeper understanding of reality.[2]

Once a theory is accepted by the scientific community, Polanyi notes, it is effectively invested with something resembling prophetic powers: 'We accept it in the hope of making contact with reality; so that, being really true, our theory may yet show forth its truth through future centuries in ways undreamed of by its authors.'[3] Notice the vocabulary that Polanyi uses here. The language of contemplation, of the embracing of a vision which enables us to transcend our mundane existence, of prophetic hope for a future fulfilment as yet unverifiable or unrealizable, of obedience to the demands of a reality which stands over against us yet cannot be demonstrated beyond doubt. The capacity for pattern recognition is described in ways which remind us of an aesthetic sensibility or satisfaction. All this is the sort of language familiar to us from various human contexts, including religious and liturgical ones; but not, perhaps, language which we would ordinarily associate with the pursuit of scientific goals and the employment of scientific methods.

Picking Up the Tools of the Trade

Once a theory or vision has been formulated, then the process of attempted verification or falsification must begin, and here at last in our imagination the scientist dons the obligatory white coat, enters the laboratory, and gets to grips with test-tubes, microscopes and all the paraphernalia associated with 'objective' experimental procedures. But even here Polanyi will not allow our imagination to proceed untroubled. To be sure, the scientist proceeds to gather data, to examine the facts and to sort them. But at no point is this process an impersonal or dispassionate one.

Most of us, who are not specialists in a particular scientific field, faced with all this equipment and with the reality to be studied would also be faced with an insuperable obstacle – we simply would not know where to begin, what to look for or how to look for it, which tools to employ for which procedures, how to extract the desired information and measurements from them, and so on. And this fact in itself makes a significant point: namely, that the process of gathering data in any scientific field is one which requires a considerable degree of training, a body of assumed knowledge, and familiarity with established techniques and methods. In order to gather the data (the facts) efficiently, the scientist uses this collection of 'tools' in the manner prescribed by the scientific community in which he or she was trained. But the use of such tools is not straightforward or easy. There are often judgements to be made concerning which precise tool to employ in a specific circumstance, or in taking precise readings from highly sensitive and sophisticated instruments. The tools themselves, Polanyi alleges, become in effect an extension of the scientist's own personality in the engagement with reality. We are hardly conscious of them as we pick them up and use them, but take them for granted, trusting them as reliable and appropriate devices for gathering the required information. We can see from all this, then, that the process of observing and recording data in the laboratory, far from being an essentially passive or impartial process in which information presents itself and is duly logged, is in fact a highly complex procedure in which the personal elements of trust, commitment and judgement all find a significant place. 'Even the most strictly mechanised procedure,' writes Polanyi, 'leaves something to personal skill in the exercise of which an individual bias may enter'.[4]

Picking Up the Tricks of the Trade

Polanyi suggests that many of the practical skills of science must be 'caught rather than taught' as we might say. There is something non-specifiable and non-analysable about them, something which can be passed on from generation to generation of practitioners only by a process of discipleship, in the relationship which develops between master and apprentice, and not gleaned from reading even the best and most comprehensive books on the subject.

Reflection suggests that many things in life are like this. Why is it that Grandma's Yorkshire puddings, made according to a decades old formula which consists in 'a handful of this' and a 'dash of that,' always seem to rise to perfection and taste marvellous, while our best attempts to follow the precise specifications of expensive recipe books result in a sorry-looking and relatively tasteless substitute? What is the knack of riding a bicycle, or casting a fly, or executing a proficient golf swing? It is highly unlikely that any of the many thousands of people who do these things are aware of the scientific formulae pertaining to their successful performance. And even if they were, such knowledge would be of no practical use to them. For the truth is that the skill of doing these things consists in more than the sum of the various parts which such analysis might reveal. And it is learned only by following the example of a skilled practitioner, and then practising under their watchful eye until we become proficient, until the knack is discovered or the penny drops.

So it is also in many respects with the training which a scientist must undergo. But such learning (and therefore any activity which is subsequently based upon it) is, of course, anything but objective in the popular sense of that word. Let us hear Polanyi again:

> To learn by example is to submit to authority. You follow your master because you trust his manner of doing things even when you cannot analyse and account in detail for its effectiveness. By watching the master and emulating his efforts in the presence of his example, the apprentice unconsciously picks up the rules of the art, including those which are not known explicitly to the master himself. These hidden rules can be assimilated only by a person who surrenders himself to that extent uncritically to the imitation of another.[5]

There is no hint of a detached impartial, passionless attitude here, then; rather authority, submission, trust, contingency, risk and commitment are the words which describe what goes on.

Telescopes and Wigs for Gentlemen

This analysis of the tacit conditions attaching to scientific engagement with 'facts' can be applied to more familiar contexts. Knowing is *never* an impersonal transaction with the world, but *always* a skilful activity in which we are personally committed from beginning to end. Each of us brings ready-made frameworks of interpretation with us to what may seem to be the most straightforward acts of comprehension. These frameworks are not universal, but are determined by our personal particularity as participants in specific human communities, and persons with particular backgrounds, experiences and expectations.

We have already alluded to the way in which every act of sensory perception involves a complex process of interpreting data whether we are concious of it or not. Thus, the statement 'I see a copy of a newspaper on the table across the room' is a factual statement intended to assert something about the world beyond ourselves. But it is far from being unpolluted by the dross of assumption, interpretation and belief. What we 'see' is determined in large measure by the mental categories which we bring to bear on the sensory data. From the overall complex of such data presented to us we are able skilfully to isolate one part or another and to identify it as a discrete object – a newspaper, a table, or whatever. But this supposes a familiarity with such concepts, a judgement concerning their applicability to this particular experience, and a commitment to the verbal symbols 'newspaper' and 'table' as capable of conveying our meaning satisfactorily to others. Such things are not simply 'given'. In a society where neither newspapers nor tables were known, such a statement would be meaningless, and observers would not 'see' the same as we do. Their report of the facts would be correspondingly different to our own.

Similarly 'facts' require not only to be identified, but to be selected and classified. The vast bulk of things which happen to us or around us day by day are not likely to be listed when someone asks for an account of 'the facts'. As George Steiner has observed: 'To remember everything is a condition of madness.'[6] We are highly selective, presenting what we consider to be relevant or significant to the nature of their enquiry. But this entails factors of judgement and evaluation. Again, it is not a mere matter of relaying something which is obvious to all who care to look and see.

A skilled dentist, looking into the mouth of a patient, will 'see' far more than the patient himself is likely to observe by peering into the bathroom mirror. She knows what to look for, and recognizes the significance of certain visual indicators which most of us would overlook. The answer to the question 'What are the facts?' is determined in this and every case by knowing the relevant questions to put to reality, thereby sifting the wheat from the chaff. Similarly, the eye of a trained criminal investigator might reasonably be expected to 'see' all manner of things which the average observer of the scene of a crime would very likely miss. What we 'see', what is presented to us, and 'the facts', then, are not all the same thing. A fact is not simply a fact, obvious to anyone who is operating in a rational manner. To a considerable extent what we shall be able to identify as 'the facts' of a particular case will depend upon who we are, and what frameworks of understanding and meaning we bring to bear on that case. Fact and interpretation are, in this sense at least, inextricably intertwined.

Facts, then, are not the pre-theoretical, value-free, pure units of given 'public' experience that popular mythology would have us believe. Such 'straightforward facts' do not exist. They were, in MacIntyre's words, 'like telescopes and wigs for gentlemen … a seventeenth century invention'.[7] Real facts are already theory-laden, quarried from the mass of our experience via a complex process of interpretation, in reliance upon tools to which we entrust ourselves and through the exercise of skills upon the performance of which the success of our quest for knowledge depends. Furthermore, Polanyi argues, factual statements, far from being essentially neutral, are precisely statements about what we *believe* to be the case on the basis of such labours. There is no absolute certainty available, precisely because every act of knowing rests ultimately upon an uncritical acceptance of certain fundamental beliefs and commitments, and is to this extent inherently corrigible. Such commitments furnish the framework within which and the tools with which we exercise our capacity to know. Statements of fact are, in the final analysis therefore, statements rooted in personal commitment and not dispassionate observations. Every statement which takes the form 'x is true' may be recast as 'I believe that x is the case' without any change in meaning. In the one case the faith component of our knowing is explicit, whereas in the other it is hidden. A statement of fact which is not cast in this passionate mode is either a lie (i.e. we do not believe it to be true at all) or else a mere empty verbal formula which says nothing (from which we withhold commitment either way).

The person who seeks a neutral, impartial point of view craves the truth. But truth, Polanyi insists, 'is but the external pole of belief, and to destroy all belief would be to deny all truth'.[8] Put differently, belief is the foundation upon which every truth claim rests. You cannot have the one without the other, you can only deceive yourself into thinking that you have.

The Dogmatism of Doubt

Another vital element of Polanyi's critique of objectivism is his careful critique of the logical structure of doubt. The tendrils of Descartes' influence are long and all-embracing, and reach through the centuries into our own age with smothering effect. The contention that it is somehow more appropriate to doubt than to believe something which cannot be proven to be true is familiar to us. Scepticism is widely perceived to be more intellectually respectable than faith or trust in unproved claims. We are urged, in the absence of the demonstration necessary to convince us, to maintain an 'open mind' rather than sliding into a 'narrow' dogmatism. The transition from the Dark Ages to the age of Enlightenment is, in many people's minds, linked directly to the emergence of a 'mature' refusal to take anything on trust, and a concomitant willingness to doubt whatever cannot be demonstrated, this being the only route to firmly based and responsible knowledge. As Polanyi notes, programmatic scepticism of this sort is a logical corollary of objectivism. It consists in the attempt to distil off every voluntary component of belief until what remains is a pure residue of objectively demonstrable fact and logically necessary truth, the stuff of real knowledge.

The person who entrusts himself to the principle of doubt, then, claims thereby to classify his dispositions correctly, affording the status of knowledge only to those which are objective and publicly available. For the rest, which are in principle dubitable, the label 'mere belief' must suffice. Indeed, in its more rigorous forms, scepticism eschews belief altogether, and prides itself on a preference for holding no knowledge at all over the entertaining of essentially dubious claims.

Polanyi engages in an analysis of doubt which reveals the fallaciousness of this typical perception of it. His basic point is that doubt and faith, contradiction and affirmation manifest a logical equivalence. In other words, every expression of doubt is at one and the same time a statement of faith in something else. The sceptical statement 'I doubt P' can be restated in a positive form: either 'I believe not P' or 'I believe P is not proven.' But these statements provoke the question 'On what basis do you believe this?' The answer, Polanyi argues, invariably reveals some framework of suppositions or beliefs which, at the time of and for the purposes of doubting P, are not themselves doubted. They provide the conditions for doubting P (believing not P), but they are themselves not doubted. If they were, then the conditions for doubting P would be removed. And doubting these suppositions would itself inevitably take the form of a belief in some alternative to them, a belief which would in turn be based on some other set of faith commitments. Thus every doubt has a fiduciary structure and is rooted in a set of faith commitments which for so long as they support the doubt, cannot themselves be doubted. The branch upon which every doubt sits is a belief. To insist on chopping this branch off in the misguided attempt to assume a wholly uncommitted position can only result in self-referential destruction, as the initial doubt itself falls to the floor.

Thus it is quite impossible to exercise in practice the sort of thoroughgoing scepticism which some have sought and have exalted as an ideal. A mind genuinely open with respect to everything would, like a box with no sides, prove in the final analysis to be empty, quite incapable of containing anything, even doubts. The more we doubt, the more we are compelled to believe and to trust in order to do so. If we shift the focus of our doubting, then we shift our faith commitments to accommodate the process. By doubting one thing we thereby uphold the claim to truth of another. The very process of doubt itself entails the uncritical acceptance of and reliance upon whole frameworks of meaning, so that far from being an exercise of a purely objective nature it is, like every act of knowing, a complex procedure rooted in and founded on commitments of all sorts, most of them beyond the scope of our awareness. Thus Polanyi notes that a truly uncommitted stance of the sort aspired to by objectivism would inevitably reduce itself to silence, since the very language in which it articulates its disbelief consists in a set of linguistic tools the legitimacy and applicability of which for the task in hand is simply taken on trust, received from a tradition of use by a particular community. Indeed, we might press the point further and insist that thought itself, since it is so closely tied to linguistic forms, would have to be set aside until the verity of these forms could be established, on the basis of criteria which would themselves have to be tested, on the basis of criteria which ... and so on *ad infinitum*.

To doubt, then, is not to avoid unproved beliefs. On the contrary, such beliefs provide the basis on which doubt is founded, by which it is supported, and in terms of which it is formulated and articulated. The nearest approximation to detached objectivity that can be achieved, therefore, is the refusal to commit oneself at length to any fiduciary stance, the willingness to move from one set of commitments to another in order to avoid permanent association with any unproved beliefs. This is the relativist pluralist dilemma. Having discovered that the quest for a view from the spectators' gallery is a quest for a non-existent perspective (for a 'view from nowhere') such pluralists have opted to become citizens of nowhere, eschewing all truth claims and affirming the equal value of each and every different point of view as a suitable habitat from within which to search further. But those objectivists who advocate the method of the rigorous and systematic abandonment of faith commitments do so in the belief that a genuinely neutral terra firma awaits them at the end of the process, and with it truth. Polanyi's analysis suggests that they deceive themselves, and urges us not to be taken in. In practice, he notes, 'Philosophic doubt is ... kept on the leash and prevented from calling in question anything that the sceptic believes in, or from approving of any doubt that he does not share.'[9] What this means in effect is that the sceptic simply confuses his own chosen or assumed beliefs with a neutral and objective point of view. The spectators' gallery of his imagination proves in reality to be a stall in the market-place of faith commitments together with the rest of us. When, therefore, he advocates 'rational doubt' as the answer to the quest for truth, what he really means is that we should see things the way they really are if only we would accept rational beliefs like his own. What is desirous, Polanyi concludes, is that scepticism should own up and face up to its own fiduciary foundations, since, he suggests, 'A dogmatic orthodoxy can be kept in check both internally and externally, while a creed inverted into a science is both blind and deceptive.'[10]

Faith and the Structure of Critical Thinking

Polanyi's contribution to our discussion thus far has been to insist that the intellectual tradition stemming from Descartes' search for certainty has falsified our view of truth by driving a wedge between a falsely conceived ideal of objectivity (as utter detachment) on the one hand and fiduciary commitment (belief) on the other. This popular model exalts the provable and demonstrable as an ideal of true knowledge, and denigrates that which cannot be proven. But, Polanyi alleges, every act of human rationality is (in all the ways that we have listed) inevitably undergirded by a fundamental reliance upon unprovable beliefs and the uncritical assumption of tools and methods with which we approach reality and seek to make sense of it. All that objectivism does, therefore, is to force such beliefs underground, or to bury them and then to deny that they still constitute the ground upon which it stands. Thus Polanyi's aim is 'to restore to us once more the power for the deliberate holding of unproved beliefs',[11] the honest recognition that the basic structure of human rational activity is that of *fides quaerens intellectum* – faith seeking understanding. There is no absolute neutral standpoint from which to conduct rational inquiry and thereby secure guaranteed access to truth. The only view which is available to us as humans is the view from where we are, from within the parti-cular frameworks of commitments and assumptions which contribute to our particularity, and from within which we seek to engage meaningfully with the world. In Polanyi's language we 'indwell' these frameworks just as we indwell our own bodies, and we can no more step outside of them into some completely objective 'elsewhere' than we can step outside of our bodies, or double-check the account which our senses render to us of the world by comparing it with the way the world actually is. This does not mean that our engagement with reality is in some sense naive or uncritical. It does not mean that we shall settle for 'any old beliefs'. But it does mean that we must think again about the sort of thing a critical enquiry actually is.

The true nature of critical rational activity does not consist in the sort of complete abandonment of beliefs, assumptions and points of view that objectivism would have us believe. It cannot be totally open-ended, but needs certain fixed points of reference, limits and boundaries within which its explorations are to be confined. If, as the history of thought suggests, these fixed points are not (as Kant suggested they were) simply given to all humans in and with the structure of their minds, thereby supplying a universal uniformity to the structure and orientation of rational activity, then we must face up to the fact that they are supplied in other ways They issue from the communities in which we live, the literal and intellectual 'languages' which they speak and in which we are nurtured; and from the specific frameworks of meaning and understanding which we acquire along the way of life through education, training and personal experience of other sorts. These are fixed points our relationship to which is characterized not by detachment and certainty, but precisely by personal indwelling and trust or faith. We take them for granted, buy into them uncritically, use them without calling them into question. We can do no other. To do so would be irrational in the extreme. Critical thinking, then, proceeds precisely and inevitably on the basis of 'fundamental beliefs' held concerning the nature of things, and by employing tools and skills in a supremely personal way. As such it is by nature an essentially corrigible enterprise, and one for the results of which we must in the proper sense take our full share of responsibility.

The way in which we each see the world, therefore – the only way in which we are able to see it – is precisely as the view from where we are. It is supremely our view. We are not able to avoid this personal perspective or to exchange it for the view from nowhere. Polanyi concludes:

> We must now recognize belief once more as the source of all knowledge. Tacit assent and intellectual passions, the sharing of an idiom and of a cultural heritage, affiliation to a like-minded community: such are the impulses which shape our vision of the nature of things on which we rely for our mastery of things. No intelligence, however critical or original, can operate outside such a fiduciary framework.[12]

As we approach the world from within this 'system of acceptances that are logically prior' to all critical mental activity and necessary conditions of it, our fundamental beliefs are themselves continuously reconsidered. As we engage with reality, a dialectical process occurs in which reality is viewed in the light of our fundamental beliefs, and our beliefs in the light of reality. But, Polanyi insists, such reconsideration is of a sort which presupposes the truth of these beliefs, precisely because they constitute the system in terms of which our thought takes place at all. In order genuinely to call them into question we should have first (having identified them) to cease to employ them as fundamental beliefs, and to adopt some other set or system of beliefs in terms of which to conduct the enquiry. This might well prove to be possible; but we should remember that the result would not be an *objective* view of our beliefs, but simply the view of them afforded by others. Again we should remind ourselves that it is quite impossible for one person to compare someone else's view of things (or the beliefs on which this view rests) with the way things really are, but only with their own view of things.

Taking Stock of Tradition

We shall, in this chapter, treat the views of Alasdair MacIntyre only briefly, since the basic direction of his critique of objectivism coincides substantially with that of Polanyi which we have considered at length. We shall have rather more to say of his community and tradition-related account of rationality later.

While Polanyi emphasizes faith as the necessary condition of all rational activity, however, MacIntyre is concerned to affirm tradition as its inevitable context. The Enlightenment quest for an objective truth which would be neutral, impartial and genuinely universal was, he argues, doomed to eventual failure because it was the quest for a non-existent standpoint. In reality, all rational activity is rooted in a set of principles (cf. Polanyi's 'fundamental beliefs') the character of which is 'inescapably historically and socially context-bound'.[13] In short, therefore, the answer to the Enlightenment's agonized question 'What is rational?' is 'It depends who you are, and to which particular intellectual tradition you belong.' Thus the idea of a single set of things which 'no rational person can deny', so beloved of a certain sort of popular polemics fades away, and what emerges in its place is a series of 'rationalities' which are context-particular.

For MacIntyre, then, rational activity, critical questioning and the search for truth are to be approached not by hankering after 'the principles which a socially disembodied being would arrive at',[14] some universally knowable set of timeless truths abstracted from particular life contexts and employed as a sort of litmus paper to test the intellectual pH of our knowledge. We can only begin our quest for knowledge from where we are. The way in which critical inquiry really works, therefore, is from within a particular 'tradition', on the basis of a particular set of beliefs, commitments and practices which provide that inquiry with its rational basis and limits. Such inquiry, MacIntyre notes, is both tradition-constituted and tradition-constitutive. We inherit a standpoint, a point of view, from which to engage rationally with the world; but in the course of our inquiry, our posing and answering of questions, our tradition itself is carried forward and transformed. The principles which provide the fixed points of reference for a particular tradition, and in terms of which an inquiry is conducted within it, are not of a self-sufficient or self-justifying sort, the 'necessary truths' which Descartes sought after. They are themselves of such a sort as in principle require justification. Or, as Polanyi puts the same matter, they are essentially 'unproved beliefs'. But for the purpose of practical rational engagement these principles are assumed uncritically, and are questioned only within limits which they themselves have pre-scribed. To proceed otherwise, to call these principles themselves radically into account, to demand their explicit justification, one would have to abandon them as principles, and thereby step out-side one's own tradition. One might even evaluate them, not *objec-tively* of course, but in terms of some other tradition with its own assumed principles, its own index of what is rational and what is not. To do this is simply to view the world from somewhere else, from another available perspective, another point of view.

Particularity and Self-Transcendence

Both Polanyi and MacIntyre deliver a fierce and unrelenting attack upon the objectivist demand for 'plain facts' and 'demonstrable truths' established by wholly objective methods. Such truths, such facts, they assure us, are a will-o'-the-wisp pursued at the cost of time and valuable energy, and captured only at the expense of self-deception. But their respective accounts of human knowing force us to reckon with a significant problem. For in denying the exis-tence of any absolute or neutral standpoint, in dismissing the pos-sibility of there being any such 'view from nowhere', both are driven to concede *the perspectival nature of all our knowing*. There is, each affirms, no view of things available to us except that granted by the tradition within which we currently stand (Mac-Intyre) or the fiduciary framework which we indwell (Polanyi). But in this case, must we not face the fact that we are trapped inside or behind our beliefs, that our tradition cuts us off from any direct contact with reality itself? If we are sealed within our various frame-works of meaning and interpretation just as surely as we are con-tained within the physical particularity of our bodies, if we are not permitted to escape these in order to sneak some Cartesian glance at the real world by peering behind the screen, and if (as both Polanyi and MacIntyre insist) we are unable to appeal to some universal (and to that extent 'objective') Kantian truths of reason, then surely the battle with scepticism and relativism is already effectively lost? If we cannot escape the limits of perspective and gain access to a universal and certain truth then surely we must concede the claim that truth (if there is such a thing) is ultimately unknowable? This is the dilemma as it was posed in the seventeenth century, and as it has stood ever since. Either absolute rock-solid provable certainty, or else the miry swamp of despondent agnosticism. We must ask why we should agree to accept the terms of such a dilemma at all.

Impulse Towards the Impossible

Thomas Nagel notes that the impulse to transcend our particular personal point of view is supplied precisely by the recognition that it *is* a point of view, a perspective, and not simply an account of the way things are. 'The recognition that this is so,' he writes, 'creates pressure on the imagination to recast our picture of the world so that it is no longer the view from here'.[15] We want, in other words, to be sure that our perspective is not deceiving us, and so we aspire to 'the view from nowhere', to a view untrammelled by perspectival factors. This aspiration (which drove the Enlightenment), Nagel argues, is admirable enough. To submit unquestioningly to appearances would be the worst sort of intellectual stagnation and decay, and would be an abdication of our responsibility in the face of the truth. But (and it is a very big but) we must not confuse the only sort of self-transcendence available to us as humans – the ability to step outside our particular perspective and to enter (imaginatively, physically or whatever) into some other point of view in order to compare it with our own – with having discovered 'the view from nowhere'. This was the great mistake of the Enlightenment, and we should not continue to make it. Such a 'God's-eye view' of things would be convenient, and may continue to be an ideal which we keep in view to remind ourselves of our limitations. But it is a view which we cannot achieve. More importantly, it is not the only view which permits a genuine self-transcendence. There are many ways in which we are able to compensate for our particularity, and to transcend it by facing up to it and exploring other possible ways of seeing things. What we cannot do is to transcend it in any absolute manner, exchanging 'the view from here' for 'the view from nowhere' rather than 'the view from somewhere else'.

The Bid for a Better View of Things

One important point which Nagel makes is that the quest for self-transcendence is bound up logically with a realist account of human knowledge; that is, an account in which 'the universe and most of what goes on in it are completely independent of our thoughts',[16] and in which human knowing consists, therefore, in a gradual exploration of and accommodation of our minds to the structure of a complex reality which far transcends our capacity to think or speak of it. His point is simply that if scepticism or relativism are correct, then there is no need to try and transcend one's particular point of view, to evaluate its worth, since every point of view is as good or bad, as true or false as all the rest. Nagel's account of knowing, then, while it refuses to endorse the objectivist model of a detached and absolute certainty, is nonetheless one in which truth is something which may yet be aspired to and known. Self-transcendence is all about making progress in the bid for truth. But, he cautions, 'If truth is our aim, we must be resigned to achieving it to a very limited extent, and without certainty'.[17]

This, it seems to me, is very close to Polanyi's outlook. He too endorses the quest for self-transcendence or, as he puts it, the attempt to transcend our subjectivity. He too ties it closely to a realist account of knowledge in which we are engaged in 'establishing contact with a hidden reality; a contact that is defined as the condition for anticipating an indeterminate range of yet unknown (and perhaps yet inconceivable) true implications'.[18] But for Polanyi we transcend our subjectivity not by escaping it and fleeing to a detached spectators' gallery from which we can observe the relationship between our view of reality and reality itself, but rather by committing ourselves passionately to a particular standpoint as the best and most reliable route to reality known to us, a commitment which has, as he puts it, 'universal intent'.

Extending Ourselves into the World

Polanyi abandons the imagery of being trapped behind or within our particularity as unduly pessimistic. One of the characteristics of post-Cartesian models of human knowing has been their tendency to conceive of the human agent as an uncomfortable duality of mind and body in which the mind (the real knowing subject) is essentially passive, on the receiving end of a constant flow of data or ideas, and isolated from any direct engagement with the world by the barrier of the body. It is this view that bolsters the sceptic's case. We are trapped behind the appearances supplied to us by our senses, utterly reliant on second-hand testimony which we cannot verify, and so on. But Polanyi chooses a rather different image of the relationship between knower and knowledge. Knowing, he argues, is precisely an activity, not a passivity. It is an activity in which the human subject indwells and employs various tools in order to make contact with and explore the world. Thus our relationship to our body, for example, is one characterized not by the constant anxiety of one forced to rely upon an untrustworthy source of information, but rather the confidence with which a skilled practitioner employs his tools in practising the skills of his trade. Other 'tools' (and again we should recall that Polanyi understands by this *conceptual* and *linguistic* tools, as well as actual technology) with which we must operate in acquiring our knowledge do not act, therefore, as additional barriers, distancing us ever further from reality, but precisely as extensions of our bodies (and thereby ourselves) into the world which we 'indwell' in order to gain further access to reality. They are transparent rather than opaque. We view the world through them, just as we view it through a pair of spectacles. Or, to use a different picture which Polanyi himself suggests, we make contact with it just as a blind person makes contact with and explores the world through her white stick. The stick acts not as a barrier preventing access to the world, but as a gateway through which to enter it. We do not focus upon, and are not aware of, the medium, but rather the reality to which it grants us access.

Conscience and Commitment

On what grounds, then, are we able to entertain confidence that the account of the world which our particular perspective grants us, via this active and supremely personal engagement with the world, is in any sense 'true'? Clearly for Polanyi we cannot know with absolute certainty that it is. But we can test it out, compare and contrast it with other available points of view and so on. And in all this we find ourselves ultimately faced with a judgement: which perspective, which account of things offers the most fruitful and satisfactory avenue of approach to reality? Having exercised our judgement in this manner, we subsequently stand in a relationship of personal commitment to our point of view. We believe it to be a reliable and satisfactory viewpoint. We cannot know it to be so in any absolute sense. We do not pretend that it is the only possible viewpoint, or that it renders an exhaustive account of things. We admit both its partial nature and its partiality. But we believe the account which it affords to be true inasmuch as it makes the most satisfactory contact with reality that we have found, an account which is more satisfactory than other views which we have considered. Further, it puts us in touch, we believe, with a reality which compels our recognition and our assent, a reality for which we are not responsible, but which places us under a responsibility to bear faithful witness to its structure and shape. This reality goes far beyond our current understanding, but what we know of it contains within it 'a host of hidden implications' which will gradually be revealed through exploration of its inherent logic. In a sense, then, we invest confidence in a particular framework or perspective because, as we occupy it, we find ourselves laid hold of from without, seized by a reality which manifests itself to us, and charged as a matter of conscience with the task of declaring this reality to our fellows. It is in this relationship of intellectual commitment to a truth which seizes us from beyond ourselves, this declaration of universal intent (the claim that what we know in this way is not merely 'the truth for us', but makes contact with an objective reality), that we transcend our subjectivity.

Commitment in Community

Thus the despair of relativism is avoided in the final analysis only, but decisively, by an act of faith and personal commitment. We take our stand on what we believe to be true, not in any arbitrary manner, but through an exercise of personal responsibility in our engagement with reality. Like Luther we declare 'Here I stand. I can do no other.' Our conscience will not permit the sort of cosmopolitan wandering from one perspective to another which suggests that none is any more or less true than the others. Yet to others who demand that we should justify our stance and show forth its truth we can ultimately respond only with an invitation to come and stand where we stand, to view the world through our eyes, and see whether the result does not make more sense than the one which they themselves are familiar with. We must be equally open, of course, to the risky business of being prepared to do the same. Our engagement with reality is not, in this respect, an essentially isolated affair, but one which occurs in and with a 'community of verifiers' as Polanyi calls it; that is to say, a community of other people who share our basic outlook, and whose testimony concurs and coheres with our own in such a way as to reinforce and confirm its basic reliability.

It is here that MacIntyre's account complements Polanyi's helpfully, reminding us that traditions are rooted in communities, and thereby reinforcing the suggestion that rationality, far from being an isolated and uniquely personal or subjective thing, is in fact an interpersonal matter as well. There is a shared fund of agreement concerning what is rational, what is moral, what is tolerable, and so on. And this shared fund may differ considerably from one community to the next. But the view of knowledge which MacIntyre entertains is not a relativist one but a realist. Traditions, he suggests, are justified by their supposed appropriateness as accounts of reality. They refer us appropriately to the world, and facilitate a meaningful engagement with it in its rich diversity. Such traditions develop, MacIntyre argues, through the eruption of 'epistemological crises' – crises, that is to say, concerning their reliability in performing this task. Something is encountered (some discovery, or experience, or alternative tradition) which forces a community to concede that its own tradition is in some respect inadequate or unhelpful. We might say that this constitutes a recognition of error. But relativism can give no meaningful account of error, or of progress from a less satisfactory to a more satisfactory knowledge. It can furnish no good reasons for preferring any one tradition (or any one stage in a tradition's development) over another. As far as it is concerned, all are equally useful and equally useless. Again, therefore, self-transcendence, the desire and the ability to progress in knowing, is bound up with the conviction that there is a reality beyond ourselves, and that we can in fact make substantial contact with it via our knowing. The conception of truth, MacIntyre insists, is integral to tradition-related rational inquiry. Thus he condemns 'perspectivism' as he calls it (the view that since all truth claims are equally valid no truth claim is really worth making). 'Genuinely to adopt the standpoint of a tradition,' he writes, 'thereby commits one to its view of what is true and false and, in so committing one, prohibits one from adopting any rival standpoint.'[19]

There are, of course, many such rival standpoints, standpoints between which there can only be conflict of one sort or another. Standpoints between which, indeed, there may well be some movement or (to use the metaphor which MacIntyre himself invokes) 'conversions', transferences of personal commitment and conviction, the exchange of one way of viewing the world and our place within it for another. An important part of our own commitment to one particular tradition or faith standpoint will be our desire to share this outlook with others, to testify to its truth, to express the universal intent attaching to it by exposing others to it, engaging in the humble task of persuasion not in order to suppress or curb the holding of other points of view, but in order that others might be free to consider ours and to explore the possibilities inherent within it as an account of the truth. As I have already suggested, the condition under which such testimony or witness must be engaged in is a willingness to consider the views held by others, not because we are not confident in the truthfulness of our own perspectives, but precisely because we are, and because we are also more committed to truth than to our own accounts of it.

The Search for the View from Nowhere Leads us Nowhere

At the end of the day both objectivism and relativism founder on the same erroneous assumption; namely that it is possible to transcend one's particularity in an absolute manner, gaining access to a view of reality which is no one's in particular, the view from nowhere. Thus perspectivism proves to be self-referentially flawed: for only on the assumption that we know what the truth really is can we assert with any certainty that no human perspective coincides with it, or that it lies beyond the reach of all perspectives! The purpose of this chapter has been to consider some alternative accounts which have attempted to break the stranglehold which the quest for this sort of absolute self-transcendence has maintained over modernity. Rational inquiry, critical questioning, we have suggested, are things which take place within the contingency of our particular frameworks of belief or traditions and in utter reliance upon them. But self-transcendence and contact with the real world of a sort which compels our allegiance, are nonetheless entirely possible. The myth of a knowledge uncontaminated by unproved beliefs, entirely liberated from the authoritative voices of tradition, must therefore be set aside, and the realities of the structure of every act of human knowing faced up to. We turn next to consider the implications of this claim for our approach to theology.

NOTES
1 Polanyi, M., *Personal Knowledge* (Routledge & Kegan Paul 1958), p. 16.
2 Polanyi, *Personal Knowledge*, p. 5.
3 Polanyi, *Personal Knowledge*, p. 5.
4 Polanyi, *Personal Knowledge*, p. 19.
5 Polanyi, *Personal Knowledge*, p. 53.
6 Steiner, G., *After Babel* (Oxford University Press 1992), p. 30.

7 MacIntyre, A., *Whose Justice? Which Rationality?* (Duckworth 1988), p. 357.

8 Polanyi, *Personal Knowledge*, p. 286.

9 Polanyi, *Personal Knowledge*, p. 297.

10 Polanyi, *Personal Knowledge*, p. 268.

11 Polanyi, *Personal Knowledge*, p. 267.

12 Polanyi, *Personal Knowledge*, p. 266.

13 MacIntyre, *Whose Justice?* p. 4

14 MacIntyre, *Whose Justice?* p. 4.

15 Nagel, T., *The View From Nowhere* (Oxford University Press 1986), p. 70.

16 Nagel, *The View From Nowhere*, p. 92.

17 Nagel, *The View From Nowhere*, p. 10.

18 Polanyi, *Personal Knowledge*, p. vii.

19 MacIntyre, *Whose Justice?* p. 367.

Part Two

Recovering Faith in Theology

— 4 —

Theologies Public and Private

In the last two chapters we have considered three basic approaches to and descriptions of human knowing. The main factor dividing these three from one another was their respective attitude towards the issues of faith and truth, commitment and certainty, and the location of these with respect to the spheres of the public and the private. Theology, whatever else it may be, is certainly a reflective activity, an activity of the mind, and therefore any account of its operations will in practice be undergirded by and closely inter-twined with a particular model or understanding of the workings of human rationality – an 'epistemology' to use the technical jargon. In the rest of this book I shall begin to sketch the outlines of an approach to theology which takes its cue from the accounts of rational activity given by Polanyi and MacIntyre as faith seeking self-transcendence through critical reflection in community. First, though, I want to illustrate and respond to some contemporary approaches to theology which embrace objectivism and relativism as the only intellectual options, in order that we may be clear what is involved in moving beyond them.

Theology as Public Property

In Chapter 1 we considered Brian Hebblethwaite's suggestion that Christian theology, if it is to hold up its head in public, must employ criteria and methods which are, so to speak, common property, acknowledged and used by the wider intellectual public of philosophers, historians, natural scientists, sociologists and the rest. The theologian cannot appeal to private authorities or experiences to support what he says. No evidence or argument the truth of which is incapable of being tested by the ordinary intelligent person in the street can be appealed to without the integrity and worth of the project being undermined, and the universal truth of the gospel message called into question. While, therefore, the theologian may, by virtue of belonging to a particular religious tradition or community, or as the result of some specific private religious experience, hold numerous firm beliefs and submit to the authority of texts or teaching offices, he may not, *qua* theologian, bring these directly to bear upon his primary task unless he can render them publicly accessible and meaningful. What I want to do in this section is to explore some different ways in which this conviction has been adopted and put into effect in contemporary theology. We turn first to the German theologian Wolfhart Pannenberg.

What is it Reasonable to Believe?

The basis on which people respond to the gospel and commit themselves to the Christian way, Pannenberg argues, must be utterly reasonable. 'In order to be in a position to trust,' he writes, 'one must experience as reality whatever it is he is supposed to build upon.'[1] In other words, it is no good inviting people to take the step of faith without first giving them a good reason for doing so and pointing them to something firm to place their foot on. We cannot expect them to make the huge and potentially risky investment of Christian commitment without being able to see that this is a reasonable thing to do, that there is a reality there to be believed in and responded to, and that such action is not, therefore, flying in the face of common sense. The potential object of faith, in other words, must be convincing enough in and of itself to prompt them to profess faith in it at all. Faith may, of course, lead them on a considerable way *beyond* the first foothold identifiable by reason or common sense, or experienced 'publicly'. But 'faith' which commits itself without some such publicly demonstrable foothold is in reality a blind leap into irrationality, a conviction wholly unrelated to and unsupported by any others that we may hold as intelligent human beings in the world. This, Pannenberg urges, is not the true nature of Christian faith.

For Pannenberg, then, the reasonableness of responding to the gospel and committing oneself to Christ must be demonstrable to those who are not yet Christians, who lack faith: otherwise no one would ever *become* Christians in the first place!

The point which Pannenberg makes here is sharpened if we consider a stark alternative to it. According to Paul Althaus, the 'truth' of the Christian gospel is not apparent to those who lack 'eyes to see' it or ears to hear. The reality in which faith invests itself, that which evokes the response of faith, that is to say, is not knowable in any straightforward way to all and sundry, not 'given' in the public sphere, but, paradoxically, is itself only discerned by the eye of faith. Even if we consider matters of fact, Althaus argues, the true significance of those facts remains hidden or obscure to unbelief, and is only recognized from the particular perspective of faith. Thus, to pick an example at the heart of the gospel tradition, the miracles of Jesus are signs of his identity as Messiah; but they function as such only when God grants the faith which enables people to grasp this true significance. There is nothing about them which, when viewed by the public at large, compels such recognition. When Christ is confessed it is not 'flesh and blood' which have revealed his identity, but the Father in heaven. For Althaus, then, it is the disposition of faith which leads to knowledge of the truth rather than vice versa. Faith is not a natural progression from knowledge or experiences available to all, but results from a special dispensation which sets us in the perspective from which the truth may be seen, and demands a response.

Pannenberg demurs. If we once grant that the truth or meaning of gospel realities is justifiable or demonstrable only on the basis of a prior decision of faith, he insists, then two things seem to follow. First, we risk embracing the relativist suggestion that things as such have no intrinsic meaning or truth, but only that with which we decide to invest them. On this way of thinking Christian faith consists in a commitment to construe certain facts and events (the life and death of Jesus for example) in one particular way in preference to other possible (and equally valid) ways of seeing them. Pannenberg is implacably opposed to this subjectivist view which, he argues, undermines the notions of truth and meaning altogether. Reality, he urges, must have an objective meaning which is publicly knowable and to which we may appeal, therefore, in our attempts to commend it to others. Second, Althaus suggests that there is a crude logical gap between the way things appear to the person in the street (the 'public' perspective) and faith's perspective – in which case, Pannenberg insists, faith has an 'absurd' character, lacking any foundations or support in our common human outlook whatever. Consequently we cannot seriously expect intelligent human beings to engage with it with any degree of sympathy or interest. Appeals to supposedly self-authenticating revelatory experiences cannot be permitted, Pannenberg suggests, where what is revealed thereby has this free-floating and arbitrary character. 'An otherwise unconvincing message,' he writes, 'cannot attain the power to convince simply by appealing to the Holy Spirit.'[2]

The truth of the Christian story, therefore, must be perspicuous at some level to the unbelieving eye, commendable by faith to reason and experience. For Pannenberg, therefore, it is knowledge (as obtained in the public domain) which leads to faith, and not vice versa.

The Spirit as the Restorer of a Rightful Mind

Pannenberg's case is carefully nuanced to take account of some obvious objections. To argue thus, he suggests, is not to deny that in many cases people are blinded to the truth, and require some sort of illumination on the part of the Spirit before they can perceive the true meaning or significance of what is before them. But, he insists, what we are dealing with here is the presence of unhelpful prejudgements which warp people's perception. What is needed is for these to be cleared away and for the objective truth of things to be able to break through. The Spirit's role, therefore, is to bring humans back to a state of reason in order that they may properly adjudge the warrant of the step of faith for themselves. Truth, viewed objectively, in other words, commends itself to reason. While such truth may not in fact be apprehended by all, it is, nonetheless, in principle available to be apprehended by all in the public sphere, and we should certainly seek to commend it to all on these terms. Once it has been seen, it may or may not lead to the further 'decision of faith'.

Look and See What the Lord Has Done!

This duly works itself out in Pannenberg's discussion of revelation. By 'revelation' he understands not a body of information about God which has come down to us somehow in textual form (scripture), but rather God's activity within history to which scripture testifies. It is through God's actions, therefore, that we know him. But events, of course, can be highly ambiguous. If, therefore, a specific series of events are alleged to be revelatory, the question naturally arises 'On what basis is their proper significance perceived, and to whom, therefore, do they function in a revelatory manner?' Pannenberg rejects any suggestion that the historical revelation is only recognizable as such by those already possessing the disposition of faith. It is not a secret 'gnosis' accessible only to an enlightened few. The fact that many do not believe reflects not the hiddenness or particularity of the revelation, but rather the refusal of unbelief to see what is given objectively in order to be seen by those who will consider it in a rational manner. 'Nothing,' Pannenberg writes, 'must mute the fact that all truth lies right before the eyes, and that its appropriation is a natural consequence of the facts.'[3] The truth of revelation, therefore, is 'a truth that is open to general reasonableness'.[4] A more blunt or confident assertion of the essentially public nature of the matter with which theology deals would be hard to find. If people employ their minds properly, and are not blinded by irrational assumptions or prejudices, and if the basis for faith is laid out competently before them, then the truth with which the theologian is concerned will be seen. It is precisely by such an 'open appropriation' of truth, Pannenberg believes, that the disposition of faith in Christ is rendered plausible and possible.

Faith, therefore, is not for Pannenberg a particular disposition or perspective from within which one must view reality in order to discern its true meaning or significance. Rather, discernment of truth through the 'open' (public) application of generally accepted tools and methods leads one to the point at which the decision of faith is rendered reasonable, but may still, in the final analysis, be resisted for moral reasons. There is an objective account of things which alone furnishes the firm foundation necessary for faith, and hence for theology. Faith is not a blind leap, but a carefully considered and reasoned judgement; not a state of 'blissful gullibility' but a venture in which the Christian 'risks trust, life and future on the fact of God's having been revealed in the fate of Jesus'.[5] The reality of this revelation, as a basis for faith and theology alike, must therefore be as certain as possible. It is no good for Christians to proclaim that the facts are dubious, or the faith which they proclaim one which, while seemingly irrational to everyone else, appears perfectly reasonable once one takes the step of faith and views it from the inside. That is the hallmark of all fanatical sects whose views intelligent humans would waste no time in condemning as manifestly ridiculous. Well then, Christianity too must pass this test. The facts on which it bases itself must prove reliable when subjected to publicly accepted canons of historical inquiry. The gospel must 'make sense' in the face of the questions asked of it by human reason. The truth of faith's claims, in other words, must be 'public truth' in the sense of being open to the scrutiny of all, and recognizable by them as truth.

Stepping Back from Faith

Another contemporary theologian who develops a case along distinct but broadly similar lines is John Macquarrie in his *Principles of Christian Theology*. Theology, Macquarrie affirms, is indeed an activity of faith, but not in the sense that it requires or demands faith as such as its necessary condition. Rather it is a critical and reflective activity to which faith naturally leads, and which must be constantly related to the concerns of faith and experience, otherwise it degenerates into an abstract and sterile intellectual exercise. Nonetheless, theology as such is distinct from faith, and operates in a mode in which a step is consciously taken back from the immediate engagement of faith and religious experience in order to achieve a critical distance from which to reflect upon this same faith and experience. Faith, then, while it lies behind theology, is itself to be set on one side in the actual doing of theology, and in effect becomes its object. Furthermore, inasmuch as theology craves a place 'in the total intellectual endeavour of mankind',[6] it must carry out its activities in a mode suited to this public office. In theology, therefore, the perspective of faith is exchanged for a public objectivity from within which faith itself is scrutinized and subjected to rigorous examination. The end result, it is hoped, will be the public demonstration of the reasonableness of the existence of faith, or even of some of its basic claims, a demonstration which carries weight outside as well as inside the community of faith precisely because it proceeds along publicly prescribed routes.

Two aspects of Macquarrie's account are especially telling; namely, what he has to say about 'experience' and 'reason' respectively as 'formative factors' in theology.

Pointing to 'Signals of Transcendence'

As we have seen, theology, for Macquarrie, is inseparable from the experience of faith. But, he insists in this context, we must not suppose that the theologian's concerns are to be identified with those of 'religious' experiences alone. On the contrary, theology must be concerned to draw on 'the whole range of human experience', and especially in a secular age when many people might disclaim any explicitly religious experience, theologians have drawn attention to what might be called "religious dimensions" in everyday experience.[7] This is a procedure which Macquarrie endorses. The theologian is able to point to 'signals of transcendence within the empirically given human situation',[8] phenomena within the given public experience of humankind which seem nonetheless to point beyond themselves and to require some transcendent source or basis. Macquarrie cites human awareness of finitude, freedom, creativity, and hope, for example, as publicly available experiences which may be appealed to as an indication that the substance of theology, far from being esoteric and inaccessible, is actually rooted in basic elements of human existence to which all may turn reflectively who choose to do so. Such features of our common existence, while they may not be experienced as 'religious' by those with no religious faith, are nonetheless there to be experienced by them, and may be identified as closely bound up with the concerns of faith and theology. Thus the theologian suggests that part of what it means to experience the world humanly includes what faith would identify as a 'religious' dimension, and that faith itself, therefore, as an interpretation of this dimension, is worthy of further consideration.

Checking the Credentials of the Christian Story

Alongside this appeal to what we might refer to as the 'boundary dimensions' of public experience, Macquarrie affirms what he calls the 'corrective' use of reason in theology without which, he argues, 'We would seem to be the potential victims of the pretensions of any supposed revelation that might seek to impose itself upon us.' What we must undertake in our theology, therefore, is, he urges, an application of 'reason' to revelation itself, or to any other source of religious authority, 'questioning its credentials, submitting it to scrutiny and criticism, removing from its content whatever may be involved in irreconcilable conflict with other well-founded convictions that may be held'.[9] The description which Macquarrie gives makes it clear that what he has in mind here is the bringing to bear of some external standard or index of reasonability which, having public warrant, enables us to sift the wheat from the chaff. 'Reason' in this corrective task operates, therefore, according to universally accepted principles. It provides an objective evaluation of the reasonableness of religious claims, thereby preventing us from being 'taken in' by the fraudulent, the outrageous, or the irrational. The concern of the theologian in applying this public index of truth is certainly not to 'prove' the doctrines held to by faith, but simply to correlate these beliefs with 'other well-founded convictions that may be held' in order to show that, whether they are true or not, they are not irrational, and their truth, therefore, must at least be entertained as a possibility.

Laying Bare the Public Roots of a Private Faith

The overall approach to theology (more specifically to what he defines as 'philosophical theology') which Macquarrie advocates is one which he describes as a 'phenomenological' approach. What this amounts to in practice is an approach which refers us to and seeks to render publicly available and meaningful 'the conditions that make any theology possible',[10] the 'structures and experiences which lie at the root of religion'.[11] These conditions and experiences, far from being the exclusive preserve of the avowedly 'religious', prove in fact to be of a quite general nature. Thus a direct link is established between theology and public existence, between 'theological discourse and everyday discourse',[12] and the former is shown to have an identifiable point of contact and departure in the latter. By starting thus, with our common humanity, with a public rationality and experience, an attempt is made to show how theology can be seen to 'make sense', to explain the hitherto seemingly esoteric and meaningless language and ritual associated with it in terms of things or questions or concerns which everyone can at least relate to, even if they do not choose to pursue the specifically Christian response to them. Once this task has been completed, Macquarrie argues, faith is shown to be entirely compatible with that know-ledge and experience of the world which is public territory, and perhaps even supported by the same. This, he avers, grants 'revealed theology' (the peculiar distinctiveness of Christianity obtained from elsewhere) a 'flying start'.

The Perceived Need to 'Go Public'

What both of these 'public' theologies share, then, is the assumption that in some way or other theology, as a human intellectual enterprise to be set alongside others, can and must prove itself, its value and its meaningfulness as defined and measured by some publicly prescribed canon of truth, whether rational, historical, experiential or whatever. Unless it can do so, unless it can commend itself to those who doubt its value, and justify its own existence by furnishing the public with compelling reasons for continuing to take it seriously, then its intellectual and academic credibility is in serious doubt. Sometimes this assumption is undergirded by the specifically theological claim that if the gospel itself is truly universal in scope, and if God really is Lord of all and not just of some, then we must suppose that his truth will be of a universal sort and therefore applicable to every culture and social circumstance, and his self-manifestation such as to be recognizable by all. To claim less than this, it is argued, is to risk reducing God to a tribal deity, to undermine his claim to the allegiance of the minds and wills of all, and ultimately to call into question the very gospel itself as a universal message of salvation.

The primary mode of such theologies, therefore, is that of advocacy or justification. Theology, we are given to understand, must play the intellectual game together with everyone else on a level playing-field, a field on which, furthermore, a common set of rules is adhered to. Any breach of these rules constitutes a foul and cannot be tolerated. Thus the theologian may not, when engaged in this public theological task, employ any tactics or draw upon any resources which are unavailable to the other players on the field. In this sense, the bringing to bear of particular faith commitments, or the appeal to private sources of authority and insight, constitute the intellectual equivalent of steroid abuse, taking the game beyond the level at which other participants can play it, and thereby undermining its integrity and the validity of its appeal to truth. Public theologies, therefore, are on the whole very strong on demonstrating the relationship between theology and truth (however that may be defined), but find themselves compelled to set commitment and particularity on one side in order to achieve this.

Theology as Private Concern

There is a penchant among many people today, it seems, to define and to designate their points of view by way of reference to that which they see themselves as leaving or having left behind. Hence such terms as post-modern, post-Christian, post-critical and so on. What this indicates, I think, is on the one hand a recognition and appreciation of the profound significance of the contribution of the last couple of centuries as an episode in the development of human understanding, and on the other a conviction (which I share and on the basis of which this book itself is predicated) that in all sorts of ways this same period has bequeathed a set of presuppositions, methods and tools for intellectual inquiry which frankly no longer convince us of their eternal usefulness, and which may and must now be set aside. Thus in this particular context the prefix post- indicates both indebtedness and intentional discontinuity.

George Lindbeck offers as the subtitle of his important little book *The Nature of Doctrine* the following clue concerning its orientation and content: 'Religion and Theology in a Postliberal Age'. In fact, as we shall see, what Lindbeck's proposal for theology seeks to leave behind is as much a part of theological conservatism as it is of liberalism. In order to understand the particular way in which he describes the nature and function of theology we must, as his subtitle hints, turn first to his account of religion. Religions, Lindbeck advises, may be construed in three basic ways, from each of which there issues a concomitant understanding of the theological task.

Faith, Belief, and Experience

First, religions may be understood as systems of beliefs concerning the world, its origins and destiny, its relationship to God, and so forth. By 'belief' in this context is intended a primarily cognitive disposition of the human person. Thus religions are based around creeds in which their particular distinctive set of beliefs or 'truth claims about objective realities'[13] is embodied. The Nicene creed, for example, would on this model of things sum up the essence of catholic Christianity. To believe (grant intellectual assent to) these articles of faith, or at least to a set of beliefs including these, is bound up with the very meaning of what it is to be Christian. To dissent from the truths promulgated therein (whether in this particular form or some other) or to advocate some incompatible account of the realities with which they deal would thus be to challenge the very heart of the particular religious tradition concerned, and to identify oneself over against, rather than within, that tradition, either as heretic or unbeliever. Theology, according to this way of thinking, is the formulation, articulation and commendation of the truths believed by a particular religious community. Doctrines are to be understood as 'informative propositions or truth claims about objective realities',[14] that is to say realities existing independently of our belief in them. The theologian deals with a vast compendium of such truth claims which have to do specifically with the situation of the human in relation to God. The truth of a doctrine, therefore, is a question of the correspondence between what it asserts or affirms and the objective reality to which it refers. Truth is a matter of descriptive reliability, of the relationship between statement and reality.

Second, religions may be understood as comparable to aesthetic, rather than scientific or philosophical, enterprises, and as having to do, therefore, with the creative response of the human spirit to the world and our situation in it. On this view it is not creeds as lists of non-negotiable beliefs which lie at the true heart of religion, but rather the symbol and ritual and myth through which this latent creativity expresses itself. These do not seek to tell us about some external state of affairs, but rather about the inner state of affairs which produces them from one generation and one culture to the next. Thus doctrines are interpreted 'as non-informative and non-discursive symbols of inner feelings, attitudes or existential orientations'.[15] The truth of such doctrines is not a matter of their coherence with some objective reality, but rather of their symbolic efficacy, of 'how effectively they articulate or represent or communicate that inner experience of the divine' (whatever that may mean) 'which is held to be common to them all'.[16]

Having described these two different ways of thinking about religion, Lindbeck proceeds to reject them, and offers a third for our consideration.

Religion as the Language of Life

Religions, Lindbeck suggests, are best thought of as entire frameworks of meaning from within which life is viewed and made sense of. They are 'comprehensive interpretive schemes, usually embodied in myths or narratives and heavily ritualised, which structure human experience and understanding of self and world'.[17] Religion is a communal affair of course, and it is thus the lives of whole communities which are shaped by these shared systems of reality and values. The system functions within community in much the same way as Kant's supposed *a priori* categories of human understanding function for the individual, except that unlike the latter it is particular rather than universal, and varies significantly, therefore, from culture to culture. Nonetheless, it functions as a set of categories which enables us, as members of specific communities, to make sense of and describe the world around us intelligibly. This suggests a helpful analogy in the nature and function of language. Try to imagine how you might begin to make sense of the world, to understand and think about it, to describe it to yourself or to others, if there were no words upon which to draw, and Lindbeck's point becomes clearer. Religion provides us with a set of mental, symbolic, practical and behavioural tools with which to approach the task of interpreting and living in our world. In this sense it makes the knowledge and experience of the world which we have possible. Without the categories or 'language' which it furnishes we would not be able to think about the world as we do, or to experience it as we do. In this sense, religion shapes our subjectivities. Like cultures and languages, Lindbeck contends, religions are aspects of community life which are given in and with our social location and identity. We are born into a tradition, and only by indwelling it are we able to make sense of life at all. This, then, is what Lindbeck dubs the cultural-linguistic model of religion.

If religion may be likened to a language then, Lindbeck suggests, the nature and role of doctrines within religion may be likened to that of grammar within language. Rather than being concerned either with the articulation and rational commendation of truth claims or the search for and refinement of symbols adequate to express an inner experience, the concern of theology is rather with ensuring that what is said and done within the life of the community is consistent with the overall framework of meaning which structures the community's life. It lays down and oversees the keeping of the 'rules', just as grammar administers rules for the ways in which a particular language may or may not be spoken. Some ways of thinking and speaking are acceptable; others are not. The criterion of acceptability is coherence with the system as given, so that what is thought and said and done in one place will be consistent with what goes on elsewhere. Thus, Lindbeck argues, the primary concern of theology is with *intra-systematic consistency*. Significantly, the question of *truth* is defined here in terms of such consistency. A statement or an action is true, that is to say, if it fits with the overall world or scheme of things provided by the framework, rather than being true by virtue of some alleged correspondence with any objective reality. Similarly a thought, statement or action will be deemed false if it contradicts the system in some way. The task of doctrine, therefore, is both descriptive (to offer a coherent account of the system in its various parts) and prescriptive (to ensure that the rules are adhered to and the system's integrity maintained).

Truth and Coherence

We can illustrate this further by comparing two statements from very different literary works. 'According to the 1911 census the population of Great Britain was 40.8 millions.' (Arthur Marwick, *The Explosion of British Society 1914–1970*) 'Captain First Rank Marko Ramius of the Soviet Navy was dressed for the Arctic conditions normal to the Northern Fleet submarine base at Polyarnyy.' (Tom Clancy, *The Hunt for Red October*) There is a sense in which both of these statements may be said to be true, but in rather different ways. The first is taken from a work of history, and as such we should normally expect it to refer us to some fact, to tell us something about the way the world actually is or was; which makes, that is to say, a truth claim in which truth is bound up with accurate reference to some actual state of affairs or objective reality. We would approach the question of the truth of this statement, therefore, by asking on independent grounds about the state of affairs it claims to refer to. The second statement is clearly not true in this sense. It is taken from a work of fiction at the outset of which we find the usual disclaimer concerning 'any resemblance to actual persons living or dead', and we should not dream of asking questions concerning its factual accuracy or inaccuracy. That is simply not the point of the statement. It is part of a fictional narrative, fact-like perhaps, but not factual. Yet this does not mean that we can simply dismiss it as untrue, unless we insist on applying inappropriate criteria of truth and falsity to it. It is untrue if it is treated as a truth claim concerning some actual state of affairs. In fact there is no such person as Captain Marko Ramius. But the statement can be said to be *true* insofar as it refers us appropriately to a set of circumstances around which the novel from which it is taken is structured. It is true, that is to say, within the world of the novel. It refers to a state of affairs within that world, and makes no claim to trespass beyond it. It is true inasmuch as it keeps to the 'rules' laid down by the author at the outset, and fits into the overall structure of the plot as he conceives it. To cite an example which Lindbeck himself offers, to say that 'Hamlet is the King of Denmark' is true within the world of Shakespeare's play. To deny that it is so is to call into question the basic structure and shape of that world as Shakespeare himself sought to establish it for his audience. Truth in this sense, then, is a matter not of accurate reference to some actual reality, but with coherence and conformity to a given and accepted framework or world of meaning.

Lindbeck accounts for the task of Christian doctrine in precisely these terms. Within the framework or world of Christian belief, doctrine functions as a regulatory tool, ensuring that the actions and statements of the Christian community cohere with the overall story. Making sure that Hamlet is not mistakenly spoken of as Thane of Cawdor; or, rather, that the church's statements concerning God are consistent with what the framework furnishes in terms of a trinitarian reference to him as Father, Son and Holy Spirit; or, again, that the actions of the community are consistent with its catholic confession that 'Jesus is Lord.' To affirm this is to proscribe certain types of behaviour within the church, behaviour which would in some way compromise the way in which Christ's Lordship is understood–in terms of self-emptying service, for example. Theology, therefore, is not a first-order discipline, but a second-order discipline; its true object is the church's talk and behaviour, rather than the reality to which these appear to refer us.

Out of the Frying-Pan ...

There is much in Lindbeck's account which is attractive, and a good deal which I find helpful and would wish to draw upon. At first sight the story which he tells concerning the irreducibly community-related and socially located nature of the ways in which humans make sense of and describe their world has much in common with MacIntyre's tradition-related account of human rationality. Insofar as it seeks to move beyond the optimistic excesses of objectivism and take seriously the genuine diversity of frameworks of under-standing and meaning this is a welcome theological development. But the problem with Lindbeck is his apparent willingness to embrace an uncertain relativism as the only real alternative to that which he leaves behind. Either show absolute demonstrable cer-tainty, or else recognize that in the final analysis there is simply a series of different perspectives, different ways of looking at things, to be reckoned with, and none can be affirmed as superior to or more valuable than others in the quest for truth and reality. These are the twin horns of the dilemma upon one or other of which modernity appears to have impaled itself, and which I sought to challenge in the first part of this book. Lindbeck, I would venture to suggest, successfully avoids one horn, only to find himself impaled on the other.

Lindbeck concedes that truth of coherence and truth of corre-spondence are not by any means necessarily exclusive of one another. Indeed, he affirms, a body of statements which are true in the sense that they correspond to reality will presumably have also to manifest coherence with one another to the extent that reality is a coherent whole. But in this case more is involved in asserting their 'truth' than an assertion of their coherence with one another. It is possible to have a vast body of statements which cohere, but which are yet strictly 'false' when measured by the criterion of cor-respondence; as, for example, in realistic fiction. 'Intrasystematic truth', therefore, 'is a necessary but not sufficient condition for ontological truth.'[18] But this also means that truth as coherence does not imply truth as correspondence. If the latter cannot survive without the former, nonetheless the former may exist quite independently of the latter. Again, a novel or a play demonstrates precisely this point.

While Lindbeck is not especially concerned to insist that religions also manifest truth of coherence without truth of correspondence, he is extremely hesistant about making claims concerning the latter. It is the former which really matters. A particular religious tradition may, he allows, make statements which are 'ontologically true', but we certainly cannot be sure or guarantee that it is so. Such correspondence is not necessary, moreover, for the tradition to be 'true' in the more constructive sense. The statements themselves, taken as ontological truth claims, are 'informationally vacuous'.[19] Their cognitive content is minimal. They may well be ontologically true for all we know; but Lindbeck espouses a form of agnosticism at this point. If they are true in this sense, he insists, then we cannot know how they are true. We cannot, as it were, trespass beyond the story which they tell in order to gauge its correspondence with the reality concerned. The story, like Hume's sense experience, distances us from reality itself. But this really does not matter, according to Lindbeck. Cheerfully acknowledging that this is so he insists that the value and 'truth' of religious statements is in no way lessened by it. We must simply construe such truth rather differently.

Faith and 'Living as if'

A much more fruitful way of thinking about the 'ontological truth' of religious statements, Lindbeck suggests, is to consider whether our uttering of them itself (and the broader network of stories and practices within which they properly belong) does not facilitate our willingness to commit ourselves to a whole way of living *as if they were true*. Thus such statements as 'God is good' and 'Jesus is risen' have the same propositional force as ontological truth claims, since they allow us to respond and to behave in ways appropriate to their 'truth' as embodied in the realistic narrative of our stories and rituals. We enter, as it were, into the stories, and live our lives as if these things were true, as characters in the stories which as yet have no ending but are constantly unfolding.

What matters, therefore, is not some supposed ability to pierce beyond the veil of our particular framework in a Promethean attempt to know absolutely. Such an attempt is misguided and doomed to failure. Rather what matters is the extent to which our framework, the story which it tells and which we indwell, 'works' for us as we seek to live our lives in a way which is somehow conformed to the shape of a reality which we cannot directly perceive. Is this story one which, as we play out our role within it, enables us to live fulfilling and worthwhile lives? Are there perhaps other stories which might offer an equally or more satisfying approach to life? Certainly Lindbeck embraces a form of religious pluralism in which, while he allows for the possibility that one tradition may in some sense be superior to others (i.e. provide categories enabling a more authentic response to reality), nonetheless insists that we cannot know it to be so in any way that would allow us to adopt some arrogant or tribalistic stance towards others and their alternatives. Different traditions, he suggests, are like children telling stories about the way things are, each with a very different construal of reality, but all lacking any decisive reason for boasting or for seeking to convert others to its own way of seeing things. Reality itself lies beyond all their construals of it, and the most appropriate attitude for them to adopt towards one another, therefore, is one in which each tradition is respected in its particularity and distinctness and valued as a different perspective on things, and for what that perspective may have to offer to the others.

For Lindbeck, then, theology within a cultural-linguistic understanding of religion is a private concern in the sense that it is practised within a particular community, lays claim to no supposedly universal rational or experiential basis, and seeks no justification from such. On the contrary, both reason and experience are viewed as in part the products of the way in which reality is construed within different traditions. Thus what is reasonable will differ from one context to the next; and the world will even be 'experienced' quite differently by members of different communities due to the way in which our subjectivities are decisively shaped by the systems of values and beliefs which are handed down to us and into which we are born. The theological task is both descriptive and regulative: setting forth the particular story which the community lives by, and ensuring that what is said and done conforms to the shape of this story. Whether the story itself is 'true' in the sense that it refers appropriately to some actual state of affairs beyond itself is, as we have seen, a question which Lindbeck considers to be unanswerable in the final analysis, and one which matters far less than the intra-systematic truth of community life, and the 'pragmatic truth' of the stories and practices which structure that life. There is commitment a plenty here, therefore, as people adhere to a particular construal of reality, indwelling it and speaking its language, committing themselves to the form of life which it demands of them. But there is truth only in a severely qualified sense. At the end of the day, the commitment concerned is rooted in pragmatic considerations. The framework concerned 'works' as a story to live by. The question of its truth or falsity in the more ultimate sense of correspondence with reality lies beyond its immediate purview. Consequently, it has no means (beyond the purely pragmatic which must not, to be sure, be treated lightly) of commending itself to others, or of furnishing reasons why its account of things should be preferred to theirs. Nor, in typical relativist fashion, does it seek any.

NOTES

1 Pannenberg, W., *Basic Questions in Theology* vol. 2 (SCM Press 1971), p. 37.
2 Pannenberg, *Basic Questions in Theology* vol. 2, p. 34.
3 Pannenberg, W., *Revelation as History* (Sheed and Ward 1969), p. 136.
4 Pannenberg, *Revelation as History*, p. 137.
5 Pannenberg, *Revelation as History*, p. 138.
6 Macquarrie, J., *Principles of Christian Theology* (SCM Press 1977), p. 3.
7 Macquarrie, *Principles of Christian Theology*, p. 6.
8 Berger, P., *A Rumour of Angels: Modern Society and the Rediscovery of the Supernatural* (Penguin Books 1971), p. 65.
9 Macquarrie, *Principles of Christian Theology*, p. 17.
10 Macquarrie, *Principles of Christian Theology*, p. 39.
11 Macquarrie, *Principles of Christian Theology*, p. 58.
12 Macquarrie, *Principles of Christian Theology*, p. 46.
13 Lindbeck, G., *The Nature of Doctrine* (SPCK 1984), p. 24.
14 Lindbeck, *The Nature of Doctrine*, p. 16.
15 Lindbeck, *The Nature of Doctrine*, p. 16.
16 Lindbeck, *The Nature of Doctrine*, p. 47.
17 Lindbeck, *The Nature of Doctrine*, p. 32.
18 Lindbeck, *The Nature of Doctrine*, p. 65.
19 Lindbeck, *The Nature of Doctrine*, p. 67.

— 5 —

Theology as Passionate Quest
for Public Truth

Unless you believe, you will not understand.
Augustine of Hippo

Here I stand. I can do no other.
Martin Luther – allegedly

The two types of theology which I have outlined thus far are ones which I consider to be unhelpful as they stand. In one we find truth craved, but pursued at the expense of commitment. In the other, commitment of a sort is demanded, but the issue of truth is left hanging as an unanswerable question. Each, I believe, has something valuable and necessary to contribute: on the one hand a conviction that there is a truth to be known which is genuinely 'public' in the sense of being ontologically or objectively true in every time and place and circumstance; and on the other hand a recognition that every human act of knowing, every bid to discover or handle this truth, rests on a basis which is inherently corrigible, on points of view which are generated by particular social and cultural locations or traditions. The tragedy is that objectivism and relativist pluralism ('perspectivism' as MacIntyre calls it) find themselves driven onto the alternative horns of the modern/post-modern dilemma. When the notion of publicness is fused with an ideal of knowledge as demonstrable certainty (resulting in the search for a truth which is 'public' in the sense that it is equally accessible to all), and when the pluralist abandonment of this ideal results instead in a relativistic agnosticism (a loss of publicness of any sort), then, frankly, the dilemma seems to be insuperable. Neither of the alternatives which it offers, I would suggest, holds a particular attraction for the Christian theologian.

What I want to return to here is the suggestion that we need not accept this choice in the first place, let alone make it. The dilemma is a false one. My conclusion in the first part of this book, drawing on the thought of Polanyi and MacIntyre in particular, was that both a genuine 'publicness' and an unashamed 'pluralism' belong together in an account which faces up honestly to the actual structure of human knowing.

Publicness and Particularity

According to a recent book by Ronald Thiemann, the challenge to Christian theology in the contemporary context is 'to develop a public theology that remains based in the particularities of the Christian faith while genuinely addressing issues of public significance'.[1] It is precisely this that both objectivism and perspectivism fail to achieve. Publicness and particularity are understood by both in ways which render them mutually antagonistic or exclusive. The challenge of developing an approach to theology in which these two quantities are held together is one which can, I believe, be met by drawing on the resources which Polanyi, MacIntyre and others provide.

Such a theology will be committed to a genuinely 'public truth' (in the sense defined above – i.e. it is the truth which is public rather than our mode of knowing or dealing with it). Yet it will refuse to pursue the will-o'-the-wisp of a para-contextual 'objective rationality' or 'universal human experience' by means of which this truth may be seized and forced upon others in the name of 'what is demonstrably the case'. The account which it gives of things will, therefore, inevitably be one which takes the particularities of the Christian tradition fully seriously, which will be rooted decisively in and shaped by this tradition and the standpoint which it offers. Yet at the same time it will crave transcendence of these particularities, believing pluralism to be a feature of human knowing rather than of the way things are beyond human knowing. And it will be optimistic concerning the capacity of humans to transcend their particularity and to establish genuine and reliable contact with reality. The knowledge generated thereby, while not aspiring to the mythical status of the 'absolutely certain' or 'proven beyond doubt', may nonetheless properly be deemed 'public truth' insofar as it claims universal intent. Since such self-transcendence begins with and relies utterly upon prior fiduciary commitment to a particular perspective or tradition as providing the most appropriate vantage point and tools for a fruitful engagement with the reality or object concerned, its logical structure may properly be described as a passionate quest for public truth, or, in more familiar and simple terms, as faith seeking understanding.

Extra-Systematic Reference and Moral Obligation

My reasons for rejecting the approaches of those theologies which I have described as 'public' will be clear enough from my conclusions regarding objectivism. Lindbeck's theological project, on the other hand, while there is much about it which I find attractive and helpful, is unsatisfactory in the final analysis because of the way in which he pulls his punches on the issue of truth.[2] It does not seem to be tolerable to rest content with an account of theology in which truth is defined wholly in terms of coherence or pragmatic efficacy, highly important though these may be in themselves. The question which his account leaves us asking at the end of the day is 'so what?' So what if all these statements and practices and forms of life do cohere with some grand pattern to which they all belong? Does the pattern itself, the framework, bear any relation whatever to the way things are in reality? Does it serve as an extension of our knowing selves which facilitates an active engagement with the world beyond it? Does it furnish tools with which to explore this world, to map its contours in helpful and reliable ways? Or does it serve rather as a Humean 'representation', an account of things which, for all we know, may be quite misleading, and beyond which 'reality' lurks wholly unknown? Consistency can hardly be the only thing we wish to ask about, either in theology or elsewhere.

What Lindbeck's position involves in effect is an abandonment of all claims to genuine publicness of any sort. Not only can we not know whether the Christian gospel is 'public truth', it does not actually matter that we cannot know, so long as the form of life which issues from it is one which 'works'. But this, I would suggest, is inadequate and unsatisfying. Many Christians, I suspect, would certainly not be satisfied with such an account. They would wish to inquire whether the particular framework of beliefs and practices which they indwell bears in some appropriate way on the way things are in (and beyond) the world. Their commitment to the framework, moreover, far from being essentially unrelated to this matter, will be bound up inseparably with it.

What if the whole framework which the Christian idiom offers to us were to be fictitious in the way that the narrative world of *The*

Hunt for Red October or of J. R. R. Tolkein's *The Lord of the Rings* may safely be said to be? Would the serious supposition that this might actually be so really make no difference to our willingness to indwell the world which the idiom furnishes? Would we be prepared, nonetheless, to live as if the account which it offers of reality were true since, while (on Lindbeck's view) we cannot know whether it actually is or not, it provides a coherent overall picture, and commitment to it seems to 'work' in practice? It seems to me unlikely that most Christians would view things in so amoral a manner. Their commitment to Christ, upon which through the ages many have had to stake their freedom and even their lives, is not for them a matter from which the issue of truth can be so readily or willingly detached. In reality, the question of the external reference of the Christian story is one which arises inevitably, and certainly one which Christians historically have taken extremely seriously. I suspect that it would seem strange to most people for it not to be so. While, for example, we may admit the intra-systematic 'truth' of the claim that Hamlet is the King of Denmark within Shakespeare's play, the question of the relationship between Shakespeare's Denmark and the Denmark of the real world is not one which most would consider to be meaningless or irrelevant. Indeed, of someone who could not identify any significant distinction between the two, and who insisted on 'living as if it were true' that Hamlet were the King of Denmark, we should probably say that they were losing their grip on reality. It is not clear that there are any very good reasons why the story told by the Christian community should not be equally open to critical questioning concerning its relationship to reality. Lindbeck's theological model is inadequate precisely because it robs us of access to any extra-systematic referent by appealing to which we may thus adjudge the relative truth or falsity of different frameworks.

Lindbeck's agnostic pluralism, therefore, is ultimately unhelpful. More importantly, it is also quite unnecessary. Its pessimism appears to be predicated in vigorous response to a crudely Cartesian ideal of truth as absolute certainty, knowledge as a subjugation of reality by the mind, and true statements as a direct and exhaustive mirroring of reality in propositional form – an ideal which Lindbeck rightly sees cannot be attained, least of all where God is concerned. But, as I have already indicated, abandonment of the quest for certainty of this sort need not entail the immediate flight to the unwelcoming haven of agnosticism which it so often has provoked. Similarly, the rejection of a crude propositionalism need not drive us into either a mute refusal to speak or else a mode of speech in which we withhold universal intent from what we say, conceding that it has no necessary purchase on reality. Knowledge does not need to be absolutely certain nor statements precise verbal representations in order for there to be true knowledge and speech which bears appropriately upon the world.

Thus relativistic agnosticism is not the only critical response to an over-confident objectivism. There can be reliable knowledge which is based not on the imperialistic wielding of certain and provable axioms, but rather on the self-transcendence of faith seeking understanding. Such knowledge, recognizing its own fragility, is characterized by a degree of humility, yet claims to have made genuine and fruitful contact with reality, and to furnish a reliable route (albeit not an absolutely certain one) to further discovery in engagement with this same reality. Were it not genuinely to believe this it would cease to make the statements which it does, and explore some other route instead. Its commitment, in other words, is of a distinctly moral and not an arbitrary sort. As Christians, we commend the Christian gospel to others because we believe that it is a truth which genuinely pertains to their objective situation.

This leads us to another point which Lindbeck fails to address in any satisfactory manner, namely the question of the source or provenance of different religious frameworks. Where does the Christian idiom come from? How did it ever come to be? The way in which Lindbeck discusses things suggests that it is simply there as a given formative factor in people's lives. But it was not always there. And the forms which it has taken over the centuries are quite varied. How, then, did it arise, and on what basis has it changed and developed over the years? The only satisfactory answer to such questions, I would suggest, must be posited in terms of some genuine engagement with a reality in response to which particular beliefs and forms of life emerged, and in continuing engagement with which they have developed from one generation to the next. Remove all reference to such extra-systematic engagement or reference as we might call it, and it becomes impossible to account either for the existence or the development of the Christian framework except by construing it in terms of purely human and historical factors. Such an account will not suffice and certainly does not reflect the way in which the Christian story itself accounts for itself. The thing of which it fails singularly to take account (and which

Lindbeck studiously avoids mentioning) is the very thing with which Christian theology begins and ends: namely the claim that an extra-systematic reality is indeed to be known here; not on the basis of human endeavour and self-transcendence alone or as such, but because he makes himself known in particular ways, times and places. The claim, in other words, that God has revealed himself. Such a claim may well be impossible to prove or to demonstrate in 'public' fashion, but it furnishes the very starting point for theological activity as a passionate, committed quest for further understanding and truth. Lindbeck's evasion of this basic issue may well reflect the fact that, once such a claim is taken seriously, the agnostic pluralism which he advocates is rendered highly problematic. For if God has indeed spoken or acted in such a way as to give himself to be known here, then to withhold or suspend fiduciary commitment to this story as public truth is to fail in one's moral responsibility in the face of reality.

The Proper Object of Theological Concern

Theology, I suggest, like every other intellectual enterprise, proceeds inevitably on the basis of certain passionate commitments. But this immediately raises the question 'commitment to what?' In the natural sciences, as we have seen, we may identify a twofold commitment: on the one hand to the reality and knowability of the object of study, and on the other to certain tools and procedures as employed within a particular community of knowing. In the case of theology, I would suggest, things are broadly the same.

The Christian theologian's task may take many forms, and involves many different objects of study. Thus at one level it involves the study of history, of texts and the cultural locations from which they issue, of forms of life, of beliefs and rituals, both in their contemporary manifestations and in their historical development. All of these things, as they manifest themselves in the life of the Christian community, provide a focus for theological questioning and reflection. More than this, the theologian is also concerned with wider issues of human existence and thought, with the contemporary state of human understanding in science, philosophy, art, the social sciences and so on. But as Christian theologian his interest does not begin or end with these various human realities as such. All of this is of vital concern, but it does not constitute the ultimate object or focus of genuinely theological activity. In the final analysis the theologian is interested in all of these things only insofar as they are believed to have a more than purely human significance. For the theologian's concern is with a reality who, in and through and in relation to all these things, gives himself to be known to humans; and in the light of whose reality, therefore, they must all ultimately be viewed. The reality of this other object (or more properly subject since it is he and not we alone who acts in our knowing of him) furnishes the theologian as such with his distinct point of departure and his overall purpose in knowing, or else the activity in which he engages is not truly Christian theology, but something else. To attend to the study of these other intermediate realities while withholding commitment to the reality and knowability of this specific object, or to handle them in such a way as to obscure this reality or to fail to take it seriously, would be to abandon the properly theological task.

The ultimate object of Christian theological concern and exploration, then, is God himself as he has given himself and gives himself to be known. The nature of this particular object, moreover, determines the ways and means via which the theologian must go about his exploratory task.

Again, however, this does not make his approach unique or peculiar. Every approach to these things, every venture within these disciplines will be shaped and directed just as surely by some set of ultimate commitments and concerns or another. The theologian's concern is driven by his particular commitment to and his desire to make sense of the Christian story and the self-manifestation of God in and through that story. It may well be the case that on occasion the Christian theologian, handling the tools, let us say, of the textual-critical or the historical trade perfectly competently, will arrive at distinct and even conflicting conclusions from his colleagues who employ the same tools and procedures, but within a quite different framework of assumptions and meaning. When such clashes of understanding and interpretation of results occur, the temptation is always to seek some wholly objective criterion of truth with which an adjudication may be reached. But if, as I have suggested, no such advantageous standpoint exists, then what we must face up to is the fact that what we are dealing with here is a clash of frameworks at the most basic level, two or more quite different construals of reality each shaped by a framework of meaning from within which the world is approached and in terms of which it is handled. The shape which an attempt to deal with such a clash might fruitfully take will be explored later. The point which I make here is simply that the theologian's interest in and approach to human life and knowledge in all its rich diversity is one which is shaped from the outset by his commitment to the reality of the God who has made himself known. This, as it were, provides him with a non-negotiable starting point, and a framework of under-standing within which to operate.

The theologian is committed first, then, to the reality and know-ability of his ultimate object of concern, namely the living God who has made and makes himself known. This commitment drives the theologian's quest for knowledge and understanding, undergirds that quest, and gives the quest its focus and concern.

Theology as a Tradition-Constituted and Tradition-Constitutive Critical Activity

Second, the theologian, like the scientist, is also located within a community of knowing and brings to his task, therefore, a set of assumptions, tools and procedures on the basis of which the object of concern has been fruitfully approached in the past. This involves attention to certain objects and places in the quest for knowledge, and the setting aside of other routes as relatively fruitless. It involves being prepared to build on the labours of other earlier practitioners, to learn from their mistakes as well as their successes. Since it is a quest for knowledge rooted in the conviction that there is a reality here to be known, and that knowledge of that reality is genuinely possible, the theologian's task also involves an openness to the possibility that earlier routes and methods and tools may have to be set aside as new discoveries are made, as reality opens itself up in new ways which demand other tools, other ways of knowing, and the revision or refining of earlier assumptions.

What this means is that the theologian operates within, and is fundamentally committed to, an established tradition of life and thought. This tradition, I shall suggest duly, is not narrowly intel-lectual, but involves many aspects of the Christian idiom, its beliefs, its practices and rituals, its art forms and architecture; all the ways in which the Christian community embodies its life under the Lordship of Jesus Christ and thereby seeks to live out the story which generates and shapes its existence. Such a commitment does not mean that the theological task is in any way uncritical or 'fideistic'.[3] On the contrary, while it belongs to and works within a tradition, its task is precisely to bring to bear on this same tradition a critical questioning in the light of that reality to which it claims to embody a total living response. Thus the tradition is both the assumed starting-point for theology and the object of its critical concern.

To those who would suggest that to begin with the assumptions and commitments furnished by a tradition in order subsequently to engage critically with that tradition is a hopelessly circular exercise two things may be said. First, if, as we have argued, there is no neutral or objective set of criteria from which to begin, then the only alternative to beginning with the commitments proper to the community of faith would be to substitute for them some other set of commitments, i.e. those of some other 'faith' perspective. To do so might be interesting, but it is not clear that it would necessarily be of any great value either to the community of faith as such, or in the pursuit of truth. But, second, while the process is, like all acts of human knowing, certainly circular in structure (i.e. certain basic beliefs belonging to the tradition are assumed at the outset which cannot be disbelieved while they serve as assumptions) it is not hopelessly or viciously so as long as the true and ultimate object of concern, and the criterion upon which critical activity proceeds, is not the tradition but rather the reality which lies beyond it, and in this case that means God as he has given himself and gives himself to be known in the midst of the community of faith. The tradition is measured and adjudged, that is to say, in the light of our ongoing encounter with this reality. Our only approach to such an encounter is through tried and tested means, through use of the tools and procedures which have rendered reliable knowledge in the past, through the life and worship of the community within and through which this reality has been known and, we believe, will be known again. Yet, precisely because we believe this reality to be knowable, because the particularity of our tradition may be transcended by an act of faith in which we commit ourselves to these ways rather than others as fruitful routes to disclosure, the tradition itself is constantly reformed and revised and transformed by this very encounter, sometimes in quite challenging and surprising ways.

Theology, therefore, is not a matter of those who are committed to a tradition asking questions about that tradition in terms of the tradition's own criteria and assumptions and allowing only those answers to be given which fit with the tradition's own already-established conclusions. That, I would suggest, is the hallmark of genuine fideism: the refusal to allow any challenging or surprising answers to be heard, an utter commitment to the form which the tradition has taken in the past and must continue to take in the present and the future. In this sense, we might venture to suggest, because Lindbeck furnishes no conditions for genuine critical activity within theology other than an insistence upon adhering to the grammatical rules of the given system, his model trespasses dangerously close to fideism and is difficult to distinguish from it in certain respects. But if our theology is a realist one – if, that is to say, we engage critically within the tradition and on the basis of it, but in such a way as to allow the reality which we engage with thereby to shape our thinking, our speaking about it, our activity and, indeed, our entire form of life – then the tradition which furnishes our starting-point (we must have a starting point) will not be immune from rigorous questioning, but will be exposed to it at every point, and will be constantly being reformed and revised in the light of its true source. A framework which, in Polanyi's sense, constitutes and acts as a genuine extension of our knowing selves in this way cannot avoid such reformative calibration. Only when and if the framework becomes opaque, and thus itself becomes both the primary object of concern and the sole criterion or arbiter of truth, can our engagement with it be such that preserves itself from all change. This happens when theologians, or Christian communities, become more concerned with their own systems of beliefs and practices than with a genuine openness to reality. Then dogmatic orthodoxy petrifies into an idolatrous exaltation of the particular framework or idiom, rather than manifesting the requisite humility and responsive obedience before reality's self-disclosure.

In the case of Christian theology, of course, the reality concerned is a personal one who acts upon us rather than we acting upon him. He is known only as he gives himself to be known, and only in the particular ways and modes in which he renders himself knowable. Thus, while I have been employing the language of quest and self-transcendence in this chapter to describe theology as an act of human knowing, this should not be taken as suggesting that theology is some sort of Promethean storming of the heavens. What may be construed humanly as 'discovery' is better thought of theologically as revelation. The claim that the Christian tradition furnishes the possibility of a genuine self-transcendence in which God is known is perhaps better expressed by saying that we believe that God has made himself and makes himself known to humans in these particular ways and forms of life, so that it is God who takes these particular places, traditions, stories, activities, forms of life and so on, and gives himself to be known supremely here rather than elsewhere. This being so, humility and obedient response are more necessary than ever if our knowing and speaking are to be appropriate and 'true'. Such humility, it seems to me, avoids the excessive and over-optimistic claims to which certain forms of theological objectivism have resorted, yet without falling into the trap of abdicating our responsibility before the truth.

The question, then, is not whether theology should be critical in its approach, but rather, on what basis ought this critical activity to proceed? For those adhering to some supposedly 'public' approach this basis is furnished by universal principles of reason or common human experience. For Lindbeck's cultural-linguistic theology the basis is provided by the shape of the tradition as given, to which conformity and coherence are demanded. A more satisfactory model, I would suggest, is one in which the basis for critical thinking is furnished by the fundamental faith commitments proper to a particular tradition; insofar as these furnish a genuine possibility of self-transcendence, reliable and fruitful contact with reality is made, and in the light of this contact and the knowledge rendered by it the tradition itself is viewed in a new light. Thus the appropriate analogy for this 'critical-realist' model of theology is not that of a circle, but, as McGrath suggests, rather a spiral, since each heuristic engagement with reality sees some form of development or adjustment or new understanding of the tradition from within which it was mounted. The tradition is not static: it moves forward.

Aspects of the Theological Task

What I am proposing, then, is a model of Christian theology as the pursuit of genuinely public truth through engagement with the reality of the divine self-giving in Jesus Christ. This engagement begins from the conviction of faith that such truth is indeed to be had, that this reality is known and may be spoken of appropriately; it proceeds on the basis of ways and means of knowing through which, it is believed, God gives himself to be known. It employs certain 'tools' (to use Polanyi's phrase) in the pursuit of its end: the scriptures of the church, the doctrinal inheritance of creeds and confessions, the living ritual of worship and prayer, the whole complex of ways in which the community's self-understanding finds expression in word, gesture and action. In and through his study and use of these various tools, his indwelling of the framework of the Christian idiom, the theologian seeks to encounter afresh daily that living reality which is their source and to which they constitute a living response. In the light of this encounter he seeks continually to adjust, calibrate and hone the framework so that it constitutes an appropriate response, a response which in some sense corresponds to that reality as a human echo of it.

This understanding of theology has certain basic similarities with that which Avery Dulles commends as 'post-critical' theology.[4] Theology of this sort, he argues,

> intends to speak about reality as actually constituted and to make statements of universal validity. It points to the deficiencies of any system that purports to dispense with faith. Recognizing that every affirmation rests upon some kind of faith, [it] frankly relies on convictions born of Christian faith. It does not pretend that its arguments can be conclusive to thinkers who do not have the same faith-commitment. It nevertheless invites the uncommitted reader to enter into the universe of faith and seeks to foster conversion.[5]

Thus it is an approach to theology which seeks to hold publicness and the particularity of the Christian tradition together.

The Christian theologian, like Polanyi's scientist, confesses the partial and commitment-laden nature of the knowledge which he offers to others. He makes no unrealistic or self-deceiving claims concerning its certainty or universal demonstrability. Yet, as one who genuinely believes himself to have encountered, or rather been encountered by, the supremely 'public' reality of the God who is Lord of all, he finds himself placed under a moral obligation to speak of this reality, to commend him to others, and to do so by commending to them the framework of the Christian story as the particular location where this God has made and makes himself known. His commendation of this particular tradition, this framework of meaning, is not intended to deny in any arrogant manner that this reality might be known in other ways and other places. But it proceeds on the basis that he has made himself known here, and that the substance of what has been learned thereby encourages the view that this place offers a more satisfactory and full-blooded encounter with him than any other, an encounter which sets all prior perceptions of and approaches to him in the shade. At the end of the day, therefore, the reception of this knowledge by others as public truth will depend upon their willingness to entertain this same standpoint, to consider this particular story and seek to view things from within it, to explore the heuristic potential which is claimed for it. Whether, in doing so, they will in fact make fruitful contact with the reality concerned depends, in this particular instance, more upon his willingness to be known than upon their willingness to know. That is the frustration with which every Christian who seeks to lead others to this reality must reckon on occasion.

According to this way of thinking, therefore, theology has a variety of tasks. At one level it is called upon to be *descriptive*, to tell the story with which faith begins and ends, to spell out the gospel in a clear and meaningful way, to interpret it and translate it into contemporary forms. It is also called upon to perform a *regulative* task, to ensure that what is said and done in the community of faith coheres with this story, that deviant modes of speech and action are clearly identified as such and proscribed, that the various elements of it are grasped in their proper relation to one another. But theology is called to do more than this. It is called to engage critically with the story itself, to test the various parts of it not simply in terms of their coherence with one another, but in terms of their ultimate correspondence to the reality from which and in response to which the story first issued and from which it continues to draw its meaning and significance. In its execution of this responsibility theology monitors and regulates the public truth of the church's language and actions. Thus it certainly has to do with the formulation and evaluation of truth claims, although these need not be understood in terms of the somewhat crude propositionalism caricatured and promptly rejected by Lindbeck. All the rich resources of metaphor, analogy, narrative, model and myth are drawn upon alongside more straightforward discursive linguistic modes, in order to refer in appropriate ways to the reality encountered by faith. Through such means theology offers to those who do not share the community's perspective an account, a way of seeing things which it genuinely believes will grant them a more satisfactory purchase upon reality. It calls them to exchange their standpoint for its own. It does so not in any boastful or arrogant manner, or by suggesting that any other perspective than its own is manifestly irrational, but because it finds itself placed under a moral obligation to do so by the nature of its engagement with reality itself. Polanyi's citation of Luther hits the nail on the head: 'Here I stand; I can do no other.' In the sentiment expressed in these words particularity and a perceived moral obligation to public truth are at one.

The Accountability of the Theologian

Two distinct levels or elements may now be discerned in the theologian's task. On the one hand he must engage with and unpack the particular story of the Christian gospel, the story concerning God and his purposes in creation and redemption, and the ways in which he has acted and is acting to fulfill those purposes. The theologian will seek to facilitate the translation of this story into words and forms of life which are appropriate for the contemporary situation of the community of faith, to regulate the various aspects of its contemporary articulation, and to ask critical questions concerning its truth or external reference. This narrower and more particular task we shall refer to as a concern for the internal coherence of the Christian tradition.

On the other hand the theologian must seek to view the wider field of human understanding and experience in relation to this same story, to ask after the implications of the one for the other, to pursue the integration of the one with the other. This wider intergrative task we may refer to as the concern for the 'external coherence' of the Christian story, the attempt to construe the wider world in terms of the particular story by which the community's life is shaped, to construct a coherent account of reality as a whole from this particular perspective. This task, I will suggest, will involve both the Christian story itself and the accounts of the world which we receive from other sources of knowledge being exposed and open to genuine revision and adjustment in the light of our attempts to encounter reality on the basis which they provide.

Thus we may say that the theologian has a threefold accountability. First, he is accountable to the tradition within which he stands and to which he is committed. Second, he is accountable as a citizen of the world to the wider human community with its questions, concerns and ways of thinking, and must seek in some way to integrate the Christian story with or bring it to bear upon or relate it to the other stories (scientific, historical, political, religious or whatever) which confront him and compete for his attention and allegiance, and which claim a place as part of the current state of human knowledge of the world. He has, in this sense, a public accountability to address issues of general human concern, although he will do so from within the particularity of his tradition, seeking to show just how the Christian story construes them. Third, and supremely, insofar as all these stories claim to provide some account by means of which the world is opened up and made accessible to scrutiny and discovery, the theologian's first commitment must be to the truth itself, to reality as it discloses itself and is known. He is accountable, that is to say, to public truth. In his efforts to evaluate other traditions than his own, and in his attempts to integrate the Christian gospel with other wider elements of human understanding at the end of the twentieth century, the question he asks will always be about the fruitfulness of the accounts offered as a framework from within which to engage with reality. His hope of attaining to a genuine integration will rest on the assumption that the world itself, as a single created reality, manifests an overall coherence and integration between its various aspects, that it really is a universe and not a multiverse.

In the next section of this book we turn at once to a consideration of what is arguably the single most significant factor in the church's attempt to maintain the internal coherence of the story which it tells to the world; namely, its continual engagement in the task of making sense of scripture.

NOTES

1 Thiemann, R. F., *Constructing a Public Theology: The Church in a Pluralistic Culture* (Westminster/John Knox 1991), p. 19.

2 A very helpful response to Lindbeck is provided by Alister McGrath in The Genesis of Doctrine (Basil Blackwell 1990).

3 The term 'fideism' is variously used. Some would use it to describe the position which I am espousing in which faith commitments (the Latin word for faith is *fides*) form an inevitable and necessary condition for theological activity. I would demur from this, and prefer to define it as a position which is rooted in faith commitments which are themselves invulnerable to any questioning, challenge or revision. As I shall suggest below, this is not the case with the model which I am developing due to its realist character. It is always vulnerable to the claims of reality upon it.

4 See Dulles, A., *The Craft of Theology* (Gill and Macmillan 1992).

5 Dulles, *The Craft of Theology*, p. 13.

Part Three

Making Sense of Scripture

— 6 —

Retrieving the Story:
Text, Authority, and Meaning

> The tide of literary theory has at last reached the point on the beach where the theologians have been playing, and, having filled their sandcastle moats with water, is now almost in danger of forcing them to retreat, unless they dig deeper and build more strongly.
>
> *N. T. Wright*

Stories, recent studies in sociology have reminded us, are very important to our identity as human beings in community. Every human community has a story which it tells both to itself and to others concerning its distinctive origins and *raison d'être*, and about the sort of place this world in which it exists is. Within communities, and the traditions or 'stories' which they seek to tell and to embody in their daily lives, Alasdair MacIntyre observes, authority will have been conferred upon certain voices, and these may often be identified in the form of specific texts or groups of texts. Such texts, as they are continually read and interpreted afresh in each generation, will exercise a formative influence upon the retelling of the community's story, its efforts to fashion, as it were, a new chapter in the story through the specific forms of thought and action which it adopts.

The appeal of the Christian church to the Bible as 'scripture' fits fairly clearly into this pattern. Here the Christian community identifies a series of texts by reference to which she gives some account of her own distinct identity, to which she returns and upon which she draws in her continual attempts to relate that identity to the questions and challenges posed by her contemporary context. The story which the Christian church has to offer, that is to say, is founded decisively upon the text of the Bible and the 'story' which it in turn tells with its classic themes of creation, sin, covenant, redemption and hope, a story told in and through a wide diversity of types of literature from numerous different authors and historical circumstances, but interpreted as in some clear sense finding

107

their focus in the particular story of the one man Jesus Christ, a story which is construed as gospel, good news, not just for the church, but for those beyond its boundaries also. Thus in preaching, in worship, in mission, in a thousand daily activities in and through which our self-understanding as a community is shaped and reshaped, the Christian community returns to this set of texts and seeks to make sense of it.

Scripture, then, we may say, is authoritative for the church in its attempts to think and to live as an authentically Christian community in the 1990s. But clearly, there is little value to be had from an authoritative text unless some sort of agreed answer can be given to the question of its meaning. As Father Brown (a.k.a. G. K. Chesterton) observes, 'It is no use a man reading his Bible unless he reads everyone else's Bible as well.' We must face the fact (obvious enough, but not always recognized) that the meaning of any text is in some sense distinct from the sum and order of the particular words which it contains. It is not enough, therefore, in reading scripture and seeking its 'authority' simply to repeat its words to ourselves and others like some sort of mantra. We are all perfectly well aware that words are very slippery things. Even the most obvious and innocent statement that we might make in daily life can easily be misunderstood or misconstrued by others, sometimes with striking effect. The same thing applies to whatever we write. We must choose our words carefully, for once they are let loose in textual form, like the Word of the Lord, they are unlikely to return to us empty handed. The problem is that what they bring back with them may not be precisely what we hoped for!

There is an indeterminacy in our use of words, whether as writer or as reader. All texts, whether some complex philosophical treatise, a sensitive note penned to a bereaved friend, or a note written in haste to the milkman, demand to be made sense of by those who read them. Their meaning must be retrieved or laid hold of. And this retrieval involves the reader as well as the writer in responsible activity, whether consciously (where the strangeness of the text is apparent to us – when it is in a foreign language, or uses technical jargon, for example) or subconsciously (where it is sufficiently familiar for us not to notice the contribution it nonetheless demands of us). Making sense of scripture, therefore, is a responsible task, something which we as Christians are called to *do*. Sense or meaning is precisely something which in some measure we *make* through a skilled and disciplined activity as readers. We must interrogate and interpret a text, we must retrieve its meaning before we can submit to its authority. As I hope to demonstrate, this is by no means so easy a task as we might sometimes suppose.

What, then, does a particular passage of scripture 'mean?' What is it about? What is it saying to us? There are a number of different ways in which Christian readers might approach an answer to this question. We might ask, first, about what we may call the surface level meaning of the text, what it seems to us to be saying at a straightforward first reading. Or, second, recognizing that these texts belonged initially to a time and place quite different from our own, we might probe deeper and pursue the question of the meaning which its words would have had for the author and his original readers. Third, we might want to explore the question of what the author's words might have to say to us today in our particular circumstances. And in with and under all of this, of course, Christian readers of scripture will seek some answer to the question 'What is God saying to us/me in and through our/my reading of this text?' Thus we are faced immediately with the fact that the question 'What does this text mean?' is susceptible in practice to more than one answer.

Texts can 'mean' more than one thing. Recognition of this fact might make some readers (especially Christian readers of the Bible perhaps) rather uncomfortable. After all, much of human existence is bound up with the reading and interpretation of texts of one sort or another. From the 'classics' of the philosophical, religious, political, and literary traditions which have shaped our culture, the more or less ancient texts which underpin our knowledge of the past, to the more mundane instruction booklet which tells us how to regulate our central heating system, the latest communication from the Inland Revenue, or the roadsign which informs us that there is DANGER AHEAD!; in all sorts of ways the structure and course of our day-to-day living rests upon our capacity to dig meaning out from texts of various sorts. But if even the most straightforward of texts are by nature capable of being read in more than one way – consider the sign found in London Underground stations instructing travellers that 'Dogs must be carried on the escalator'[1] – then how are we to decide which meaning to alight upon? Which meaning is the 'true' meaning, the authorized version? Who, we might ask, has the copyright on the meaning of a text?

This is the main issue which occupies practitioners in the field of so-called literary theory. The church, in its attempt to allow scripture to function authoritatively within the community of faith, clearly cannot afford to avoid or even to delay careful consideration of the answers which they offer. The question 'where or what is the meaning of a text?' demands to be faced and wrestled with by those committed to the truth of a gospel which comes to us chiefly through a scriptural witness. A human reading of texts lies at the very heart of the church's existence. It would seem, therefore, to be incumbent upon all who read these texts as scripture to reflect on the nature of the task itself. We all bring some hidden assumptions about how meaning is to be retrieved from the text of scripture to our reading of it. This chapter is designed to help us to consider some alternatives, and thereby, perhaps, to bring our own out into the open for a fresh examination.

Looking Through the Transparent Text

We all know what a window is for. It serves two basic functions. First, it lets light into a building, and second, it enables those on the inside to look out and see what is going on in the world around them. Let me introduce you, then, to the dominant approach to scripture over the last five hundred years or so in which, in various ways, the text might reasonably be likened to a pane of glass through which light streams to the reader and through which, crucially, the reader is in turn invited to gaze in order to look at something else lying beyond or behind it. We do not look *at* a window. We look *through* it. So, on this view, the meaning of the biblical text is sought not in the text itself, but in some sense beyond it, in the text's essential transparency.

Scripture as a Window onto History

In the wake of the Reformation, while various ways of reading scripture were in practice tolerated, the dominant approach was that which supposed that its true meaning was to be had in what we may call its 'literal' or 'plain' sense; the sense, that is to say, which its words seemed to bear directly to the reader who approached them with no more than a good dose of common sense. What the text seemed to be saying or to be about, that is to say, was what it was in fact saying or about. The esoteric and heavily allegorical meanings attributed to it by medieval Catholicism, a grasp of which required the interpretative mediations of the church's teaching office, were now widely discredited. A fundamental feature of scripture was held to be its perspicacity for all readers. Scripture, it was believed, was God's Word to all people, and therefore its meaning must be within the grasp of all people. God, knowing all things, would not be half so foolish as to entrust its message to the clergy alone! The thing to do with scripture, therefore, was to translate it into languages which people could read, and distribute it as widely as possible that they might do so.

To this was attached another supposition. What the text of scripture was doing, it seems generally to have been supposed, was rendering to the reader a straightforward and and reliable account of actual events and states of affairs in God's world, and of God's dealings with his world. The meaning of scripture was in this sense identical with the meaning of the events themselves, the 'history' which it was its function to open up for us, a history stretching from creation to the last days, and having its central focus in the life, death and resurrection of Jesus Christ. In recounting this unitary story, scripture offered a precise and trustworthy picture of actual characters and their actions, of events which had happened and those which had yet to happen.

This was a way of thinking, we should note, in which while the text of scripture was certainly greatly valued, it was so precisely as one might value a carefully placed window providing access to a view otherwise hidden from sight. In practice it was not the window itself which was important, but the historical and theological landscape to which it granted privileged access. Scripture's purpose was to lay bare the panorama of human history, to tell of things which we could otherwise not hope to know about the human past and future, and, vitally, about God's purposes for humankind. Thus the plain sense of scripture was for the most part taken as a reliable historical reference from which its true meaning was inseparable. What one saw as one looked through the window was, in an uncomplicated way, what was really (historically and actually) on the other side. Scripture's authority for the church, therefore, lay in its provision of a 'factual' account of the story of God's dealings in the real world, and thereby its granting of an opportunity for Christians to locate themselves confidently within that same world.

An Optical Illusion Unmasked

This confident and uncomplicated approach began to break down with the development of historical consciousness from the mid-eighteenth century onwards. Scholars began for the first time to seek to submit the biblical documents to the same sorts of literary and historical analysis that other ancient texts were routinely submitted to. When this was done, what happened in effect was that what had once seemed fairly clearly to be a unified historical and doctrinal story in scripture began to fragment before the reader's very eyes. The world of the text's 'plain sense', the 'real world' of God's dealings with humanity within which the pre-critical reader had sought to locate himself, now fell victim to an earthquake which initially all but reduced its familiar landmarks to rubble.

Thus, for example, by locating the biblical documents within their appropriate literary genre it could now be seen that the true nature and purpose of many texts had simply been misunderstood by earlier interpreters. Texts containing *prima facie* historical material were seen to be of another literary type altogether, so that to ask or expect them to answer genuinely historical questions was actually seriously to misunderstand them, and perhaps to miss entirely the message which they were seeking to convey through the use of such established literary conventions as symbol, story, parable and so on.

Increased familarity with the specific historical and cultural background to the texts also served to prompt some basic rethinking of their original meaning. In particular, there was a growing awareness that while the Christian community had for generations read its Old Testament as a book about Jesus Christ (at least in the sense that its meaning was taken to be bound up with a prospective reference to events lying beyond its own immediate purview), these ancient Hebrew texts would certainly not have been read or understood in this way by the community within and for which they were written. Where their original or historical meaning was concerned, that is to say, there was usually no need to look beyond the more immediate historical and political circumstances of Israel's life. The recognition that this might be so was of profound consequence for the Christian reader. For it had hitherto been taken for granted that the proper meaning of these texts (and the 'historical' events to which they referred) lay in their status as the early chapters in a single story, the denouement of which was only reached in the New Testament. If it was now seriously to be reckoned with that the author of Isaiah 53 (to pick an obvious example) might not have been intending to refer his readers to Jesus of Nazareth but to some rather more contemporary figure, or that the basic nature of the entire Hebrew Bible was not so much that of a 'prequel' to a classic Christian sequel, but in some sense that of a classic in its own right, then the genuine coherence and unity of the 'history of salvation' traditionally traced through the various books of Christian scripture was placed in question.

It was the application of such methods to the Gospels, however, which made the greatest impact. One of the first things to emerge from careful study of these documents was a frank denial of the supposition that they constituted in any sense simple and historically precise 'factual' descriptions of the things which Jesus did and said, and of the things which happened and were done to him, during his life and ministry. They were not a primitive verbal equivalent of the home video or the photojournalist's portfolio, recording it 'as it really was'. The authors, far from being eyewitnesses who simply reported what they had seen and heard, were in fact very careful editors who used existing sources and traditions in quite distinct ways to produce sophisticated theological retellings of the story of Jesus. The sources themselves, it could be seen, had developed over time in the telling, a development which could often be traced by comparing one Gospel with another. At every level of the gospel narrative, from the selection and ordering of events in the plot, the details recorded in the accounts of those events, and the theological significance discerned in them, distinct editorial perspectives may be discerned. Sometimes these distinct perspectives are so different from one another that it is even possible to speak of alternative ways of thinking and speaking about Jesus, his mission, his death, and so on.

Enough has been said to indicate that what happened in and through the dawning of this new historico-critical awareness and approach was that the world of the biblical text 'indwelt' by precritical readers shifted on its axis and much of it seemed to crumble irretrievably around their feet. What they had assumed they were looking at through the window of the text proved, on closer and more expert inspection, to be something quite different. The historically and doctrinally unified world beyond the pane could be maintained, it seemed, only so long as the question of the original meanings and historical development of the biblical texts was ignored. Once this question was asked and answered through careful research and scholarship this same world proved to be a clever trick of the light, or an optical illusion created by looking at the glass from a particular angle.

What the historical critical approach to scripture did, then, was to prise apart three quite distinct levels of 'meaning' which pre-critical readers had conflated on the assumption that they were in fact one and the same: the 'plain' or 'literal' sense, the reference of the text to actual historical events, and (lying in between these two) the 'original' meaning intended by the author or editor of the text. Between these three, gaps of as yet undefined proportions now yawned. Once this separation was effected, it was clearly no longer possible to view the question of the meaning of the text and its function as authoritative scripture in the same way. The naive commonsensical assumption that the plain sense of the text rendered a direct, reliable and coherent picture of historical actualities (the way it really was) had proven illusory. How, then, could the text any longer serve as a firm and authoritative basis for locating one-self within the world as God's world? How was its authoritative meaning for the community of faith to be construed? The anxiety provoked by the eruption of such questions was of a similar magnitude to that stimulated by Galileo's telescope. It was also to provoke some essentially similar responses, resulting, in the short term at least, in a misplaced quest for some new basis for biblical certainty.

Scripture and Historical Reconstruction

The initial response to such anxious questioning was one which can be seen, in retrospect, to share the basic assumption of the pre-critical approach. The point is neatly made in some words from John Barton: 'Christianity is not in the last resort about relations between texts, but about events in the real world: the Word of God did not for us become incarnate in a book, but in a life.'[2] In other words, the real point of scripture, what it is 'about', is God's dealings with humankind in history, and its meaning is bound up, therefore, with *the meaning of the events* in which this history unfolds, events in the life of Israel and the life of Jesus through which God in some sense reveals himself and his purposes to us. Where the distinctively 'modern' approach differed, of course, was in its frank recognition that this meaning could no longer be found on the surface of the text. What was to be seen there was deceptive, and one must probe beneath it, engaging in careful historical detective work, pressing beyond the literal sense, beyond even the *original sense* of the text, and through a careful handling of the evidence and clues provided there, uncovering the deposit of meaning-laden history which lay behind it. We must build our theology and our life as the Christian church on the 'solid ground' of what actually happened. It is here that the genuine unity and coherence of the meaning of scripture could now be identified; not, that is to say, in what the texts themselves say, the various and diverse human perspectives which they offer, but, in Pannenberg's words, 'only behind them, in the figure of Jesus who is attested in the very different writings of the New Testament in very different and incongruous ways'.[3]

Like its pre-critical counterpart, then, this is a view in which scripture functions as a window onto the meaningful acts of God in history. We look through the text itself to discern something which lies behind it. What is now realized, however, is that the task of looking is one which must be approached with great care, for what appears at first glance in the glass is not readily identifiable with what is really there. The glass must be carefully wiped and our eyes adjusted to the conditions in order to eradicate the tricks of perspective and the light, so that we can make out the shape and dimensions of the factual reality which lies on the other side.

The assumption upon which this approach has generally proceeded is that its results will generate a reliable and agreed factual account of the history of Israel and the life of Jesus, and thereby undergird contemporary Christian faith and understanding with something resembling a solid foundation. But in practice it is not at all clear that the task of leaping over the yawning gaps from text to author to 'the facts' is one which can render this degree or sort of certainty. 'The facts of the Bible as elucidated by criticism' have an irksome tendency of turning out to look very different when the historico-critical tools are handled by different practitioners. Thus, for example, as is well known, the numerous attempts in the nineteenth century to offer for consideration scientific accounts of 'the life of Jesus' on the basis of the gospel narratives, far from providing a solid bedrock for faith as was intended, simply served to demonstrate the inherent fragility of historical inquiry and the provisionality of all its results.

Meaning and the Author's Intention

Recognition of this had led others to seek the authoritative meaning of scripture not in history as such, but in the meaning which the authors and editors of the biblical texts found there and intended to convey to their original readers through what they wrote. The recovery of this might be supposed to be a somewhat less ambitious and more manageable task. It may not be possible to arrive with any degree of certainty at the facts lying behind the text, but the text itself is in our possession, and with the aid of his-torico–critical skills we can subject it to careful examination and retrieve its original and authentic sense. Again we should note that in this approach the text is something that we look *through* rather than look at. The question which we ask as we do so has now changed. It is no longer 'What happened?' but 'What does the writer *think* about what happened?'. The words on the page now become clues to guide us in the retrieval of this psychological 'fact'.

This is the view taken, for example, by Klein, Blomberg and Hubbard in their recent book *Introduction to Biblical Inter-pretation.*[4] The question of the meaning of any part of the biblical text, they suggest, is identical with the question of the author's intended meaning. What did he intend his readers to understand from his words? Once we have answered this question we have answered the question of the text's meaning for the church, for we may assume that 'the writers or editors of the Bible intended to communicate to all people in the same way'.[5] Following the liter-ary theorist E. D. Hirsch[6] they concede that the text may indeed be understood in other ways as it is applied within other contexts and to new and different situations, but they designate these 'signifi-cances' which should not be confused with its *true* meaning, and must be set alongside the meaning itself in order that their legiti-macy might be evaluated. 'The meaning of a text,' they insist, 'is: *that which the words and grammatical structures of that text dis-close about the probable intention of its author/editor and the prob-able understanding of that text by its intended readers'*[7] and it is with uncovering this meaning, therefore that the task of biblical interpretation should be concerned first and foremost. For all prac-tical purposes, then, the author's meaning is the authorized version. For these three biblical scholars the importance of this careful dis-tinction is heightened by the claim that it is only the true meaning, and not the various later 'significances', which is inspired by God, since it alone is encoded within the actual form of the text in its original historical setting. The task of the biblical interpreter, there-fore, is to decode the text, and thereby to retrieve the hidden inspired meaning of its human author.

Other ways of thinking are possible. Thus, for example, John Barton, while he shares a similar approach to the question of the

meaning of the text, sees no need to invoke inspiration as a category. For him the original sense is vital for the church inasmuch as
it provides a normative 'record of the roots' of Christian belief, an
unchanging written deposit in which is captured the ways in which
the first Christians thought about Jesus and his significance, and
against which, therefore, the church today may check the authen-
ticity of its own beliefs. Here Barton follows Krister Stendahl's
sharp distinction between an essentially historical and 'descriptive'
approach to the biblical text (concerned with uncovering the 'original meaning') and a more theological task of discerning the text's
meaning for the church in its current circumstances (what he calls
'translation'). As Francis Watson observes, the assumption here is
that while the latter 'meaning' may only ever be provisional, the
former is something objective and fixed, and hence, once retrieved,
it 'gives us means to check whether our interpretation is correct or
not'.[8] This makes the task of 'translation' an altogether more manageable one, since, as Watson puts it, 'We can all join in and check
each other's results against the original.'[9] The descriptive approach
to scripture provides, as it were, an objective historical litmus test
with the aid of which we may check the chemistry of our present-
day readings and the faith which is rooted in them. Thus it is precisely the original sense of the text, its cultural and historical
particularity, which matters, for it is in this that the authority and
value of the Bible resides. The 'Christianness' of our contemporary
readings of the text is a matter of their relationship to the authentic or primitive Christian belief which we find reflected in the original sense.

This insistence that the 'proper' meaning of a text is identical
with what its author intended, while it has received considerable
support from literary theorists such as Hirsch, probably represents
in any case what most readers suppose to be the case most of the
time. We read, common sense suggests, in order to find out what
the writer thinks, and also, perhaps, thereby to find out something
about the thing or event which she is thinking/writing about. That,
I take it, is what most of us suppose ourselves to be doing when
we read the newspaper, or the letters which the postman brings, or
the road sign which flashes past us at speed on the motorway with
information concerning the next exit. The situation may be somewhat different, of course, when we read a work of fiction or a
poem. But even here, if some dispute concerning the meaning of
a phrase or a paragraph arises, what most readers instinctively find

themselves asking is 'I wonder what the writer had in mind here?' It is for this precise reason that tradition dubs the writer the 'author', that is, the one who authorizes the meaning.

But why should it be so? A moment's reflection suffices to challenge the over-hasty response that it is simply 'obvious' that it should be thus. Terry Eagleton, in his invaluable book *Literary Theory: An Introduction*,[10] points out that the assumption has no very obvious justification save its 'common sense' acceptance by most readers. 'There is no more reason in principle,' he writes, 'why the author's meaning should be preferred than there is for preferring the reading offered by the critic with the shortest hair or the largest feet.' Once it is conceded that other meanings are to be had from a text, then the question naturally arises concerning which should be preferred or granted priority. What the 'common sense' view amounts to in practice is a public conspiracy to protect private property. We (the reading public) agree, that is to say, that the meaning which shall be granted the status of 'authoritative' shall be that which the writer intended her readers to understand. We allow her the copyright, not just at the time of writing, but for so long as the text shall survive and be read.

The attractions of such a view for a Christian approach to scripture are obvious enough. For what this identification of writer as 'author' does is to provide a degree of fixity which the interpreter of the text (biblical or otherwise) may seek to lay hold of. A norm for interpretation is established, and the anarchy of a situation in which a welter of different meanings is identified, none of which may be considered any better or worse than any other, is avoided. This concern is especially understandable where a text or set of texts is expected to function authoritatively for the life of a community. Interpretative anarchy might be supposed to lead in this case to loss of communal identity and eventual despair. Not, of course, that the legitimacy of different interpretations of the biblical text could ever be denied within the church. Were this to be so then all preaching would have at once to cease, or at least there would be no genuine need for it. All that would be required would be a single 'authoritative' commentary in which the single authoritative meaning of the text were laid out for consideration. But in practice all Christians recognize that the text must be read and applied afresh to new situations, within new contexts which bring new questions to it. That is what is taking place both in pulpits and works of theology. But the question must be faced whether, in this task, there can be identified any fixed criteria or principles for evaluating the 'meanings' which are retrieved in this ongoing task, or whether, on the contrary, anything goes. Thus, whether in its more conservative/biblicist or liberal versions, the concern to uncover the original sense of scripture is essentially a historico-critical bid to identify an immovable textual basis for Christian existence, to furnish an authoritative reading of the text alongside which the legitimacy of others may be gauged. What we must do, it is suggested, is to compare our contemporary readings, applications and 'significances' with the real thing – the meaning which the author had in mind.

The Text as Common Ground?

This may be a laudable intention, but there are some serious problems with it which we must take careful note of. Those who practise this approach often seem prepared to invest a considerable (perhaps surprising) amount of confidence in its results. The author's meaning, it is generally supposed, is, like the physical text itself, a publicly accessible and establishable fact. While it may take a considerable amount of effort to uncover it through historico-critical attention to the text, the original meaning may nonetheless be laid hold of in a way which is demonstrable and accessible in principle to all readers. Hence for Stendahl, for example, the 'descriptive' task 'may be carried out by believer and unbeliever alike'. It is an objective quantity in the sense that it is bound up with the author's relationship to the words on the pages of his text. What the text 'means', therefore, does not vary from age to age or place to place, but is fixed, and may be recovered. Such an assumption is necessary if this original sense is to serve as an objective standard of comparison, and thereby to render a firm basis for adjudicating between competing contemporary interpretations or significances.

As Stanley Hauerwas has pointed out, this assumption unites the critical approach to scripture with its pre-critical counterpart. There is a meaning 'in' this text, and it is one which may be retrieved by anyone who cares to take the requisite amount of trouble to do so, whether by the simple application of common sense, or the more complex application of historical sense. The Bible, in other words, is in some sense common ground as well as holy ground.

The main criticism levelled at the pre-critical reader was, we may recall, that he mistook what he saw as he looked at the text for the text's real meaning which in actuality lay concealed beneath the surface. The literal meaning which, it had been supposed, was obvious to all readers, was thus shown to be deceptive, and the task of penetrating beneath it to the authentic sense was begun in earnest. But it may be argued that the move from 'what the Bible clearly teaches' to 'the assured results of higher criticism' is not so much a move beyond naivety as a shifting of the focus of that naivety. For in reality the results prove not to be so assured as some have supposed. (Any reader doubting this is invited to consult any two commentaries on a given passage of scripture and to compare their conclusions.) The question which some recent developments in the theory of interpretation have raised, therefore, is whether the historico-critical approach is not equally prone to confuse the results of its own interpretative labours in a simplistic way for 'the meaning of the text itself'. There are two very good reasons for suspecting that this might be so: on the one hand the problematic nature of the text; and on the other the problematic nature of the reader.

The Importance of Getting the Joke

What the emergence and development of historical consciousness has impressed upon us in no uncertain terms is the fact that reading texts from times and places other than our own is not so simple or straightforward a matter as might at first be supposed. Even when such texts have been helpfully translated into modern English (a task of interpretation, we should note, in the execution of which the opportunities for distortion and misunderstanding of the original are already legion) there is yet a further task of 'translation' to be done by the competent reader. The reason for this is that, notwithstanding their apparent innocence, all texts are written in a form of code. Writers write what they write for particular groups of people. Within such groups or communities there is invariably a shared fund of popular knowledge upon which both writer and readers may draw. Thus a writer may well allude to events, texts, themes, practices and so on, which are never presented or explained directly in his words, but which form what is sometimes called the 'pre-understanding' which he assumes will be present and to which, therefore, he addresses himself.

To pick an obvious biblical example, when Jesus told a parable about a landlord and the tenants occupying his vineyard he could take it for granted that those who heard the story would be familiar with the rich imagery in the Old Testament of Israel as the vineyard of the Lord. Once this pre-understanding is appreciated, the story which Jesus tells becomes one about God, the various recalcitrant kings of Israel, the prophets whom God sends to call them to account, and, provocatively and enigmatically for his hearers, God's own Son whom he sends knowing that he will be put to death. If this pre-understanding is absent, then this meaning will simply be missed. The hearer or reader simply will not 'get it' because the wealth of associations which the story is intended to trigger off are not there to be triggered. The same phenomenon is observable in the case of 'in jokes', the humour of which is really only apparent to the initiated who know the hidden significance of a certain phrase or allusion. To be an outsider when such a joke is shared is to miss the point, to be excluded from the fun. These are very specific examples where such irony is accepted. But there is a sense in which all human communication (verbal or textual) manifests some such irony. We always say much less than we mean, and we take for granted a body of understanding and associations through which the words we use will send signals dashing in all directions to our hearers or readers. Writers, in other words, play into the hands of readers' expectations. Such expectations are part and parcel of the communicative process itself, and the absence of them leaves it incomplete or damaged. Put differently, the pre-understanding which the writer assumes on the part of his readers is in effect something which the readers must bring to the text in order to retrieve its intended 'meaning'. Meaning, we might say, is a transaction between a writer and his readers in which both must contribute something.

The problem which faces the contemporary interpreter of historically and culturally distant texts, therefore, is that he or she does not belong, is not party to the shared fund of pre-understanding, and therefore lacks the vital equipment which will enable the text to be fully translated or decoded. That is why training in historico-critical method consists basically in an attempt to familarize the student to the greatest possible degree with such contexts, to enable her to step sympathetically into the shoes of a typical first-century Jew, or an Elizabethan artisan, or a Victorian aristocrat, or whoever, in the hope that in so doing she may begin to 'get the joke' in the Gospels, in Shakespeare's plays, in Dickens' novels and so on. That is why commentaries on the Bible spend so much time telling us about the social, political, religious and other conditions within which the texts emerged, since familarity with these, it is supposed, will enable us better to align ourselves with the original reader, to see through his or her eyes. We are being initiated in part into the original community of readers, granted access to the shared fund of knowledge, the pre-understanding which provides, as it were, the reader's contribution to 'the original meaning' of the text.

The Problem of the Private Thesaurus

Let us suppose, for the moment, that it were possible to do this with some degree of success and to 'become' in effect a contemporary of Paul or the Gospel writers for the sake of reading their material. This is still, we should have to recognize, a considerable way short of laying hold with any degree of certainty of the author's intended meaning, although it may get us a good deal closer than we should otherwise be. The point is this: in order to know exactly what the author 'had in mind' we should have to do much more than become one of his contemporaries. We should have, in fact, to be able to see inside his head, and this is something to which not even the most competent historical critic may aspire! There are, as I have just indicated, what we might call social constraints on language and meaning. In other words, it is not possible for us to make a word or a sentence 'mean' something which bears no relation whatever to its everyday uses in a particular context, just because we intend or will it to mean this. There are boundaries placed around the possible uses to which words can reasonably be put, and shared pools of association from which meanings may legitimately be drawn. Yet at the same time we are perfectly well aware that words and sentences can nonetheless bear quite different meanings or nuances to our neighbours. We say something to someone. We know what we mean. But the words are received differently and we find (perhaps) that we have given offence without having intended to do so. And the main reason for this is not hard to find. For, while it is true that those who are contemporaries and neighbours share a certain 'pre-understanding', the sharing only goes so deep. Once we dig deeper what we find is that the associations which particular words, phrases, images and so on have for each of us are shaped decisively by the specific experiences which we have had in life; our childhood, our upbringing, our social status, our education, and so on. So that while a particular word may signify a certain amount to two or more people in common, beneath the surface the streams of association will run deep and diverge, perhaps quite significantly.

George Steiner in his helpful book *After Babel* explores this phenomenon and concludes that each living person draws in effect
upon two quite distinct sources of meaning. First, there is the 'current vulgate', the shared pool of associations and significances
which exists at the surface and is the stuff that makes communication possible at all. This is the tip of the iceberg which is visible to
all those who belong. But then, hidden beneath this, there is also
what Steiner refers to as a 'private thesaurus' which each of us possesses, and which has been compiled through the radically individual set of experiences and associations which go to make up our
unique human personality, and which lurks in our subconscious.[11]
Thus, he suggests, when we communicate with others we do so
only 'at the surface'.[12] What any two people 'mean' when they utter
or hear the same words, therefore, will overlap only to a certain
extent by virtue of their sharing in the 'vulgate' of a particular
human group. Were a full account of their meaning to be possible
it would appear at once that the words in question 'meant' quite
different things to each. What Steiner suggests, therefore, is that
there is in practice a process of translation involved in every act of
human communication.[13] We seek to attune our ears to the associations which a word has for the person speaking, to dig beneath
the surface level and to invade their private thesaurus. To the extent
that we are successful, genuine communication occurs. To the extent
that we fall short, there will be failure and misunderstanding. Even
though we hear their words, we shall miss what they are saying to
us. But, since none of us has the capacity actually to become someone else for the purpose of grasping their meaning, we can do so
only with a hope of partial success, and there will always be an
extent (sometimes quite considerable) to which we misunderstand
what they are saying. Such is the slipperiness of words and meanings even among those who claim to 'speak the same language'.

What this drives us to concede, therefore, is that the attempt by
historico-critical scholars to retrieve 'the author's original intended
meaning' from the biblical texts is in the strict sense a lost cause.
Not even Paul's mother or his best friends could hope to achieve
this with any degree of finality or certainty. We cannot simply take
the words which Paul uses and pin down precisely 'what they
would have meant to a first-century Palestinian Jew'. It would be
convenient if we could, but in reality language is not like that. The
relationship between words and meanings is much more open-
ended, so that 'There can be no determination of all "the functions

words can serve" at any given time.'[14] This being the case, it appears at once that the most which historico-critical tools can do is to enable us to penetrate to some degree into the *generalities* of their use, to become conversant in the vulgate, the popular conventions and ways of thinking which would have governed the author's use of language at the surface, and thereby to begin to reconstruct the *probable* meaning of the words used by him. Perhaps in doing so we shall be able to discern ways in which his own particular use transcends the vulgate, to see how he deploys words in distinctive ways in order to bring to expression those resonances and associations which are peculiarly his own. But we shall never fathom his intended meaning completely. To do so would be a denial of his distinct personhood, and an abandonment of ours.

The Text as Looking-Glass

The actual results of historico-critical retrievals of the original sense of the biblical text do not encourage excessive optimism concerning the sort of certainty which attaches to them. As has already been indicated, comparison of any two commentators on the same passage of scripture is likely to reveal clear disagreement even over fundamental matters, rather than a basic consensus. We have seen that there are good reasons for this inherent in the slipperiness of historical texts themselves, and the difficulties created by historical distance. Cracking codes is an awkward business. But literary criticism has come increasingly to recognize that it is not only the text which is problematic in the quest for meaning; we as readers are just as big a variable in the problem of pinning down the text's sense.

Confessing our 'Readerly Guilt'

Terry Eagleton puts the matter neatly. The reader, he reminds us, 'does not come to the text as a kind of cultural virgin, immaculately free of previous social and literary entanglements, a supremely disinterested spirit or blank sheet onto which the text will transfer its own inscriptions'.[15] On the contrary, each of us is possessed of 'readerly guilt', our readings are affected from the very outset both by the pre-understanding which we inherit from our own social and historical context, and by the 'private thesaurus' bequeathed us by our personal pilgrimage through life. We cannot help but be shaped by these things. What we see when we look at the text, even when we do so with the aid of historico-critical tools, will still be precisely what *we*, as socially and historically located readers, see. We are not capable of ceasing to be the particular readers that we are. We can no more step out from behind our pre-under-standing to see 'the text itself' or the 'original meaning itself' than we can leave our bodies behind and view the world from a God's-eye perspective. To suppose otherwise is again to lay claim to the view from nowhere. But we cannot do it. We cannot become socially and personally disembodied time travellers, able to step into the shoes and see the world through the eyes of readers of other ages and other places at will. We may strive after such empathy; we may even go some way towards attaining it. That is what the task of translation and interpretation is all about. But at the end of the day we shall not escape our own historical and personal situation.

When we read a text, therefore, we do so as those who bring to it a particular set of assumptions, questions, expectations, most of which will be wholly subconscious and therefore all the more influential upon our reading. From within the 'privacy' of our own mental set we set out to try and make sense of what we read. And 'make sense' is precisely what we do. The meaning which we retrieve from it will be in substantial part a product of the pre-understanding which we bring to bear upon it. What we should seek to do as interpreters, of course, is to become aware of our own pre-understanding, to take stock of it and to transcend it in a bid to become aware of the pre-understanding of the author or original readers, to view the text from a perspective distinct from the one which we habitually occupy. But, as I have already indicated, we can never do so absolutely since pre-understandings (both the author's and our own) run deep and are irreducibly personal. 'No two human beings,' writes Steiner, 'share an identical associative context. Because such a context is made up of the total-ity of an individual existence, because it comprehends not only the sum of personal memory and experience but also the reservoir of the particular subconscious, it will differ from person to person'.[16] Furthermore, no statement ever means precisely the same twice, even when made by the same individual. What a word 'means' for us changes and develops with each new use of it. This being so, it follows that in order for any interpretation to retrieve the *precise meaning* of the original, the interpreter would in effect have to 'become' the author at the exact moment of writing.

What all this leads us to admit, therefore, is that the meaning which we retrieve from a text (historical or contemporary) will never be absolutely identical with the meaning which it had for its author, or, indeed, with its meaning for any other reader. Meaning is in constant metamorphosis. This is so precisely because meaning is not something wholly objective, but the product of an interaction between two sets of variables – the signals transmitted by the author, and the wavelengths to which our readerly receiver is tuned. To borrow again from Eagleton's inimitable stock of images: 'The meanings of a text do not lie within [it] like wisdom teeth within a gum, waiting patiently to be extracted'.[17] So we should query the view which suggests that sufficient training in theological dentistry will equip us to uproot them, and recognize instead that the meanings we extract will always be in part at least a product of the readers that we are.

It is here, I think, that the genuine risk of naivety in historico-critical approaches is exposed. For while such approaches have been ready enough to acknowledge the historical particularity of the text and author, they have not always taken fully seriously their own particularity, and have often aspired to the role of socially disembodied time traveller, unhindered by presuppositions and assumptions. This is to see the speck in the eye of the text, while overlooking the plank which distorts one's own vision. The result of such naivety is that one is able to make clear-cut and convenient distinctions between 'the original meaning' and other interpretations and significances, and to compare the latter with the former as if it were some sort of wholly objective and factual control or norm for interpretation. But the original meaning which even the best historical critic comes up with is itself an interpretation, a reconstruction. It may be a more or less efficient one. But it is certainly not 'the original meaning' as such. It cannot be. We cannot, as it were, lift ourselves up by our bootstraps out of our personal and cultural frame of reference and discover in some absolutely objective way what the biblical writers had in mind. The distinction between 'what the text means' and 'what the text means to me' is to this extent a wholly misleading one.

At this point the notion of the text as transparent, a window through which we may gaze with our vision unhindered to see something which lies beyond or behind it, begins to wobble dangerously and is best set aside as a basis for approaching scripture. The suggestion which is emerging is that the text may in fact prove to be a partially reflective surface, so that what we see as we consider it or look upon it (its 'meaning') is in some sense and to some extent always going to be a reflection of what we ourselves bring to it. Meaning, rather than being anterior to the text and observable through it, is, it now seems, something which *happens* as we read the text and which is, therefore, like the knowledge of the Lord in which the psalmist rejoiced, new every morning.

The Metamorphosis of Meaning

Recent developments in literary theory have come increasingly to recognize and to lay stress upon the role of the reader in the event in which meaning happens, rather than attending primarily either to the author or to the supposed referent which lie behind the text. The reader, it is now more often acknowledged, it vital to the text. Without her the text remains inert upon a shelf. It has no 'meaning,' because it 'means' nothing to anybody. Only once it is picked up, dusted off, opened, and read does it begin to mean something. What it 'means', many would now want to suggest, will depend at least in part upon the particular context within which it is read, and even upon the particular reader herself.

In one particular school of thought this swing of the pendulum has gone so far as to suggest that 'meaning' really has very little at all to do with the author, his circumstances or literary intentions, but is determined entirely by the reader. Thus one American advocate of the so-called reader-response approach to the text, Stanley Fish, argues that texts do not have or possess permanent meanings which it is the job of the interpreter subsequently to discover or retrieve. Rather, meaning is the word which we use to describe what happens to us as readers when we read texts. Put differently, 'The reader's response is not *to* the meaning: it *is* the meaning.'[18] What this boils down to is the suggestion that when we approach a text what it will mean for us will not be determined in any way by the text itself or anything 'in' it, but entirely by the expectations, associations, questions and significances which we bring to it.

Behind this view there lies an unashamed philosophical scepticism and relativism. Human beings, the ways in which they understand the world, the languages which they use to describe it, are, Fish believes, wholly conditioned by particular historical and cultural perspectives. Occupants of different social and historical contexts (different communities) will 'construct' the world differently and in discordant ways. The perspectives which they occupy will be so diverse, that is to say, as to be incompatible. There will be no significant overlap between them. Thus, speaking utterly different languages (both literally and metaphorically) they will be unable to see things in the same terms, or to mean the same thing even when they employ the very same words.

In the case of texts, which may pass physically unchanged from one historical or social context to another, what this implies is that it will be quite impossible for a reader in one context to enter sympathetically into the 'meaning' which a text might have for a reader in another context. What Fish denies, in other words, is that we are capable in any way of transcending our historical and social locatedness. Because meaning, as we have already suggested, is never absolutely stable or fixed, because it is strictly never the same twice, he concludes that there is no fixity or stability whatever; that there can be no overlap, no point of contact, between what texts mean for readers in different contexts. Here, as so often elsewhere, disillusionment with a false objectivism capitulates all too rapidly to total relativism. Meaning, like truth, becomes what we make of it. There is no 'real' or authorized meaning. There is only an infinite series of different meanings all but one of which may have little directly to do with anything which the author 'had in mind'. Since we cannot in any way know what the author had in mind we must make a virtue out of a necessity, and insist that what really matters for us is not some strange antiquated and inaccessible 'original sense', but what the text says to us in our particular circumstances, as readers with particular needs and wants and questions.

Pushed to its logical conclusion, especially when we taken into consideration what Steiner has to say about the 'private thesaurus' which each reader consults in reading, this could result all too easily in the view that what a text 'means' is entirely in the hands of individual readers and what they choose to do with it, a view embraced by adherents of the more radical 'deconstructionist' school of thought. Fish himself carefully avoids such rampant individualism by insisting that our expectations and responses as readers are fundamentally shaped by the communities to which we belong. What a word or phrase 'means' for us, in other words, is constrained and guided by what our shared communal rules of discourse permit it to mean.

In various ways, I believe, Fish's reader-response approach to the question of text and meaning is one which Christian readers of the Bible cannot dismiss too quickly. But, as I shall suggest in the next chapter, the thoroughgoing relativism which undergirds it renders it highly problematic for a community which seeks to place itself genuinely under the authority of a set of texts. For in the end of the day what Fish suggests is that what we see when we look at the text is little more than a reflection of our own corporate image, of a meaning which we as a community of readers 'authorize'. But a man who consults his own reflection in a mirror for guidance is in little danger of hearing anything he does not want to hear. Except in the world of fairy tales he will very likely remain undisturbed in his conviction that he is 'the fairest of them all'. The truth may be rather different.

The Stained Glass Text

We turn finally in this chapter to consider an approach to texts which seeks to rescue their 'meaning' from the greedy clutches of referent, author and reader alike. The chief characteristic of 'formalism' in its various guises is its insistence that what a text *means* is a question which may be answered only in terms of the text itself, and not by inquiring after what lies behind it, or by exploring the emotional responses of individual readers or communities of readers to it. The text, it is argued, once written and made public, must be treated as something which has a life of its own, an object in its own right, an object possessed of a clear form or structure which can be appreciated for its own sake. It constitutes a self-contained, coherent, and integral whole which may be explored and enjoyed by the reader without any specific knowledge of the author or the particular historical circumstances in which it was written, just as the average tourist may marvel at the flying buttresses and vaulted arches of a great cathedral without any information about either the architect or the builders. Its meaning is a matter of the way in which its various components are related to one another, the way it is constructed or crafted, its finished form as a work of art. A text may thus in some sense be said to create its own 'world of meaning' which is *sui generis*; there is no need to refer beyond it to the real world, to its author, or to anything else in order to access this meaning. The text itself constitutes an entire and self-enclosed 'system' in terms of which the meaning of individual words, phrases or whatever within it is to be determined. Since form or structure is something fixed in the physical text as such, the meaning of a text may therefore be said to be objective and permanent, and there to be grasped by anyone with an eye for literary architecture.

This notion first emerged with the so-called New Critics in the 1930s who applied it primarily to the form of the poem. Before long, however, similar ideas were being applied more radically to works of drama, to novels, and ultimately to literary texts in general. Meaning was being saved from the contingency and inherent fragility of historico-critical results on the one hand, and the apparent subjectivism of reader-oriented models on the other, and offered to the reading public as something objective and scientifically establishable. Interpretation, it was now held, was essentially a matter of literary pattern recognition. Texts were ultimately reducible to the discrete literary building blocks out of which they were constructed; universal myths, types and figures which recurred over and over again in new guise, literary structures which could be seen to operate in accordance with identifiable universal rules and mechanisms. The interpreter, armed with a basic knowledge of these rules and little else, could happily retire to his study, clear the clutter of historical and philological reference works from his desk, and engage dispassionately in the task of laying bare the 'objective meaning' of a text.

Formalist theories and methods have found an increasingly receptive attitude among those concerned with the interpretation of biblical texts. There has been no shortage of those willing to adopt or at least to borrow the tools of 'structuralism', for example, as providing a fresh approach to the question of the meaning of the Gospels, epistles, and various Old Testament texts. In more general terms, the influence of some of the less radical manifestations of formalism (or at least some essentially similar ideas) may be traced in two distinct but closely related developments in Christian approaches to scripture; namely, canonical criticism and narrative criticism.

Think of the collection of books which any person may happen to have on their bookshelf at any given time. In such a collection there might be some novels, some historical texts, perhaps a collection of poems, a dictionary, and so on. The books have something in common insofar as they are part of the same collection, but in reading them we do not really take this into account. We take each book from the shelf in turn and treat it as a distinct entity, allowing its meaning to be determined by all sorts of things, but not normally by its relationship to the other books on the shelf. This, we might suppose, is a somewhat arbitrary factor and irrelevant to the understanding of any particular volume. This is, in a sense, precisely how the historico-critical method urged readers to think of the collection (or canon) of books which make up the Christian Bible. The canonical critic, however, urges us to construe things differently. Instead of thinking of it as a collection of different volumes, the canon of scripture can and should, he argues, be thought of as one large text, the various parts of which relate to one another not as discrete works on a shelf, but rather as chapters in a single work. Once this interpretative step is taken, the question of the meaning of a particular text has to be addressed in a quite distinct way. For, to pursue the analogy, a particular chapter from a novel cannot properly be understood in isolation, but only when one relates it to what precedes and follows it in the overall structure of the plot as a whole. More than this, whereas historical inquiry may well uncover earlier and more primitive forms of a text or portion of text, or provide some account of the actual course of events lying behind the text, the canonical critic sets this aside as interesting but strictly irrelevant for the question of *the text's meaning as scripture*. What matters is *the final form of the text as we have it*, both in its individual parts and its overall structure and shape.

What canonical criticism does, then, is in effect to insist upon treating the Bible in its entirety as one large and self-contained literary work with a coherence and integrity of its own. The meaning of any passage within the text is to be discerned through its place in the work as a whole, and not traced back to its original historical location or to the author's intention. The text has a life and a meaning of its own in which the meanings of individual parts of it are swallowed up and transformed. Thus, for example, the meaning of Isaiah 11.1–10 as scripture is not the meaning which it would have had for the original reader, or for the prophet himself, but rather the meaning which it has as part of 'the world of the text' in which the same prophecy is understood as fulfilled in the figure of Jesus of Nazareth. Meaning is a matter of the relationships between themes, events, figures and lines of development of the 'plot' within the contours and structure of the text as a whole. This does not make historical attention to the text irrelevant, but secondary so far as the meaning of the text as *scripture* is concerned.

Narrative criticism urges a similar attention to the text as such and as a unitary whole. Thus, for example, Hans Frei, whose work *The Eclipse of Biblical Narrative* was the major stimulus for theological reflection in this area, argues that historico-critical scholarship made a huge mistake when, having rightly prised apart the plain sense of scripture from its historical reference, it then proceeded to identify the *meaning* of scripture with the latter rather than the former. On the contrary, Frei insists, the meaning of the biblical texts is bound up inseparably with the story which they tell and the particular form in which they tell it. The bulk of scripture comes to us in the form of 'realistic narrative,' a history-like (but not necessarily factually precise or 'historical') medium the point of which is not to direct us away from itself to some more ultimate reality behind or beneath itself, but rather to provide a 'narrative world' into which we may enter and in which we may dwell. Once we see this, 'There is neither need for nor use in looking for meaning in a more profound stratum underneath the structure (a separable "subject matter") or in a separable author's "intention", or in a combination of such behind the scenes projections.'[19] To behave thus is to expend our interpretative energies unravelling a beautiful and carefully woven tapestry, the story depicted in the folds of which gradually disappears into piles of brightly coloured thread on the floor as we search for the 'meaning' somewhere else than in the tapestry itself.

What the reader is offered in the Bible taken in its literal or plain sense, according to Frei and others who have pursued his insights further, is just such a tapestry; a story, or rather a whole series of stories which nonetheless manifest an overall coherence and unity and render to the reader a realistic narrative world into which she is invited, as it were, imaginatively to step. It is a world in which God is actively involved, in which he has acted decisively for the salvation of a sinful human race by himself becoming human and embracing death on a cross, in which he has poured out his Spirit upon all flesh in redemptive and sanctifying power, and a world which now awaits and longs for the final revelation of his glory in the return of his Son as Judge and King. This, we may now say, is the meaning of the text. This is what it is about. Pre-critical readers were naive in their supposition that this story was simply a straightforward 'historical' account, a rendering of the real world and 'what actually happened' in its history. We now know that this is not the case in any obvious sense. But we may let that matter go, and hold instead to the narrative sense of the biblical text as the significant consideration for a reading of it as scripture. What lies behind or beyond the text is no longer considered to be the primary thing.

Instead it is to the story depicted on the surface that we must look for the text's meaning – the history-like narrative world which it presents for our consideration, and within which it invites us to locate ourselves as characters, participants in the fashioning of the story's next chapter.

What we have here, then, is not the transparent text through which we are invited to look to see something else; nor the text as mirror in which we discern the meanings which we as readers bring to it; but rather the text as stained glass *at which* we are called to look in order to discern its meaning. It is the story depicted in the brightly coloured shapes on the surface which is the important thing. This is the world of meaning within the horizons of which we must seek the meaning of any individual part. With stained glass, of course, there is a self-contained aspect which makes the question of what lies on the other side of it wholly irrelevant. Even to ask the question is to miss the whole point of what the window is designed to achieve. But, if the point of the text as narrative is to invite us to indwell the world offered there for our consideration, to make it our world, to become its citizens, then a question naturally arises about this 'formalist' approach to scripture. What is its relation to reality? How is the world depicted here related to the world in which we live? Why should we commit ourselves to it rather than other possible construals of reality? It is at least worth pondering the question just how long a community which, by some historical accident which we may safely leave our imaginations to contrive, found itself drawing for its sense of corporate identity upon the narrative worlds offered by Terry Pratchett or Mills and Boon would actually survive! It would seem, in other words, to be entirely relevant to inquire why precisely these particular texts and the story which they tell were identified and chosen, and just what they have to offer by way of a purchase on the reality of the human situation in the world. This question will not go away while we continue to take seriously the question of truth in our attempts to think theologically. We shall return to it in the next chapter in which I shall begin to sketch a provisional approach to an understanding of the Bible as the scripture of the community of faith.

NOTES

1 See Eagleton, T., *Literary Theory: An Introduction* (Basil Blackwell 1983) p. 6.
2 Barton, J., *People of the Book?* (SPCK 1988), p. 34.
3 Pannenberg, W., *Basic Questions in Theology* vol. 1 (SCM Press 1970), p. 37.
4 Klein, W., Blomberg, C., and Hubbard, R., *Introduction to Biblical Interpretation* (Word Books 1993).
5 Klein, Blomberg and Hubbard, *Introduction to Biblical Interpretation*, p. 132.
6 Hirsch, E. D., *Validity in Interpretation* (Yale University Press 1976).
7 Klein, Blomberg and Hubbard, *Introduction to Biblical Interpretation*, p. 133.
8 Stendahl, cited in Watson, F., *Text, Church and World* (T. & T. Clark 1994), p. 30.
9 Stendahl, cited in Watson, *Text, Church and World*, p. 30.
10 Eagleton, T., *Literary Theory: An Introduction*, p. 69.
11 Steiner, G., *After Babel* (Oxford University Press 1992), p. 47.
12 Steiner, *After Babel*, p. 181.
13 Steiner, *After Babel*, p. 207.
14 Steiner, *After Babel*, p. 142.
15 Eagleton, *Literary Theory*, p. 89.
16 Steiner, *After Babel*, p. 178.
17 Eagleton, *Literary Theory*, p. 89.
18 Fish, S., *Is There a Text in This Class? The Authority of Interpretive Communities* (Harvard University Press 1980), p. 3.
19 Frei, H., *The Eclipse of Biblical Narrative* (Yale University Press 1974), p. 281.

— 7 —

The Greatest Sermon in the World:
The Bible as the Community's Scripture

The Bible is the greatest sermon in the world .... It is the
preacher's book because it is the preaching book.

P. T. Forsyth

One of the benefits of travel, they say, is that in coming home one
is able to see the familiar with fresh eyes. I hope that our whirlwind
tour of different answers to the question of how meanings attach
to texts may achieve something similar, and perhaps provoke some
creative rethinking of our approach to meaning in the Bible. I want
in particular to explore the cash value of some of the insights
gleaned in the previous chapter for an understanding of how the
Bible functions as the scripture of the Christian community (rather
than, say, a resource for research into Jewish antiquity or the history of religious thought). Is there a distinctively Christian way to
read the Bible, and if so what does it look like? Does Christian faith
make a difference to the meanings we retrieve from the text? and
so on. This in turn will create a natural context for some brief discussion of the vexed question of the 'inspiration' of scripture.

The Slipperiness of Scripture

The thing which a study of literary theory impresses upon us most
forcefully is the fact of the uncomfortable indeterminacy of words
and meanings. Language is mercurial in its capacity to slip between
our fingers just when we think we have its meaning firmly within
our grasp. This ought to make us altogether less self-confident than
some of us often are in our claim to be laying hold of the 'Word of
God' as we read and interpret the biblical text. If we are, if God
really has committed himself to a relationship with humankind the
synapses of which are in some way tied up with human retrieval of
meaning from texts, then a study of language and meaning certainly does not encourage the sort of brusqueness which claims

135

confidently to have God's word pinned down neatly, and packaged for our consideration. Gone forever will be simplistic references to 'what the Bible clearly teaches', as if all one had to do were to look and see with the minimum of effort. The Bible does not often wear its meaning obviously, like a flower waiting to be plucked from its stem. On the contrary, if we are to hear what it is saying to us then we must learn to listen. We must engage seriously and responsibly with it, often wrestling with it at length before we may demand its blessing.

Even when we have done this, through careful attention to such resources as lie within our reach – commentaries, dictionaries, and so on – the results of our reading will and can never be precisely the same twice. For we, as those who handle and 'make sense' of it, are never the same twice. The sum of our actions and experiences changes from second to second, and with it the precise 'meaning' which a word or phrase may bear for us. A passage of scripture never addresses us in precisely the same way twice therefore. Each reading adds something fresh to our understanding of it. Meaning, we might say, is a communication in which there are two poles to be considered. There is the text itself, possessed of a relative objectivity in as much as the words on the page remain constant, and these words were cast in this form by an author or editor with a particular meaning in mind (even if we cannot retrieve this absolutely), and the range of their probable meanings is in some sense dictated by the cultural and linguistic context within which he or she wrote. And then on the other hand there is the irreducible individuality of the reader, belonging to a different cultural framework, and informed by a unique set of personal particulars, social, experiential, psychological and so on. And meaning takes place in the interaction between these two poles.

What we must say, therefore, is that there is an inbuilt variable in the task of reading and interpretation; a variable which renders all talk of 'assured results' highly problematic, even in the most academic or scientific of contexts. For even our attempts to transcend our particularity and to discover the 'original sense', however successful they may be, are always the product of a process into which a degree of indeterminacy is inevitably built and from which it cannot wholly be purged without us ceasing to be the particular readers that we are. My reading of Paul's meaning in Galatians is always going to be *my reading* (i.e. Paul's meaning as it appears to me) no matter how carefully I pursue it; and it will never be *absolutely identical* with yours or with Paul's own. The question to be asked concerns the degree of overlap that we may reasonably expect there to be. Thus the retrieval of meaning from texts is rather more risky (and altogether more dynamic and exciting) than either 'what the Bible clearly teaches' or 'the assured results of critical method' can cope with.

There will be those who will suggest that, if it is truly thus, then God has left his church in an impossible circumstance. Indeterminacy, for such people, is always a terminal condition. Unless some rock-solid, absolutely certain basis or foothold can be provided for our efforts to interpret the Bible then, they will maintain, our readings can only ever be arbitrary and unassured; constructed uneasily in the midst of a slough of interpretive despond, and likely at any moment to sink with a gurgle, and without trace. This same desire for textual surety manifests itself, it seems to me, in the fundamentalist appeal to the clear teaching of an inerrant scripture, the historico-critical appeal to scientifically established and objective results, and the Roman Catholic provision of an infallible interpreter of the text. In each case the responsibility for meaning is lifted conveniently from the shoulders of the reader.

Others will embrace a radical relativism of meanings with brave spirit, equally convinced that where there is no absolute certainty there can be absolutely no certainty; that the only permanence which meaning may have is that which we (or the community to which we belong) choose to bestow; and that meaning, therefore, like a fleeting liaison, should be enjoyed while it lasts. In a sense this also shifts responsibility for meaning from the reader, since he is freed from any constraints laid down by the text itself, free to do with it what he (or his community) likes.

The Taming of the Text

This radical polarizing of two equally despairing alternatives is both unnecessary and, for the purposes of a Christian understanding of how God speaks through scripture, distinctly unhealthy. To take the latter point first, both objectivism and pluralism effectively muzzle and domesticate the text, albeit in quite different ways. Thus those who, whether from a biblicist-fundamentalist or an historico-critical perspective, insist that the real or 'true' meaning of a passage of scripture is firmly established and laid bare in their commentary upon it, succeed in practice only in confusing the two.

In doing so, they render themselves quite immune to any alternative readings of the text. They 'have' the text. They are no longer genuinely open, therefore, to consider it afresh, or to hear it speaking in any other voice than the one which they have now trapped, tamed, and packaged for observation. But other readings, other interpretations, are always possible. It is for each to commend itself by careful argument and persuasion in the face of others and in the light of the objective form of the text. But we should never take the fatal step of identifying our interpretations (however careful they may be) with the text itself, or with 'the meaning of the text itself'. To do so is to bestow upon them a finality, a sufficiency, which lifts them above the text and out of reach of its criticism. Far from establishing the text's authority, therefore, this is a strategy which effectually overthrows it, and enthrones our interpretation in its place.

The flight to complete relativism, however, is equally ill-advised. For here, too, there is a cleverly disguised attempt to control the text, to handle it with a cheery confidence precisely because any danger of its asserting itself in unexpected ways has been precluded in advance. By abandoning the quest to discover the 'true' or original meaning, by conceding the claim that the only meaning available to us as readers is a meaning which we construct out of materials which we bring with us to the text, this approach is equally effective in preventing the text from exercising any genuine authority. There is nothing in the text which constrains our interpretations. Such constraints as bear upon us come from the interpretative tradition within which we stand, from our particular perspective as readers. Unable to transcend this particularity we are incapable of hearing any strange or uncomfortable voice speaking from the text. We are protected from doing so. The meanings which we retrieve from it are those which our context authorizes. In other words, the text means what we will allow it to mean. In effect, we draw the text's teeth before we bravely place our head into its mouth in the task of interpretation The net result of such relativism is that the text has no real bite! We are granted, and can offer, no reason for preferring one meaning or reading of the text over another, save that in fact the community to which we belong recognizes this one as orthodox, and proscribes that as heterodox. The rules by which we interpret, in accordance with which we make sense of scripture, that is to say, cannot claim any legitimation from the text itself, since all knowledge of the text itself is deemed illusory. But nor, of course, can these rules and authoritative interpretations feel any real challenge from this same inscrutable text. When it roars they will, if they so choose, hear it as a purr and offer it a saucer of milk. It is difficult, then, to conclude otherwise than that on such a scenario the authority of the text has been subjugated to that of the interpretative community.

Cultivating the Art of Hearing

In place of these alternatives it seems to me that we must look again at *what actually happens* in the process of reading, and recognize it as a process in which there is both determinacy and indeterminacy, givenness and variation, genuine objectivity and an irreducibly 'personal coefficient' on the part of the reader. This being so, it follows that we are faced neither with the possibility of an absolute certainty nor the inevitability of arbitrary interpretive flux. It is somewhere in the complicated area between these two that all genuine communication occurs. We speak, and we hope that others will hear what we are saying. As George Steiner argues, the logical structure of every act of communication between humans is precisely the same. Whether we are listening to a neighbour's account of yesterday's cricket match, or poring over an ancient document with lexical tools to hand, the nature of what is happening is precisely the same. An act of translation is involved in both cases; an effort (conscious or unconscious) to align our own horizon of understanding with that of another to the greatest extent possible, to become those 'with ears to hear'. To the extent that we fall short of achieving this completely (as we invariably do) there is misunderstanding and its attendant difficulties to be reckoned with. Thus, as the German linguisticist Wilhelm von Humboldt saw long ago, 'All understanding is at the same time a misunderstanding, all agreement in thought and feeling is also a parting of the ways.'[1] There can be little doubt that the task is altogether more difficult, and misunderstanding correspondingly more likely, when there are linguistic and cultural as well as personal differences between transmitter and receiver; but, Steiner insists, we need not be so pessimistic as the born-again relativist suggests. 'We *do* speak of the world and to one another,' he writes. 'We *do* translate intra-and interlingually and have done so since the beginning of human history. The defence of translation has the immense advantage of abundant vulgar fact.'[2]

What Steiner points us to is the fact that the boundaries between cultures and communities are no more hard and fast than those which differentiate us from one another as distinct human persons. The attempt to make cultural and linguistic lines of demarcation absolute is therefore rather arbitrary, no matter how fashionable it might be. Our identities as members of particular communities represent but one level of identity on a spectrum ranging from our shared common humanity to the uniqueness of our own personhood.

The notion that the members of a particular community share a common language is thus true, but only to a degree. They also individualize that language, assembling their own private thesauruses from which the meanings which they retrieve from speech and text are in part drawn. If, then, notwithstanding such barriers, communication is possible between individuals, if translation can and does occur across the gaps created by our individual privacies, then we need not despair of hearing voices speaking to us from other cultures, other times and places. Meaning may be fragile, may break in transit if not handled with care, but it is a legitimate freight. This being so, the attempt to hear such voices, to discern the original sense of a text, is both legitimate and, within limits, possible.

Steiner offers an account of the task which takes fully seriously both its value and its inbuilt limitations. We begin with faith; 'an investment of belief, underwritten by previous experience ... in the meaningfulness ... of the ... text.'[3] We trust, in other words, that there is a meaning to be had, something 'there' to be laid hold of. We cannot prove that this is so. We may, in the end of the day, end up talking only to ourselves. Then, second, there is an act of aggression, an invasion of the world of text and author in which we 'go out and get' the meaning in order to carry it home captive. Through careful historical, cultural and linguistic study we immerse ourselves in another world, seeking to become connoisseurs in a process which, contrary to the popular ways of presenting it, 'is not a science, but an exact art'.[4] Third, we introduce the newly retrieved meaning to our own world of understanding, a circumstance which cannot leave that world unchanged. There is, to use Steiner's own metaphor, the ever-present risk of infection from imported cargo. We may find ourselves forced to reckon with new and uncomfortable ways of looking at things. (It is this which relativistic refusals to acknowledge the possibility of translation preclude, but which a reading of scripture as in some sense God's Word to his people might be supposed likely to produce.) And then finally, there is what Steiner calls the stage of 'restitution', in which the interpreter or translator seeks faithfully to offer some account of the meaning which he brings home in terms familiar to those unable to make the intellectual journey for themselves. He attempts to 'say again' in his own tongue what is said in the original. But the result of this linguistic mediation is only ever partial and provisional. It is at best uncertain. The degree of success will depend on the one hand upon the accessibility to scrutiny of the original context of meaning, and on the other upon the skills of the one who seeks to practice the art of hearing.

The Blessing of Babel

In this unstable balance between objective and personal, determinate and indeterminate, Steiner suggests, there is to be found the genius of language which both provides sufficient stability for genuine communication to occur and sufficient instability for language actually to refer to a world of experience which is complex, ever-changing, and open-ended. Words and their meanings are solid enough to be traced and handled, but malleable enough to be moulded and shaped creatively to meet new circumstances and new realities. Similarly, it seems that God may just have known what he was doing when he committed himself to language as a medium within which his self-communication to humans might substantially occur. On the one hand, there is the abiding objective physical form of the text of scripture which, taken together with the several original contexts in which it was fashioned, constitutes in some sense an objective 'given' – a source of meaning or meanings there to be sought after and retrieved. We begin with the supposition that God's self-giving to humans is in some direct way tied up with what the human authors and editors of this textual package wished to convey to their readers. We want to know just what they had in mind. Insofar as our interpretations of scripture are approximations to this objective sense there will be an identifiable continuity between them, even though they will never be identical. In our task of interpretation we commit ourselves in faith to the retrieval of this meaning, the 'gospel' which shapes our identity as a church. We stand under a moral obligation to the text, which stands over against us, which comes to us from beyond and judges us as well as encouraging and confirming our insights and understanding.

On the other hand, the inherent instability of texts, the fact that every interpretation is strictly a new interpretation, bestows upon the task of reading scripture a freshness and vividness, and again a responsibility to submit our readings to an objective text which we must admit lies ever beyond our capacities to pin it down precisely. Whether we are engaged in the task of exegesis (What, so far as we can tell, did the text mean then?) or exposition (What is the meaning of the text for us today in our changed circumstance?), the event of interpretation is one which must be engaged in repeatedly, for the results are only ever provisional. We may be mistaken. Our insights are only ever partial, and they may need to be adjusted substantially. We must return to the text again and again and submit our interpretations to it, never resting content that we have the meaning pinned down for good. If we fall into the latter trap we cease to be faithful in our submission to the authority of scripture as such, and exalt our best readings of it instead. But this very indeterminacy and flux (so long as it is held in balance with what Tom Wright has called a 'critical-realist' commitment to an objective presence of meaning to be retrieved) far from being a pathogen in the church's life, may in fact be the very thing through which the ever-new freshness of the divine address meets us. The task of making sense of scripture should be more like facing a roaring lion than engaging in an archaeological dig on the inert remains of a 'text-osaurus' whose get-up-and-go has long since got up and gone. God speaks, and when he does so he speaks to us as the particular people that we are, in the particular circumstances that we are. What he has to say will, we may suppose, manifest some sort of identifiable continuity with what he has said to others in the past and in other situations, but it will never be simply identical. The indeterminacy of reading lends itself to just such a situation. The meaning of scripture is, in this sense, new every morning, just like the knowledge of the Lord of which it is in some way the vehicle.

Just a Story?

Of all the various possible approaches to the Bible which we have mentioned, the category of narrative seems to have the most to offer as a basis for understanding the way in which the text functions as the church's scripture. What the Bible *does* when we read it in its extant form, as its declared progression from 'Old' to 'New'

Testament suggests, is to tell a unitary story about the world in which we live; a story of creation, fall, promise, fulfilment and redemption; a story which has its narrative centre in the life and actions and fate of one man, Jesus of Nazareth. It is the story of God's dealings with his world and with his creatures in and through the particular histories of Israel and Jesus the Christ. It is this story – the gospel or good news focused in Jesus – upon the basis of which the church today fashions its identity, and in conformity to the contours of which it seeks to live its life. To be a Christian is in some sense to have one's own story shaped in a decisive way by and taken up into this other larger story of God's redemptive action in the world.

But the language of 'story' can bear unhelpful and misleading connotations. The word conjures up faint images of childhood. How many of us can recall sitting white-knuckled and incredulous in front of the TV set, watching breathlessly as the hero of some serial fiction reached the fate of yet another episode apparently doomed to some unspeakable end designed to guarantee that we would be there to tune in at the same time next week? At such times my childish anguish was often in need of motherly reassurance in the form of the time-honoured formula: 'Don't worry, it's only a story.' Only a story! At the age of nine I was glad to hear it. But can we greet the construal of the Bible's message as 'story' with the same relief or reassurance? Or does it rather leave us feeling the precise opposite; somewhat uneasy, and with a hunch that we need something rather more firm or substantial than 'just a story' around which to build our lives?

Suspicion of the category of story or narrative has been heightened by the way in which its advocates have sometimes denigrated traditional historico-critical approaches to the biblical text. The meaning of this text for the church, they have urged, is not to be had by dismantling it in order to get at the 'facts' (assumed to be the true and therefore the meaningful bits) lying behind it. To do this is, as it were, to murder in order to dissect, and then to find that the soul of the thing on the slab is not able to be laid hold of by such means at all. The meaning is to be found precisely in the living entity as a whole, the narrative of the finished text with its carefully crafted plots, ironies, tensions and releases. This is the story which the writers and editors intended to tell, and to which we must attend in our reading. To indulge in textual archaeology is precisely to lose the meaning which matters most for the church.

This, I think, is an entirely valid point to make once we accept the narrative function of scripture for the church's faith. There can be little doubt that the result of historico-critical labours has often been to reduce the text to its constituent parts only to discover that they could not subsequently be reassembled into anything with any very practical function. To unravel that which the writers have woven together so skilfully and painstakingly for our benefit would seem in many ways to be a piece of interpretative vandalism. But the question of history will not go away because it is bound up inseparably with the question of the story's truth. Is this *just* a story, or is it in some sense a story which is *true*? and if the latter, then how exactly are we to understand its relation to the truth? This question forces itself upon us once we admit that the story which the Bible tells is not identical in any simple or straightforward way with 'the way it really was'. As Francis Watson observes, 'The question whether or not a story is a true story is posed by all kinds of readers, sophisticated and unsophisticated, adults and children, and cannot be dismissed as an illegitimate attempt to subject an autonomous narrative world to extrinsic reality.'[5] Is the story of salvation which the Bible tells a true story? Does the narrative world of scripture bear any positive relation to the real world in which we live? After all, there are other narrative worlds on offer. Readers of J. R. R. Tolkein, fans of *The Archers*, and devotees of *Neighbours* will all vouch for this fact. It is even possible for those who immerse themselves regularly in such narrative worlds to lose sight occasionally of the boundaries between these admittedly fictitious narratives and the world of their own lives. This is precisely what the Christian is urged to do, to live as one for whom the biblical story has become her own story. Is the story narrated here true, then, in a way that these others may be supposed not to be? If not, then it is surely irresponsible to urge anyone to live 'as if' it were, to live life, in effect, structured around a sacred fiction rather than reality?

Faith and the Real World

To put the matter in this way is to suggest that we are capable of setting the narrative world of scripture alongside 'the real world' for purpose of easy comparison, and thereby evaluating its truth. But our investigations of truth and knowledge earlier in this book have suggested that this is not so. The 'real world' in which we live is the world as we construe it, as it appears to us from a physical perspective rendered by our senses, and an intellectual perspective offered by the particular tradition to which we belong and by which our knowing is largely shaped. Like our reading of texts, our knowing of the real world is a compromise between what is 'there' on the one hand and our personal perspectives on the other. We cannot get at the world 'as it really is', for we cannot cease to be physically, socially and historically located beings. We may move to view reality from somewhere else, either actively or imaginatively; but in doing so we shall simply have adopted another perspective upon it. In the final analysis, we commit ourselves to that perspective which seems to us to offer the most satisfactory account of the reality which lies beyond ourselves. The real world, in other words, is something which we commit ourselves to in a step of faith.

The point I want to make here is simply that our knowledge of the world is shaped in large part by the 'stories' (explicitly religious or otherwise) which are told by the intellectual traditions to which we belong. To suggest that we might set the 'real world' alongside the 'biblical world' for comparison, therefore, is misleading. In reality it is to advocate the setting up of some other story (some alternative perspective on our world) as a standard by which the biblical story might be adjudged relatively true or false. Yet precisely what the Christian is called to do is to allow *this* story, in its broad outlines at least, to determine his outlook on the 'real world', to become a standard by which other stories, other perspectives on human life and its purpose, are evaluated and adjudged. That, it might be argued, is what faith is all about; it is commitment to the story which the Christian community tells about the way things are in God's world. The Christian is one who believes this story, who integrates it into his world view, and thereby deploys it as a basis for living in the world.

If, however, we have no objective standard or neutral vantage point from which to establish the truth of the story which the Bible tells, if we can no more compare it with 'the way things really are' than we can step outside our skins and compare the way something looks to us with 'the way it actually looks', then are we not forced to concede the relativist's claim that our allegiance to it, and our urging of others to commit themselves to it, is a matter of mere convention? Some accounts of scripture as narrative seem to come close to this. The Bible tells a story which offers us a satisfactory basis for living in the world. When we adopt this story, and live 'as if' it were true, things seem to work. There are other stories, and there may well be others which offer an equally satisfactory account of things, or in accordance with which we may live our lives contentedly. But we commit ourselves to the Christian story as the one which works for us. The question of its truth in any absolute sense lies beyond our purview. If, in the final analysis, it should prove to be a fiction, then all we can say is that it has been a convenient fiction with resources to shape and supply a community's life. What more can we either ask for or expect?

This sort of willing relativism, with its ultimate embrace of uncertainty concerning the truth of the gospel message, will not, I believe, suffice to sustain the life of the community of faith in its task of mission and witness. Yet what can we reasonably offer in its place? We cannot, without a genuine sacrifice of the intellect, return to the pre-critical supposition that scripture simply 'tells it as it really was'. The story told in the Bible's pages, whatever its precise relation to actual historical events may be, is certainly not a simple relating of facts *per se*. How then should we think of it in relation to this vexed question of truth?

Story and Sermon

What I suggest is that we should supplement the language of story (which remains entirely legitimate) with that of sermon. For in a sense that is precisely what we are dealing with from first to last in the Bible; one great sermon in narrative form. A sermon, of course, is designed chiefly not to furnish accurate detailed accounts of historical events. It may well include reference to things which have happened, but the way in which it deals with them will not be concerned so much to provide a simple factual transcript of the sort which contemporary historians might recognize as the stuff of their trade, but to evoke and to nourish faith. The Bible is a book written from the vantage point of faith in order to produce and to sustain faith in its readers. It is a book which *preaches*. What it preaches about is, of course, very often things which it believes actually to have happened. It tells a story which is rooted in history. It refers us to actual events in the history of the Middle East, in the history of Israel, and in the history of the man Jesus. But it does not just provide a factual description of them. It goes much further, and weaves around the facts an interpretation which it offers to us for consideration, and for commitment. The story which it tells cannot simply be identified, therefore, with 'what happened'. There are players in the story, and one in particular, whose agency cannot be observed in the way that other things might be. Yet his involvement and activity provide the events which occur with their proper meaning, if the biblical story is to be believed. This key player is, of course, God himself, who is not permitted as a character in the story which the historian might tell concerning the same events. Yet at every point the way in which the biblical writers tell their story is driven by a concern to show God's hand and purposes at work in what takes place. They tell the story as those with 'eyes to see and ears to hear'. There were and are, it must be frankly acknowledged, other ways of interpreting and telling the story. There were those who spent considerable time with Jesus, and who yet failed to recognize in his person and activity what the biblical writers paint clearly and boldly for us on every page in bright primary colours – that, in Jesus, God is present and active among human beings in order to fashion salvation for humankind. It is from this conviction that the story in the Bible is told, and it is this same conviction which it hopes to communicate to others, that they too might perceive the truth which lies hidden beneath the level of the mundane and the directly observable. We cannot suppose that they are simply describing things as any intelligent observer present at the time would have perceived them. They do a great deal more than this. That is their whole point.

What, then, may we say of history and its importance to the meaning of the biblical text? I think the first thing that we must say is that it is important. The biblical writers root their message in history. Their claim is precisely that God has acted and has acted in particular ways in and through particular events and characters in history. Christianity is an historical faith in this sense. From this it follows that we cannot abandon all interest in the quest to discover 'what actually happened'. If, for example, the Bible points us to some event as pivotal to God's saving activity in his world, and historical study could demonstrate conclusively that this event never actually happened, then the story which the Bible tells would be called radically into question. To put the same essential point into sharp focus we may cite James Barr's observation that while historical knowledge of Jesus may not be the only thing which matters for faith, few Christians would be content to commit themselves to a Jesus whom historians revealed to have been the equivalent of a used-car salesman of his day! History, then, is important for Christianity. The biblical text does point us beyond itself to actual events in our world, and to this extent it must always retain a certain vulnerability to the results of historical study.

The second thing to remind ourselves about history, however, is the fact that its results are, like everything else, subject to the variations and accidents of perspective. The historian has no privileged access to the past. He cannot see things 'as they really were' simply by adopting the tools of historical science. From the evidence at his disposal he must select, order and weave together an account of it. In this sense, as Paul Ricoeur suggests,[6] there is an ironic similarity between the work of the historian and that of the writer of fiction. The historian in a very genuine sense 'makes' history with the materials at his disposal. He fashions an historical narrative which tells the story of what he believes to have happened. In even the most objective and scientific of his engagements with the past, his own personal bearing as knower will shape what he does. He will strive to transcend it, to get at the truth of the matter, but, as we have seen again and again in this book, there can be no absolute self-transcendence of the sort which some seem to suppose. In other words, the ways in which a Christian historian and a non-Christian historian construct the past may differ (perhaps even decisively) as a direct result of their respective outlooks on the sort of place the world is. The way in which they fill in the gaps left by the evidence, the things which they are prepared to recognize as 'facts', the interpretations and likely inferences which they are prepared to allow, will all be influenced by their overall commitments in life. I make this point simply to indicate that while Christian faith may well be vulnerable to historical investigation at least in certain significant respects, historical investigation is also vulnerable to faith. The matter is not so simple as first appearances suggest.

Third, and most importantly, historical study, even when pursued by those influenced in some significant way by the Christian tradition, can never render that which faith discerns in the events of the past. By definition, the methods and conclusions of the historian exclude from the outset all consideration of the things which faith reckons the most important elements of all. The historian may, perhaps, confirm that Jesus was crucified under Pontius Pilate. But history as a discipline could never confirm or deny that which matters most in the biblical telling of the story of the crucifixion;

namely, its significance as an event in the life of God, a moral event in which the Son offers himself freely to the Father in the empowering of the Spirit. The claim that God was in Christ reconciling the world to himself is central to the plot of the New Testament story. Yet it is a claim which lies beyond the legitimate scope of historical judgement. Likewise, the historian might in principle confirm the likelihood that at some early stage in her history Israel escaped existence as an enslaved nation by traversing a treacherous stretch of water which duly engulfed her hostile pursuers: but history could never confirm what the eye of faith discerns in this event; namely, the mighty deliverance of God himself, liberating his chosen people into a new life of covenanted existence.

In the scriptural accounts, then, the everyday and the sublime, historical and suprahistorical levels are woven together in a seamless robe which relates the story of God's dealings with the human race. We are offered, as it were, a theological counterpoint in which the two melodic lines of 'what actually happened' and 'what what actually happened means for humankind' can often not even be distinguished as they rise and fall and cross one another, creating rich harmonies, dissonances and resolutions as they do so. The two certainly cannot be separated without the loss of this harmonic structure in which the whole meaning of the piece resides. In this story there may indeed be much 'history', but there is no *mere* history. The whole point of the story is to tell of things which refuse to fit into the historian's mould, to trace meanings, significances, actions which are discernible to the eye of faith, but hidden to all mundane observation. This means that it is always possible for them to be construed differently, for a different interpretation or construction to be placed upon them. To those lacking eyes to see and ears to hear, even the most remarkable of Jesus' actions and teachings remained an enigma, while to the eye of faith they were the manifest saving irruption of God's kingdom into the world. And it is this 'faith's eye perspective' that the biblical writers offer to us for consideration. The story is told by various different commentators. They view its substance from distinct perspectives, and discover in it varied significances. What is contained in the scriptural story, therefore, is certainly not a simple verbal rendering of 'the way it was', but a multifaceted yet coherent theological interpretation of the meaning of the histories of Israel and of Jesus Christ intended to provoke and to nurture faith in its readers. This rich theological tapestry is presented to us as an account of God's dealings with his world, an account 'written in order that you may believe that Jesus is the Christ, the Son of God, and that believing you may have life in his name'. It is in this sense, then, that we may helpfully think of scripture as, in Forsyth's words, 'the greatest sermon in the world'.

Written in order that You may Believe

If we return now to the question of the truth of the biblical story, we must say at once that we do not find in its pages the sort of unsullied factual accuracy which some have habitually exalted as an ideal of truth. The Bible offers us a very distinct perspective on those historical episodes which it does contain; and, of course, while its focus is certainly in history, scripture contains an awful lot more than historical material in any case. Its portrayal of the world in relation to God comes to us through literature of all sorts; poetry, sacred fiction, ethical treatises, saga, prophecy, and so the list might continue. The question of the truth of this portrayal, of the narrative world which it offers for consideration, therefore, is in essence a question about the truth of an overarching *interpretation* of history as the theatre of God's creative and redemptive acts. As I have already indicated, such truth, if it be such, is strictly indemonstrable. The horizons of the story stretch far beyond those recognized by science, history and other human disciplines. Other interpretations of the world will always be possible. There is no way of proving the superiority of the Christian story to other available 'stories' told about our world – the Marxist, the humanist, the Muslim, the Buddhist, and so on. If the story is true, therefore, its truth is certainly not 'public' in the sense of being available for verification by all and sundry. It does not invite disinterested observation, but faith and commitment. It appeals on every page to realities and agencies hidden to the unbelieving eye, realities and agencies around which the very stuff of its story is woven. Christians may believe that their story makes better overall sense of the world than any other, but they cannot expect others simply to see its truth as something given in, with, and under experience of being human in the world, as if the interpretation were manifestly true once it has been pointed out to them. Other construals of reality are possible and exist. Recognition of this legitimate plurality of stories is what differentiates the post-critical understanding of scripture as narrative from its pre-critical and critical counterparts, both of which wished to furnish a truth which was in some way historically, experientially or rationally unavoidable.

But to deny to the Christian story as it is told in scripture the sort of truth craved for it by some is not to abandon all claim to its truth, or to embrace a relativism for which the truth of the story, being wholly unknowable, is finally a matter of little concern. We cannot, as Christians, rest content with an indifference which either eschews truth claims altogether as a form of intolerance and prejudice, or else feels no need to pursue the matter beyond the level of asking the pragmatist's question about whether it 'works' as a story to live by. The church does not offer the gospel to the world and invite the world to embrace it and to live merely 'as if' it were true. Christ did not invite his disciples to take up their cross and to follow him on the road to Calvary for the sake of a convenient fiction. Yet nor, as we have seen, can we present our story as one which is obviously or demonstrably true if only the world would stop and look and think for a while.

Instead, the church may offer to others a way of seeing the world, a way of interpreting it, for this is essentially what scripture offers to the church. Garrett Green refers to biblical narrative as a construal of the world 'as ... 'rather than 'as if ...' The writer who looks at something *as* something else,' Green suggests, 'is signaling awareness of other, different ways of viewing the same object.'[7] Yet he is also drawing attention to his own way of seeing it, suggesting his way of seeing things as an alternative to other ways, and, more often than not, commending this way as in some sense better or more satisfying than others. The story which the Bible tells invites its readers to see the world differently. It asks us to use our imaginations as well as our minds; to trace in the mixed fortunes of a small group of nomadic tribes the hand of the one who created and sustains the entire universe; to view the violent execution of a man charged with political insurgency as the self-offering of the Son to the Father in a redemptive sacrifice for the sins of the world; and, having located ourselves as characters in the continuation of the very same story, to identify the world in which we live, with its wars, its tragedies, its apparent meaninglessness, as the world which God made and 'saw that it was good', the world for the salvation of which Christ conquered evil and defeated death, and into which he released the transforming power of the Holy Spirit. Sometimes this will demand the use of our imaginations not only to supplement, but in some sense actually to contradict the appearances of the situation as presented to us by common sense or experience. Yet this is a ploy well known to and well used by the historian, the scientist, and the detective, notwithstanding the talk of simple observation and deduction usually associated with those occupations. It is their capacity to 'see things otherwise', to see beyond the mere appearances to other possibilities, which enables them to break through to discover the truth, often flying in the face of common sense and committing themselves to a hunch or an intuition in order to do so. Imagination and commitment are far from being the opposites which popular discussion might lead us to believe. Imagination might be the very thing which enables us to penetrate to a truth which otherwise remains hidden, and to which we may only hold in faith. The writer to the Hebrews refers to faith as the 'conviction of things not seen'. Hans Frei, writing about the resurrection narratives, makes a strikingly similar point: 'Commitment in faith and assent by the mind constrained by the imagination,' he writes, 'are one and the same.'[8]

Faith and Citizenship

In other words, the invitation to faith which the Bible offers is precisely an invitation to interpret the world in this particular way rather than others, to identify our world as the world about which this story is told. The writers offer to us a narrative account the contours, characters and lines of development of which provide a framework for making sense of our world, its *raison d'être*, its past, present and future. We are called not simply to enter the world of the text in some sort of imaginative retreat from reality, but, having entered this world, to recognize it as none other than our own, and to begin the complex task of refiguring our own world in the light of this narrative presentation of it. Like David when presented with Nathan's parable we are intended not only to get excited about the story, but to make the identification in which the penny drops, and we see ourselves, our world, as the one about whom the story speaks. And then we must get on with the business of rethinking our world in accordance with the story, making the adjustments, intellectual, moral and otherwise, which it demands of us. For, as Tom Wright points out, the story which the Bible tells is an open-ended story, a story which has yet to be completed. And one way of thinking about conversion or coming to faith is to see it as the point in our lives where our own 'story', the narrative which we relate to others in order to identify ourselves, the way in which we understand ourselves and our place in the larger scheme of things, collides with the story of the gospel and is taken up into it, so that we now find ourselves to be characters in the subsequent chapters of that story. Here, if anywhere, is where the insights and emphases of reader-response approaches to text and meaning may be fruitful; for the way in which the Christian approaches the text of scripture is precisely with the expectation that in reading it there will be a challenge to faith, action, change and so on. The text speaks to us as a living voice today, and not merely a record of some ancient address to others. Our reading of it cannot be as impartial onlookers, but will have what is sometimes called 'self-involving force'.

As Christians, therefore, we live as those who identify our world as the same world about which the Bible speaks, and whose identities are shaped by the plot and its major players. That this truly is so is something which we cannot demonstrate to our unbelieving fellows. We cannot point to it, or offer decisive proof. We can only tell the story, offering an account of the world here and now which has its roots deeply buried in the soil of the story which the Bible tells, an account which makes sense of the world in ways which are consonant with the broad contours of that story, and which locates it and ourselves in the chapters which are, so to speak, still being written. We interpret the world as this world. That is the task to which both evangelist and theologian in their different ways are called, inviting people to image the world in this way rather than others, to step into the narrative and consider the world from within it, to see whether it does not make more sense than other alternative stories told about it. This is and must be essentially an appeal to the imagination, an invitation to construe the world differently, to entertain the possibility that things are other than we have hitherto supposed. That is why the affirmation that it is so, the discovery that the story is true, entails a *conversion* in our thinking, a radical change of mind, as well as a change of will and of behaviour. As Frei says, our minds are constrained by our imagination to think differently about our world and ourselves; that is what faith is.

Conviction and Constraint

On what basis, then, do we commit ourselves to the biblical story? What is it about these texts and the story which they tell (as opposed to others) which renders them worthy of so vital a position in the church's life? There is an answer to this question which rests content with a degree of arbitrariness in the matter, or which turns it into a logical tautology. To call these texts scripture, it asserts, is *de facto* to ascribe authority to them. Hence the reason why Christians treat scripture as authoritative is precisely because part of what it means to belong to this particular community is to ascribe authority to these particular texts. The texts are authoritative in the sense that they function authoritatively in the church. The story which they tell is deployed as a basis for living in the world. Their authority, in other words, is constituted by the church's use of them as scripture, and not by any inherent quality which they possess.

Now it is no doubt true that most Christians afford authority to the Bible in the first instance because they perceive that this is something which Christians do, and which the tradition demands of us. As a starting point that is fair enough. Discipleship invariably involves receiving certain practices and assumptions from others in an essentially uncritical manner. But that will not suffice as an account of the way in which the church has thought about the matter. One might reasonably suppose that historically speaking the reason for any community ascribing authority to particular texts and conferring upon them what is sometimes termed 'classic' status has little to do with arbitrary or rash judgements, and everything to do with the discernment of some genuine intrinsic value or insight which the texts, or the stories which they have to tell, possess in terms of enabling or resourcing a meaningful existence in the real world. In order to sustain the community's life, indeed, one might equally suppose some such quality to be necessary.

In actual fact this would seem to be the case within the church. For when people arrive at the point of making a commitment of faith, of identifying the story told by scripture as the story by which they will henceforth shape their lives, and thereby locating themselves within the community of faith, they do not do so arbitrarily or upon purely pragmatic grounds. As St Paul was quick to recognize, the story which Christians have to tell is not one which is likely to win admiration or assent from the community at large. There are other more comfortable, or more intellectually stimulating and satisfying stories abroad, by comparison with which this story may be adjudged foolishness or a scandal. No doubt the church has often reduced or mitigated this scandal by the way in which it has told the story; but it has an awkward habit of reasserting itself when the scripture is read and taken seriously. A story which has as its central theme the recalcitrance and sinfulness of humankind, which tells of our guilt before God and our need of his forgiveness, is unlikely in most ordinary circumstances to win friends and influence people. We prefer more optimistic or 'enlightened' stories about ourselves.

Those who tell *this* story, therefore, do so mostly not from choice, nor merely because they have inherited it from the community to which they now belong; but from a faith which is seized by the conviction of its truth and urgency as a perspective on human existence. They find themselves addressed by the story directly in such a way that they cannot deny its truth. Like David long ago they find themselves confronted by the challenge implicit in Nathan's words: 'Thou art the man!' And in the moment of hearing they know that it is indeed so. They are, as it were, laid hold of by a truth which they cannot demonstrate or prove, but which they can no more deny than deny themselves. There is a conviction here of a sort which leaves them morally obligated in the face of this truth. They can do none other than stand up and be counted, change their minds about the way things are with the world, bear witness and tell the story to others both in word and by living it out. They are constrained by the truth, and must respond to it. In the moment of faith they cease to be onlookers and become participants in the story, those who indwell the world it describes, rather than some other world.

How, then, does this happen? Whence are we to trace the authority which prompts this sort of response? There are various levels at which this question would have to be answered. Perhaps the most significant among these, however, is the traditional claim that in the reading and interpreting of these texts within the church, something is taking place which goes beyond a simple human reading of texts, something in which divine as well as human agency is involved. The claim, in other words, that as we read and interpret, God speaks to us, that scripture is in some sense Word of God, an 'inspired' text.

Authority and Inspiration

The claim that in the Bible we have to do with an inspired scripture can be understood in a number of distinct ways. For some it means no more and no less than is intended when any piece of human literature (or music, or art) is said to result from 'inspiration'. When we say this we recognize that the work in question is of a special sort; that it plumbs the depths of the human situation to an extent which is not true of all other texts; that it speaks to us in ways which enlighten us morally or spiritually, or which enhance our self-understanding, and so on. Such 'classics' (as they are generally termed) are identifiably great literature, both inspired and inspiring. For some theologians the notion of the inspiration of scripture is satisfactorily articulated in these terms. We need go no further in the search for its authority, which is akin to that of any great literature possessed of the power to inspire and to shape human thinking and activity. While, however, we need not doubt that the Bible contains some 'classic' literature in this sense, it would seem to be pushing things rather far to suppose that literary greatness may be invoked to account for the authority of scripture as a whole. For we must remind ourselves that large portions of the text of scripture issue not from the hands of religious and literary genius, but from ordinary men and women seized by the compulsion to tell the story of God's saving activity in their lives and the lives of others. We must frankly admit that much of the result is not great literature! Yet Christians find the mundane and (in a literary sense at least) uninspiring bits just as authoritative for faith as those parts which might easily find their way into an anthology of the world's great poetry and prose. It would seem, then, that the inspiration which the church ascribes to its scripture must be differentiated from that which issues from the muse.

More commonly, perhaps, talk of the inspiration of scripture is intended to convey the thought that the biblical writings have their own origin in God (and are related to his self-revealing and redemptive purposes) in a way which is not true of other human texts. Yet even this can be taken in quite a variety of ways. For many Christians this theological judgement concerning the *origin* of the texts is closely tied to a particular understanding of the way in which they came into being and the nature of their contents. What I have in mind is what is sometimes called the 'prophetic model' of inspiration in which the writer is thought of as serving effectively as a passive channel of words and sentences dictated directly by God. He is a secretary who reproduces efficiently the precise verbal formulations delivered to him, and presents them in textual form for the church's consideration. Like the Old Testament prophets, all that is channelled through him in this way must be prefaced with the formula 'Thus says the Lord!' This way of thinking tends to be complemented by an understanding of scripture as in effect a set of inerrant propositions, divinely delivered truths on a whole range of different subjects, historical, ethical, theological, and so on. After all, if 'inspiration' means that God himself dictated these particular words in this particular order then there can be no room for errors or mistakes of any sort. God is all-knowing, and he is a God of truth. This being so we can trust absolutely the propositions with which he has furnished us as 'divine truth'.

It seems to me that this popular model of biblical inspiration is just as untenable as that which would set the Bible alongside Shakespeare not only on the average household bookshelf but in terms of its nature and significance. One fails to take seriously the reality of scripture as the product of ordinary human processes of reflection and writing; the other tends to reduce any authority which it has to the authority of merely (albeit superlative) human literature, and thereby to rob it of any uniqueness as a set of texts which is in some sense inspired by God. Significantly, both models view the authority of scripture as being located in some fairly obvious way in the qualities of the text as such, whether as a set of infallible divine propositions, or as the noblest expressions and insights of the human spirit. What I now want to suggest is that if we seek elsewhere for the locus of the text's authority, we may also arrive at a more satisfactory understanding of the nature of its inspiration.

Written under the Influence?

One of the chief problems with the notion of an 'inspired' author sitting down under the direct influence of the Holy Spirit to produce an 'inspired' text is that it fails fundamentally to take seriously the actual process by which the biblical documents were formed. Many if not most of the books which make up our Bible were not 'written' in the straightforward sense of that term at all. Instead they came into being through a long and complicated process in which existing traditions, both written and oral, were taken up and combined, woven together, adapted and reinterpreted as their meaning for situations in the life of the people of God at particular times and in particular places was sought. The gospel writers, for example, draw on existing accounts of the ministry of Jesus as Luke openly admits (see Luke 1.1), and the way in which they use these manifests a perceived freedom to refashion even the words of Jesus to facilitate the effective telling of the story for particular categories of readers, and the creation of significant theological capital. Thus Paul Achtemeier writes: 'Far from having one fixed meaning which remained the same for all time, the sayings of Jesus were evidently regarded as capable of quite different meanings in different situations, and the author who collected those traditions used them to make the theological point he or she thought necessary for those who would read that Gospel.'[9] This, Achtemeier argues, is symptomatic of scripture as a whole. What the biblical tradition represents, he suggests, is precisely an ongoing and dynamic process of the interpretation and reinterpretation of events (and duly the traditions and texts in which those events are conveyed to subsequent generations) within the life of the community of faith. Events in the life of the nation of Israel or the life of Jesus which were deemed formative for the identity of the community are related time and time again (the Exodus and the crucifixion/resurrection being the two most obvious examples). But each time they are related there is a new slant given, a new way in which the story is told. And the reason for this is that the story is told to a new audience which faces a new situation. The telling of the story, if it is genuinely to shape and to infuse with energy the church in its daily living, must bite into the actual situation in which the church finds itself, with its particular agenda of questions and problems and expectations. The question which the teller of the story must always ask afresh, therefore, is 'What does this story mean for these people in these circumstances?'

That the biblical authors took this question absolutely seriously is demonstrable from the nature and content of their writings. What we have in our Bibles, therefore, is not a collection of one-off texts produced in the heat of an extraordinary and spiritually intense 'composition under the influence', but the end-products of a long and complex process of communal interpretation. Our authors are for the most part editors who have taken up and collated materials handed on from the past in order both to address their particular present and in turn to transmit them to the future. What they do with these materials manifests (as I have suggested it always must) both continuity and discontinuity with the past. The story which they tell is identifiably the same story as that which was passed on to them by their forebears; yet because it is interpreted by them afresh, and from within a new context, it cannot but result in a meaning which will be more or less other as well as the same. There is a slippage of meaning as well as a stability. And this slippage is not a pathological factor, but the inevitable result of the traditions being 'made anew' within the community's life, being interpreted within the developing and changing circumstances of that life. The conviction of the biblical authors, therefore, Achtemeier concludes, is that 'a rigid adherence to the form that sacred traditions assumed in the past is precisely the wrong way to honor the Word of a God who is living, and who is thus the God of the present and the future as well as of the past.'[10] 'He is God of the future, and is free to re-create the meaning of the past by what he does in the future.'[11]

'All of our Biblical texts,' Achtemeier writes, 'are therefore the products of the interpretation of the will of God as that is illuminated in a new time by earlier traditions. Struggling to understand new revelations of God's purpose for them, Israel and the church turn to older traditions to find some clue to how they may cope with such a dynamic God. Our Scriptures reflect that process, and enshrine that quest.'[12] This being so it is impossible to think of inspiration any longer as a sort of divine dictation to a particular author. To identify the final product as inspired apart from the entire religious, theological, and literary process which culminates in it is arbitrary in the extreme. More satisfactory is Achtemeier's proposal that we should think of inspiration as that activity of God's Holy Spirit in and through the entire process, and thus in and through the life of the community of faith at large, which in due course produced these particular textual deposits. Inspiration, then, is a matter of the 'en-spiriting' of the community of faith in its attempt to make sense of the traditions handed on to it, and to reforge its identity in the present in the light of those traditions. The scriptures of the church are the product of just such a process.

Inspiration, Community and Interpretation

This view of things does not encourage us to treat scripture as a once for all and final repository of divine truths which we may quarry at will to discover inerrant data on any subject under the sun. Perhaps no one has ever thought of it like this; but some popular perceptions certainly seem to come close. Once we grasp the nature of scripture as the inheritance furnished by the efforts of the community of faith, in the power of the Spirit, to make sense of the story which it has heard and received, and the implications of retelling and living out that story in a constantly changing world, a number of conclusions suggest themselves to us.

First, the Bible is not intended to be a divinely dictated encyclopaedia furnishing us with an alternative science, history, cosmology and so on, but (as 2 Timothy 3.15–16 – the most frequently cited and most frequently misused text in this regard – makes utterly clear) as a resource which will be effective in shaping the life and identity of the Christian community in relation to God's wider purposes of creation and redemption.

Second, the Bible is not intended to be (and in fact cannot be) a final word beyond which nothing more needs to be said. On the contrary, its very nature reminds us that the message to which it bears witness must be rearticulated (and hence reinterpreted) in every age afresh. In and through attention to the text and the story which it tells, the church seeks out the meaning of this story for the particular circumstances in which it finds itself. In a very real sense, therefore, what goes on in the preaching and other theologizing of the community of faith is a simple continuation of the process which led to the formation of scripture in the first place.

Third, if we are to take seriously the notion that the biblical text is 'inspired' and hence authoritative, then we must reckon also with the suggestion that this inspiration extends in some sense beyond the limits of the text to our attempts to make sense of it. An inspired text as such would be of little use to the church. What we need to know is what the text means; but meaning, I have argued, is a relationship with both an objective and a subjective pole. The decisive disadvantage of some notions of inspiration and infallibility in which these nouns refer to qualities of the text as such is that as soon as we lay our fallible human hands on the text and make sense of it what results is a meaning tainted by the uncertainty of our all too human contribution. It is as if God does his bit by providing a pure and unsullied text, but then leaves us in the lurch by demanding that we overcome our inherent weakness and sinfulness before we may possess its meaning perfectly. It should come as little surprise, therefore, that the twin errors of Catholicism and Protestantism have been on the one hand an attempt to provide an infallible papal interpreter to accompany the infallible text, and on the other a naive refusal to differentiate between text and meaning. In place of these, our revised estimate of the nature of the inspiration of scripture provides a suggestive alternative; namely, that the very same Spirit who was active over the generations in shaping and forming the community from which these texts issued is present today 'en-spiriting' our contemporary efforts as the community of faith to read and make sense of them. If we take this model seriously then we are able to say that it is not only the text of scripture, but its *meaning* which is in some direct sense inspired, which is another way of saying that God speaks to us through these texts. The Spirit, in other words, bridges the gap between objective and subjective, text and interpretation, enabling and directing our response, and fashioning the community's understanding and life anew in the process.

We can now begin to see what it is that differentiates a Christian reading of the biblical text as scripture from other possible readings of it. The church turns to the text seeking an event in which, as the text is interpreted, it speaks authoritatively for the community. This event happens. That it does happen is something to which the community bears witness, but it is something which lies utterly beyond the community's own control. God addresses us, meets with us in and through our reading of these texts. He guides and directs our thinking, challenges and provokes our behaviour, strengthens and sustains our faith as we read and interpret. Yet none of this is simply coincident with the physical possession and contemplation of the text as such. We may read this text and find it silent and remote. We may have its physical form, yet remain outsiders in relation to the narrative world which it describes. But for those to whom it speaks, for whom the world of the text opens up as a reality into which they are drawn, the text is a source of meaning and direction not in and of itself, but because it serves as a channel of our personal knowing of the God whose story it tells.

It is precisely here that moral conviction of the truth of this story, and hence its authority, is rooted. God speaks. He convinces us that things between himself and the human race are in reality much as they are in the story. We are drawn into the world of the text precisely as we are drawn into a relationship with its central character. As this happens, we find ourselves confronted by many of the same realities and experiences as are narrated in the text. Suddenly sin, guilt, grace, reconciliation, the power of God's Spirit, the risen Christ and so on are not mere elements in a narrative world, but constituent part of our own world, players and factors to be taken into consideration in our daily living and our attempts to make sense of our own situation. In this moment it is as if the apostles and prophets, far from being historically and culturally distant figures, were contemporaneous with us – their meaning making contact with us as we recognize the landmarks of the world which they describe in the contours of the world as we now experience it. We cannot, of course, demonstrate the truth of this perception to those who cannot see it. We may only describe it in the hope that they also may see it. One cannot prove the beauty of Bach's harmonies to the tone-deaf. But nor are we isolated in our construal of the world 'as' the world depicted in scripture. Those who see things thus enter the community of faith, becoming fellow citizens of this world with others for whom it constitutes 'the real world'. There is what Polanyi calls a 'community of verifiers' who confirm that the substance of our perceptions (or readings) concurs largely with their own. This is why it is so important to remind ourselves that the reading of scripture should not be an isolated or individualistic thing, but a corporate activity, rooted in the received wisdom of the community's tradition, tested by the insight and experience of others within the community, that in and through all this God's Word to his church in the distinctiveness of the present and the particular circumstance may be discerned.

NOTES
1 Cited in Steiner, G., *After Babel* (Oxford University Press 1992), p. 181.
2 Steiner, *After Babel*, p. 264.
3 Steiner, *After Babel*, p. 312.
4 Steiner, *After Babel*, p. 311.
5 Watson, F., *Text, Church and World* (T. & T. Clark 1994), p. 25.
6 See Ricoeur's essay 'The Narrative Function' in Thompson, J. B. ed., *Hermeneutics and the Human Sciences* (Cambridge University Press 1981), pp. 274–305.
7 Green, G., ' "The Bible as ...": Fictional Narrative and Scriptural Truth', *Scriptural Authority and Narrative Interpretation* (Fortress Press 1987, p. 88.
8 Cited in Green, ' "The Bible as ..." ', *Scriptural Authority*, p. 92.
9 Achtemeier, P., *The Inspiration of Scripture* (Westminster Press 1980), p. 83.
10 Achtemeier, *The Inspiration of Scripture*, p. 87.
11 Achtemeier, *The Inspiration of Scripture*, pp. 86–7.
12 Achtemeier, *The Inspiration of Scripture*, p. 89.

— Part Four —

The Transformation of Tradition

— 8 —

Looking to the Past
and Facing Up to the Future

*Every man who possesses real vitality can be seen as the re-
sultant of two forces. He is first the child of a particular age,
society, convention; of what we may call in one word a tradition. He is secondly, in one degree or another, a rebel against
that tradition. And the best traditions make the best rebels.*
                                                    Gilbert Murray[1]

Tradition is one of those 'light-the-blue-touch-paper-and-retire-to-
a-safe-distance' words. In the current climate it is likely to evoke
quite different responses from different people, whether in the
sphere of religion, politics, art or whatever. Tradition, traditional,
traditionalist – these are words which will have very positive associations for some, and prompt outright hostility in others. Matters are
more complex than this of course. It is entirely likely that people
who rebel against the associations attaching to such words in one
area may yet warm to them in another, and vice versa. The appeal
to so-called 'traditional values', for example, must surely rank high
on the list of successful advertising gimmicks, playing on our nostalgic capacity to reconstrue the past (such that it always seems
preferable to the present) and persuading us that while we can
never return to it we can at least buy a portion of it for old times'
sake. Yet many of those who are swayed to purchase the products
thus promoted (from brown bread to life assurance policies) might
well reject appeals to 'traditional values' in other spheres as an
unwarranted and romantic attempt to cling to or reintroduce a now
obsolete and outdated approach to life. The description 'traditional', it seems, may conjure up warm images of something familiar, secure, tried and tested, enduring and able to be trusted; or else
it may speak to us of a staid unwillingness to change, an attempt
to deny the inevitable march of time, to live in the past rather than
the present, and to preserve its ways of thinking and behaving at
the expense of progress. The point is that the old days may either
be for us the good old days or the bad old days, depending on the

particular issue we are considering, and the perspective which we occupy. Our attitude to appeals to tradition will vary accordingly.

The perception lying behind all this, of course (which I want in part to challenge in this chapter) is that tradition is something fundamentally oriented towards the past and its ways. A 'traditionalist' approach to something is thus defined as one which in some direct way is modelled on the past, which seeks to preserve and protect some fragment of the inheritance of the past and to keep it unstained by the perceived pollutants of the present, whether the thing in question be a set of moral values, a style of musical or artistic composition or performance, or a seventeenth-century prayer book or translation of the Bible. It is something essentially static rather than dynamic, resistant to change, rather than promoting or facilitating new developments. The old ways, the traditionalist is convinced, are the best ways, and we should abide by them, rather than jumping on every passing bandwagon or being swept along by each new wave in the tide of changing fashions. By contrast, the essence of 'modern' or 'progressive' ways of thinking and behaving is often thought to be characterized by a programmatic setting aside (or even complete rejection) of much if not all that tradition has to offer, beginning with a clean slate, unhindered by the clutter of inherited assumptions and practices, set free to think and to act responsibly in accordance with the demands of the present circumstance.

This sort of polarity is easy enough to observe on the theological scene. Here the spectrum of available views and approaches appears to range from those on the one hand who are seemingly unwilling to do more than receive an authoritative doctrinal inheritance from the past, and to protect, preserve and cherish it in order that it might in due course be passed on safely to the next generation (like a piece of precious bone china that has been in the family for centuries), to those on the other hand who view themselves as engaged in an attempt to drag the church kicking and screaming into the modern age, casting off the shackles of what they see as an unhealthy and stifling dogmatism, and bringing even the most ancient and cherished of Christian beliefs and practices into the daylight provided by reason and the current advanced state of human understanding. Advocates of what is often (misleadingly) dubbed this 'liberal' approach (as opposed to the conservatism of traditionalists) will often claim the moral as well as the intellectual high ground, setting out their stall in direct opposition to what they perceive as the relative 'intellectual dishonesty and naive credulity'[2] of those who cling to tradition and resist the open-minded and painfully honest scrutiny of 'critical thinking'.

This unhelpful (and I shall argue mistaken) polarizing of attitudes towards theological tradition has its roots, like so much else in our modern context, in the intellectual developments of the European Enlightenment.

The Assault on Tradition

Tradition had, of course, already been the victim of one serious theological assault at the time of the Reformation, an assault made in the name of scripture. Theology, it was held, must be subject not to the human authority of the church's various creeds and traditions, but must submit itself directly to the authority of the God who has spoken in the Bible. As we have already seen, matters are by no means so straightforward as that simple statement of the matter would suggest. The Bible must be read and made sense of, and our reading of it is without exception moulded and influenced by the traditions (theological and otherwise) within which we stand as interpreters. The idea that it is possible to step back entirely from these influences and achieve a pure reading of the text, therefore, is one which must be shown up for the self-deception that it is. Whatever the Reformation principle of *sola Scriptura*[3] might mean, it cannot mean that. Simple appeals to 'what the Bible says' are always the sign of (no doubt unconscious) subservience to an interpretative tradition, not liberation from it. That which we mistakenly think we have escaped from is in reality free to exercise all the more influence over us, and is therefore all the more potentially dangerous.

At the Enlightenment, the concept of tradition was subjected to a further assault; this time in the now familiar name of reason. Reliance upon the received authoritative prescriptions or pronouncements of others, whether in theology or elsewhere, was stigmatized as a superstitous and intellectually irresponsible attachment to mere 'dogma'. The mature and responsible person was the one who would refuse to accept or subscribe to the mere say-so of those in positions of authority, but would think things through for themselves, being prepared to challenge even the most basic and widely held beliefs in favour of an honest scrutiny in which the weight of evidence was openly considered, and conviction apportioned accordingly. Any belief which could not be substantiated on such a rational basis must be set aside. Experts and authorities, those who embodied the intellectual tradition of the past, became figures of suspicion. Rather than simply believing what they had to say, the genuinely free and responsible thinker must deploy his critical faculties, allowing no dogma to go unscrutinized, cutting himself free from the influences of tradition in order to test and to try its offerings in accordance with the objective arbiter of reason.

It is not difficult to identify the origins of modern liberal theological sympathies in such attitudes. The central concern or motive of liberal theology according to one proponent of it is 'to make the Christian faith *intelligible* and *credible*, *comprehensive* and *convincing* to intelligent, informed and honest minds of each successive era'.[4] In truth, however, the real distinctive of liberalism lies in the assumptions which it harbours concerning how best to achieve this laudable aim. The assumption that it is more intellectually honest to doubt than to believe or commit oneself to something which one cannot be absolutely sure of; the unrelenting appeal to 'reason' as an independent authority to be set advantageously over against both scripture and tradition; the suggestion that the most responsible thing to do with theological tradition, therefore, is initially to rebel against its authority, to test its worth, and only to afford it respect when one can establish the truth of its offerings on other independent grounds, and thereby commend its truth to those who do not belong to the tradition; these are the now familiar characteristics of the liberal theological tradition.

From Heirs to Slaves

But in that description, of course, the cat is out of the bag! For it reminds us of what is certainly the case; namely, that liberalism, with its methods and assumptions, is itself an intellectual tradition whose adherents frequently manifest a passion and conviction unsurpassed in intellectual life. Far from being the free intellectual spirit of popular perception, therefore, the liberal is, like everyone else, heir to a set of assumptions and ways of thinking and doing things which he or she simply takes for granted. In particular, many of those adjudged theological 'conservatives' would complain that their liberal colleagues are far too quick to assimilate the latest intellectual fashions and fads and then to deploy them as a supposedly 'objective' standard for 'critical' thinking, often at the expense of standards, beliefs or practices which have survived the test of centuries (a fact which by no means guarantees the truth or legitimacy of such beliefs and practices, but might be thought to put a large part of the burden of proof on those who would seek to overturn them). The terms 'liberal', 'open,' and 'critical' need, therefore, to be examined very carefully. Where the authoritative voices of modern culture are concerned it must be admitted that very often there is only dogmatism, uncritical assimilation and a closed-minded subservience to be observed among proponents of 'liberal' strategies. Frequently it is only *with regard to the received tradition* that they are liberal, open and critical. Where the spirit of the age is concerned they must often be adjudged conservatives of an unrepentant variety.

This is offered by way of an observation rather than a criticism, although it carries a powerful criticism closely in its wake; namely that theological liberalism is heir to the Enlightenment's greatest self-deception as well as many of its undoubted benefits; the sup-position, that is to say, that it is possible to liberate oneself com-pletely from tradition, and to be genuinely critical in respect of all things. Those who think that they have done so, like those who say they have no sin, deceive themselves, and, far from being the self-proclaimed champions of intellectual honesty, the truth is not in them! Like those who suppose that they have discovered in some simple and absolute sense 'what the Bible teaches', those who reckon themselves free from the limits and influences of intellec-tual and cultural tradition have in reality ceased to be its heirs only to become its unwitting slaves, rebelling and running away from the tradition which spawned and nurtured them into the arms of some other set of influences (more than likely the passing intellec-tual fashion) the existence of which they refuse to recognize, and which is therefore able to rule them with all the more ease.

We return here, then, to the point established earlier in this book; namely that all rational and critical activity takes place within the context provided by some set of assumptions and commitments or other, some cultural and intellectual 'tradition' which offers a per-spective on things, a standard by which to adjudge other ways of seeing things. Such traditions are socially and historically located and, as socially and historically located beings, we inevitably belong to particular human groups or communities who adhere to a specific set of such beliefs and practices. What appears to us to be reasonable or acceptable or credible will be what our particular tradition judges thus. Our thinking about life, the world and everything will inevitably be done in a way which draws upon and is shaped and determined by some such tradition. It will provide us with the many fixed points of reference which we need in order to function intellectually at all. If, at some stage, we find ourselves driven to modify or even to reject part of the inheritance of our particular tradition then it will not be because we have achieved complete liberation from such influences and determining factors (a completely 'open' mind), but because some other set of influences (the perspective on things offered by another tradition) has drawn us within its sphere, and has seemed to us to offer a more satisfying account of reality, or a more potentially fruitful way of approaching it. We can never escape from such influences altogether into the Enlightenment wonderland of a socially and historically and spatially unlocated 'free critical thought'.

All human thought, even that which is most critical and radical, relies, for its tools and the sense of just how, when and where to wield them, upon the support structure of an intellectual and cultural tradition – a vast body of knowledge and assumptions shared by the community within which we live and move and have our being. Try as we might, there is no way of escaping from this situation. We can be critical towards one set of beliefs or practices only by assuming the validity of another. There can be no absolutely uncommitted or totally open-minded approach to life.

The Inevitibility of Indoctrination

Basil Mitchell substantiates this point in a discussion of indoctrination–another word likely to evoke sharp (and as Mitchell shows often unconsidered) responses.[5] Indoctrination might usefully be defined as the effort to inculcate upon others a belief or set of beliefs (doctrines) which they do not fully understand, and the reasons and justification for which they are themselves quite unable to give. As those who are subject to indoctrination they are wholly reliant upon the authority of those who instruct or inform them.

Now, when we describe indoctrination in that way it is highly likely that we shall evoke (in ourselves and others) an immediate suspicion and discomfort concerning the entire process. Surely, we shall ask, such an approach is utterly unworthy of intellectually responsible people? If we were willingly to submit to it we might well soon find ourselves subscribing to all manner of weird and wonderful beliefs, most of which would bear little relation to the real world. The whole idea of indoctrinating people is one which we associate instinctively with peculiar religious cults and 'fundamentalist' groups who refuse to allow their passionately held beliefs to be scrutinized in a rational way. The results, from the extremes of Waco and Islamic suicide bombers to the more harmless but equally sad instances of families broken up by the alleged 'brainwashing' techniques of groups such as the 'Moonies,' are ones which most of us would prefer to see eradicated from our world. In fear of any proliferation of such 'irrationalism' we are driven willingly but unthinkingly into the arms of those who would have us believe that the only intellectually responsible alternative is to examine all things 'rationally', by which they mean that we should be obliged to explore for ourselves the logical and evidential basis for things before investing ourselves in them personally. The rational person, on this view, is the one who can give good reasons for holding the beliefs which he or she does hold, and thereby commend them to others as rational things to believe. Indoctrination, on the other hand, is a process whereby those whose beliefs probably lack rational warrant force those beliefs upon others gullible enough to swallow them, on the basis of the supposed authority of the teacher or guru concerned.

This sort of attitude (which I suspect is fairly common in our society) shows just how deeply the Enlightenment bug has bitten. To be sure, the Enlightenment protest against all forms of authoritarianism, and its demand that people should be free and willing to think about things for themselves rather than submitting meekly to any and every belief or prejudice served up by the political and religious establishment for its consumption, needs to be heard loud and clear in such situations as Waco and Iran, and wherever a religious, political, ideological or other authority has become authoritarian to the detriment of a reasonable and reasoned approach to life. The Enlightenment may not have been all light casting out darkness, but there can be little doubt that here as in many other respects it had a fundamentally important contribution to make to the quality of human existence. Its mistake (and it was a considerable mistake) was that it reacted too sharply; it sought (in the intellectual and religious as well as the political realms) to depose authority from its throne and to exalt in its place a libertarian model of freedom which has proven to be as much a curse as a blessing. Thus it rejected dogma and indoctrination in favour of a

171

supposedly entirely open, 'free' critical approach to knowledge. But, as I have already suggested, there is in reality no such thing as thought which is 'free' in the sense of being entirely undetermined by any influence or authority whatever. The perpetual danger lies in the risk that we shall abandon an established and known authority only to succumb unawares to a devil we do not know – more than likely some passing intellectual fad or fashion.

Mitchell confirms this in a shrewd analysis of the process of education; a process of which, he argues, indoctrination forms an inevitable and vital part. Think for a moment about the way in which small children learn: whether language, arithmetic, the rules of a game or whatever. The process involved is one in which they copy, or take on trust, the things which their parents or teachers do and say, gradually assimilating the structure of beliefs and practices for themselves until they have become second nature. This is particularly obvious in the way in which a child learns to speak, where the capacity for explaining why and wherefore does not exist until the language has actually been learned. But it applies to all learning situations. And while, as anyone familiar with small children knows, there are no students more keen to discover the answer to the question 'Why?', the truth is that we mostly do not seek to explain *why* 2 + 2 = 4, *why* 'the book what I got' is an incorrect expression, *why* the Norman Conquest happened in 1066, at least in the first instance. Later on, some attempt at answering such questions may be made. But in the initial stages of education we concentrate on furnishing the rules and the data and the skills which enable children to function in the world, and if we stopped to justify every fact, every truth claim, every rule that we offered to them, we should never make any progress whatsoever. And so we do not do so. We intend and expect only that our children shall accept on trust and authority the things which we offer to them as true, until, perhaps, they reach a stage at which they are able to formulate the question 'Why?' with sufficient informed intelligence to lay hold of the answer (assuming that we are able to give it!). In other words, on the basis of the definition offered above, what we do to our children in their earliest years is to indoctrinate them!

Taught to Believe?

Okay, you may say, that is fine for children. But surely they are a special case, and the whole point which the Enlightenment philosophers were making was that we need to 'grow up' intellectually: and that we cannot continue into adulthood, therefore, adopting the same attitude of passive acceptance with respect to the beliefs, opinions and truth claims offered to us by others, no matter who they are. We must learn to take responsibility for our knowledge and beliefs, and, as consumers in the market-place of convictions, to test before buying lest we end up with inferior goods.

It is certainly true that there are differences in the expectations which teachers may legitimately have of adults and children in the learning situation. But, Mitchell insists, those differences do not and cannot extend to a refusal by adults to be indoctrinated. On the contrary, even those who aspire to the greatest heights of intellectual and practical achievement, whether as natural scientists, surgeons, lawyers, philosophers, economists, psychologists or whatever, begin their training by being initiated into an authoritative tradition of orthodox beliefs, axioms, and convictions concerning a particular sphere of reality and what are deemed (by the intellectual community or practical guild concerned) appropriate ways of dealing with it. And these beliefs and methodological procedures are ones the reasons or evidence required to justify which lie wholly beyond the student's or apprentice's reach at this stage in their education or training. Undergraduate notebooks are packed full of such material. In this respect there is little difference in principle between the 4-year-old who guilelessly accepts the claim that 2 + 2 = 4 and the 19-year-old who scribbles furiously in lectures in order to preserve on paper the confident dogmas of his professor ('Mark was in all probability the first of the four canonical Gospels to be written' etc.) – dogmas which he does not as yet have sufficient knowledge or skill to establish (or to question) for himself.

Mitchell sums the matter up nicely. 'There is,' he writes, 'a revealing phrase sometimes used by scholars describing their own student days: "At Oxford (Princeton, Heidelberg) in my day we were *taught to believe that* ..."'[6] Taught to believe. In that phrase the indoctrinative heart of all human education is expressed. All learning, at whatever level of intellectual achievement, begins with the uncritical acceptance of facts, truth claims, methods which furnish the conditions, the materials and tools, for learning anything at all. And these things are handed on faithfully by the intellectual elders of a tradition of learning and practice into which we enter as mere novices.

Respect, Rebellion and Responsibility

But of course the matter cannot stop there. Learning does not stop with the assimilation by indoctrination of a tradition; it merely begins there. Our intention in handing on to our intellectual heirs the authoritative inheritance of our own learning and acquired wisdom is not that they should remain passive and dependent, but that they might be enabled to engage with the world and its complex realities for themselves, becoming skilled handlers of the ideas and the practices which we have bequeathed to them, and laying hold for themselves of the reasoning which lies behind them. It is perfectly legitimate to construe this as a sign of intellectual maturity as opposed to a relatively immature dependence upon the word of others. (We should face the fact, nonetheless, that all of us remain in this sense immature in many spheres of human understanding. That is why we employ 'experts' to do for us the things in which they are skilled and we are not. My own relationship to the internal combustion engine – among many other things – is of precisely this sort.)

Furthermore, we anticipate that the state of understanding will not remain static, but will move on as human resourcefulness in fathoming the depths of reality progresses, or as social custom changes the ways in which people think and behave. And those who are our apprentices today will in due course become those whose skilled handling of the tradition may well lead them in the future to challenge, revise, develop and even, in certain cases, to reject part or all of it. Thus education equips the student (indoctrinatively) with sufficient knowledge and skill to enable him to stand on his own two intellectual feet, to transcend the indoctrinative phase, to interact critically with the received tradition for himself, and thereby either to arrive at sufficient reasons for continuing to uphold it and to pass it on in turn, suitably developed, to the next generation, or else to abandon it in preference for some other way of thinking and behaving in response to the world. Authoritative traditions thereby furnish the conditions which both enable their perpetuation and development to meet the demands of the future, and ensure the essential transitoriness of any particular form they may take. The same conditions make such traditions vulnerable in principle to rejection and death.

The sort of legitimate and necessary indoctrination of which we have been speaking, therefore, is not opposed to or preventative

174

of critical, reflective and even radical thinking. And in this sense it is quite distinct from another sort of indoctrination which we might define as the effort to inculcate upon others a belief or set of beliefs which they do not fully understand, and to do so in such a way that they are subsequently either unable or unwilling to reflect critically upon it, to challenge and transform it, or to reject it in favour of some alternative set of beliefs. In actual fact, those who are subjected to this latter sort of indoctrination are generally unable even to reckon seriously or sympathetically with points of view which differ significantly from their own. Their attitude to that which is other than their own way tends to be hostile and belligerent, and not infrequently resorts to the device indicated in preachers' notes by the initials AWSL – argument weak, shout louder! But that, of course, is symptomatic not of confidence in the truth of one's views, but rather of a deep down insecurity which refuses to enter into genuine dialogue with others for fear that its own inadequacies may be uncovered. It is this sort of indoctrination which discourages rather than facilitates a responsible and honest enquiry into the warrant for and truth of its own beliefs, and which can all too easily result in the unpleasantness of religious or ideological ranting, the dangers of increased suspicion and alienation between members of different political, national or racial groups, and even the deluded and tragic behaviour of a group such as the Group Davidian Sect.

The answer, however, is not to shun authority and tradition altogether at the outset in preference for a supposedly free and critical alternative to it, but rather to recognize (and thus to be able carefully to regulate) the inevitable and proper place of authority and tradition as the matrix within which all truly responsible critical thinking takes place. Paradoxically, it is our commitment to what the tradition offers us – our faith and trust in it, our willingness to be nurtured and to develop within it – which liberates us ultimately to step our beyond simple dependence upon it into a mature engagement with the reality of which it speaks. It is only in the light of such an engagement that either the strengths or the inadequacies of our tradition will become apparent to us as critical thinkers in our own right. Perhaps then our mature response will indeed be to feel compelled to rebel against it; but we shall surely do so only after much careful consideration and with a sense of respect and gratitude for all that it has been and has given to us. To want to rebel at the outset, to push aside the wisdom of the elders of our discipline and of those who preceded them, and to do so in the name of freedom and responsibility is a sign of impetuous intellectual adolescence rather than maturity.

Voices of Authority in Daily Living

Thus far we have spoken of the way in which we are dependent upon an authoritative tradition whenever we seek intellectual maturity and responsibility in a given area of human understanding or enterprise. We cannot, that is to say, entertain the so-called principle of radical doubt in a consistent and comprehensive manner even in those areas where our knowledge is most advanced and expert. But as human persons none of us is limited to engagement with any one narrow intellectual tradition. We may be nuclear physicists, psychiatrists, or artists, but the totality of our life extends way beyond the limits of our work in the laboratory, consulting room, or studio, and involves us in knowing and acting in a whole host of different spheres and circumstances. We deal daily with the real world in all its rich diversity, and none of us is capable of achieving the level of professionally informed critical engagement in more than one or perhaps, exceptionally, a handful of those areas. In order to function as rounded participants in daily living, therefore, each of us is forced in practice to rely upon the accounts of reality offered to us by numerous different traditions – scientific, philosophical, political, practical, religious and so on. The precise combination will be different in each case; a reflection of the fact that within the larger community of the society in which we live, each of us belongs to a variety of different groups or communities whose identity is bound up with their adherence to some shared tradition or way of thinking and acting. In most we shall of necessity be content to aspire to nothing more than the status of novice. And out of the patchwork of these various individual traditions and their authoritative voices is composed the quilted picture which each of us builds up of reality, and which informs and shapes our attempt to live meaningfully in the world – a picture for the larger part of which we are unable personally to provide anything resembling a precise rational justification. For that we rely upon and trust others whose skill and training lie elsewhere than our own. In other words, the Enlightenment principle of a wholly open and critical approach to thinking, a determination to take nothing on authority but to test everything before buying, is impossible to sustain in practice. Real life just is not like that!

Think for a moment about the practicalities of the matter. Someone who consistently refused to commit themselves to any belief or any action for which they could not provide adequate rational warrant would have to stay in bed in the morning, for, as a moment's reflection will confirm, daily life is chock-full of uncertainties, trust, intellectual risk and actions based on probabilities. The truth about us as human beings, in other words, is that we do submit to voices of authority other than that of pure reason. We cannot escape doing so. In deciding whether or not to smother my limbs and torso in a protective sun-cream before braving the tropical twenty-two degrees of a British summer I do not first feel obliged to undertake the necessary education and research which would enable me to verify for myself what scientists are increasingly saying about the depletion of the Earth's ozone layer and its likely consequences. Am I shirking my responsibility as a reasonable human being, or submitting meekly to authoritarian influences? Maybe. But that is how I and most other humans actually live our lives from day to day. From the offerings of the weather forecaster and the news headlines, the stories which my wife and children tell me about the sort of day they have had and the people they have met, to these more ultimate and far-reaching voices which offer an account of the meaning of human existence and our place within it, we are constantly barraged by voices which clamour for our attention. From the morass presented to us we select, log and invest trust in some, while quietly discarding the rest, as we engage in the ongoing process of building up a coherent and reasonably comprehensive picture of the world in which we live. Tomorrow we will get out of bed and live our lives on the basis of that picture, inadequate and mistaken in many respects as it may be. It is the best picture that is available to us at this point, and we have neither the expertise nor the time to be able to test and verify every aspect of it personally. In fact, by far the larger part of it is directly dependent upon information, assumptions and ways of seeing things received in one way or another from others; those who have gone before us, and those in community with whom we live our lives. The pertinent question, the decision which we have to make, is not *whether* we will submit to such voices, but rather *which* voices we will submit to, and at what points and under what conditions shall we feel able or obliged to challenge what they are saying to us.

The quest for a critical perspective which in some way escapes all this is thus essentially a bid to escape from the particularity of our locatedness as human persons in community. It is symptomatic of the sort of rampant individualism which craves autonomy from any sort of reliance or dependence upon others, which would create a social and intellectual vacuum in which to exist and to think 'clearly'. But we cannot do so. In thinking as in every other aspect of life we are faced with the vulgar fact of our interdependence as human persons. A totally 'free' (i.e. autonomous) thought, liberated from all inherited influences and determinations, or a critical thought which is genuinely critical with respect to anything which it cannot itself demonstrate to be the case is a self-deception which simply leaves those who embrace it as an ideal cruelly exposed to the manipulation and buffetings of the spirit of the age which they mistakenly embrace as the voice of 'objective reasoning'. Having abdicated their status as heirs of one tradition, they become instead slaves to another, yet all the while believing themselves to be free. If there is anything worse than slavish adherence to a tradition, it is surely slavish adherence which is unable to recognize itself as such.

We must abandon the Enlightenment ideal of autonomous critical thinking, therefore, and face up to the inevitability of our locatedness within and indebtedness to some tradition or other. We are born and raised within a human group which has inherited a vast body of knowledge and forms of life from its past. In order to think, to communicate, to live at all we rely wholly on our freedom to participate within this shared tradition of thought and action, the bulk of which we are never in any position to verify personally. In order to do so we should have quite literally to rewind the video of human history and trace through and check every step in its multi-faceted development for ourselves. In reality, we are able to operate as intelligent and socially adept human beings only because we are prepared to take a considerable amount of the tradition on trust. And, as Mitchell points out, ironically we are never more reliant on such trust than when we use what the tradition offers to us in order to think critically about some aspect of it, or to critique some other tradition. Reason, we might say, is parasitic upon tradition. It feeds upon and flourishes within an intellectual context which provides it with a framework of fixed points of reference from which it draws its sense of direction and meaning. Tradition, in other words, is the parent of critical thinking, the womb within which it may develop and grow, rather than its antithesis.

Tradition and Transition

Once we see this, the fallacy of polarizing so-called 'traditionalist' and 'critical' (or 'dogmatic' and 'liberal') approaches to theology or anything else becomes apparent. An approach which insists upon rebelling against the tradition which spawned and nurtured it *for the sake of rebellion*, as if rebellion were in itself a good and necessary thing and all past beliefs and practices must be overturned or put on ice until verified *de novo*, is manifestly ridiculous and impossible to achieve. In theology, as in all other disciplines, what we want are what Mitchell calls 'good rebels', those whose acquired ability to take their stand within the tradition has lent them a vision and the wherewithal to transcend it as and when their dialogue with reality compels them to do so, thereby contributing to the healthy development and progression of the tradition itself, and securing it for the next generation. True freedom with respect to tradition, I would suggest, lies not in complete autonomy from it (the quest for which results only in our unwitting enslavement) but rather in a mature ability to discern the extent of our indebtedness to it, and yet a genuine willingness to hear other voices, other stories, and to be prepared in principle to revise (or even in some extreme cases to reject) our own tradition in the light of our engagement with reality.

Thus, a fearful clinging to the past – rejecting out of hand alternative and new ways of seeing and thinking, refusing to enter into discussion with them, being closed to the possibility of learning anything whatever from them – this too is a ridiculous attitude to adopt, and one equally impossible to sustain consistently. We cannot, however much we might like to try (for whatever misguided reason), live as occupants of some previous age. We cannot escape from our own location in history and see things as our ancestors saw them. We may wish to preserve what they have passed on to us; but its meaning for us in our context will be significantly, if not totally, distinct from its meaning for them in theirs. We cannot stop the march of time and the changes which it brings. As we have seen in relation to the question of texts and their meanings, continuities survive the passage of time only at the cost of a degree of discontinuity and development. We can either face up to this, and seek to manage, respond to and help to shape such development, or else we can pretend that it is not happening, in which case we shall deceive ourselves into thinking that we are preserving the

179

tradition, whereas in truth we shall be starving it of the oxygen of the present which it needs in order to survive.

Tradition, then, is not something which is essentially static and backward looking. It it looks to the past and seeks to learn from its inheritance; but it looks equally to the present and the future, seeking in the acquired wisdom of former generations appropriate ways and means of dealing with new challenges and circumstances; seeking to adapt itself, so that its voice may be heard speaking in the language which today's generation can hear and understand; committed to the view that what it offers is of lasting value, but open in principle to the revision and adaptation which ongoing engagement with reality and new discoveries may compel it to accept. In the next chapter we shall explore what sort of thing is involved in this continual process of development and adaptation of the Christian tradition.

NOTES
1 Cited in Mitchell, B., 'Faith and Reason: A False Antithesis?', *Religious Studies* 16, p. 144.
2 Saxbee, J., *Liberal Evangelism* (SPCK 1994), p. 8.
3 By scripture alone.
4 van Dusen, H. P., *The Vindication of Liberal Theology* (Scribners, New York 1963), p. 27, cited in Saxbee, *Liberal Evangelism*, p. 8.
5 Mitchell, B., *How to Play Theological Ping-Pong* (Hodder & Stoughton 1990), pp. 88–97.
6 Mitchell, *How to Play Theological Ping-Pong*, p. 143.

— 9 —

Transmission and Translation

The tradition in which we live does not stand still. It is constantly changing, and we have a role to play in guiding the direction that those changes shall take.

Maurice Wiles

The basic calling of the Christian is to serve Christ by bearing witness to the gospel. This testimony is directed primarily, of course, to those who do not consider themselves to belong to the visible church. It is intended to facilitate the discovery on their part that they do nonetheless belong to Christ by virtue of his redemptive activity in their behalf, and to draw them in thereby to full participation in the life of God's people. Without this basic missionary activity the church would perish, for it is the chief way in which, within God's own purposes and activity, its extension into the next generation is secured.

The responsibility of handing the gospel on to others is something which also arises within the boundaries of the Christian community itself. Here too, within the life of God's people, there is a continual process of 'witness' involved, although it is witness through participation, rather than by confrontation or collision with an alien tradition. Children are raised within a context where certain beliefs and practices are the accepted norm; they are 'taught to believe' the basic truths of the gospel message, and to engage in forms of life which express and are consonant with those same beliefs. At some stage along the way they will reach the point where they find themselves compelled to question or test the tradition. Sometimes (especially during adolescence when so many things associated with childhood and dependence upon parents are set aside) there will be a rejection of or distancing from the tradition in preference for some other set of beliefs or (more likely) practices which do not belong legitimately within its parameters. In other cases, the process will result in a strengthening and confirming of their identity as committed members of the tradition.

In various ways, then, whether through the osmotic acquisition of new members via various types of missionary strategy, or the faithful propagation and nurturing of the community's youngest participants, the Church is concerned essentially with a task of transmission, a task with the faithful acquittal of which its own future as a distinct community is inseparably bound up. But just what is it that we are called thus to transmit, to pass on to others? The short answer to this question is 'the tradition'; but that hardly suffices. Perhaps the time has come, therefore, to unpack this term a little further as it applies to the context of Christian life and theology. What precisely does the term 'tradition' refer to?

Interpreting the Story in Word and Deed

At the heart of the tradition is the Christian gospel itself, the story which the church has to tell concerning God's creative and redemptive engagement with humankind; a story of sin and salvation, guilt and grace, despair and hope, and a story which reaches its climax in the crucifixion and resurrection of Jesus Christ and the subsequent outpouring of God's Spirit into the world. It is this story which, in the telling, has the power to change lives and to reshape our thinking and acting in decisive ways. It is, in Paul's memorable phrase, 'the power of God for salvation to every one who has faith'.[1] This story is preserved, of course, chiefly in the scriptural inheritance of the church. The Bible, in other words, provides the textual vehicle for the transmission through the ages of the prophetic and apostolic witness to God's saving activity in Christ. And this story, in its various forms and stages of development in scripture, is passed on to us not simply so that we might venerate and cherish it as something sacred, but so that we might in turn pass it on to others and thereby secure its extension into the present and the future.

Scripture, therefore, far from being a distinct entity set over against 'tradition' as some accounts of the matter would suggest, is in fact an integral part of the tradition itself, albeit a part which is granted a special and distinct status and function within the tradition. But the gospel which scripture transmits, the story which we receive in our reading of the text, does not come to us naked and unaccounted for. Within the community of faith that story is told and retold, and in the telling the story must constantly be translated, interpreted and made sense of for those who are unfamiliar with its central characters, the main lines of its plot, the language and conceptuality of its original context, and so on. Thus most of us read the Bible in modern English translations rather than struggling with the Greek and Hebrew originals, and our attempts to make sense of its contents are aided and enhanced at every step by commentaries, Bible-study notes, sermons and other interpretative tools. And these are designed to make our reading easier and more beneficial, furnishing us with helpful illustrations and explanations, interpretative wisdom passed on by those who have wrestled long and hard with the text for themselves. At every stage in our reception of it, the story itself is offered to us not as pure text with which we may do as we like, but together with a running commentary which offers us an account of its meanings as discerned by and submitted to within the community of faith. The transmission of the gospel, in other words, always involves more than the textual vehicle of scripture alone. It is invariably accompanied by a rich tapestry of forms of thought, understanding, expression, and indeed forms of life, deemed appropriate to convey the meaning and significance of that story within a particular human context.

Here, then, we may identify a second stratum of the tradition. First there is the gospel story itself as offered to us in its textual form in scripture. And then there is the constant attempt by the church to make sense of that story, to interpret it and unpack its significance. This can be seen happening at a whole variety of different levels. There is the very technical level of the formulation of authoritative creeds and confessions, precisely worded attempts by theological experts to distil the meaning of the heart of the Christian story in conceptual and symbolic form. Very often it is this credal inheritance which is meant when reference is made to 'tradition' and, of course, it constitutes a very important part of it. But the tradition in our sense extends far beyond this to the grass roots of the community, embracing all the multiple ways in which the meaning of the Christian gospel is made manifest and embodied there. Alasdair MacIntyre reminds us that an intellectual tradition will always manifest itself in far more than narrowly intellectual ways in the community whose identity is bound up with it. Thus, 'beliefs are expressed in and through rituals, and ritual dramas, masks and modes of dress, the ways in which houses are structured and villages and towns laid out, and of course by actions in general'.[2] And in the church we may certainly say that the gospel story is 'told' not only in creeds and confessions, commentaries on the Bible, works of theology, sermons and other more or less intellectual modes of transmission, but equally (and arguably more effectively in terms of the average person in the pew) through the vehicles of liturgy, the words of hymns and choruses (perhaps the most efficient communicator and instiller of doctrine available – for better or worse!), symbolism, the 'ritual drama' of baptism and the Eucharist, 'popular' Christian art and music, church architecture, and so on. All of these feed into and inform the ways in which Christian people understand and give expression to their faith, and the ways in which they interpret the gospel story and seek to respond to it. As such they constitute an important part of the tradition which informs our reflection as Christians. But we may go even further than this.

In Chapter 7 I suggested that the basic function of scripture within the church was to tell God's story, to present a narrative account of the world and our place within it which informs and shapes our existence as those whose faith is in Christ, the central player in the story. We locate ourselves within this account, this way of seeing things, and live our lives in accordance with it. We make sense of the world from within the perspective afforded by our place as characters within the story. In so doing, I indicated, we are in effect writing the next chapters of the story, extending it into the present and the future. Another way of putting this is simply to say that the way in which the Christian community 'interprets' its gospel is not limited to intellectual accounts and explanations of the story itself, nor to the various aspects of specifically 'churchly' existence mentioned above, but extends to the entirety of the forms of thought and activity adopted by Christian people in the world. The church's attempts to be the people of God in the world, that is to say, to continue the story, provide the most poignant commentary on the meaning of the gospel which it has to share with others. We are called not only to tell the story, but to live it out. In this sense the 'tradition' broadly defined, that body of beliefs, assumptions, practices and forms of life which furnishes the starting-point for the ways in which Christians exercise their responsibility to think and act in the world, may be said to embrace the entire concrete existence of the community of faith insofar as it constitutes an interpretation in concept, word, symbol, and action, of the gospel story.

That which the church is called to transmit, then, is the story of the gospel faithfully interpreted in word and deed in the life of the community of faith. That is what is handed down from one generation to the next, and handed out to those who stand as onlookers to the community's life. The Christian hope is that those who hear and see and experience this lived proclamation in all its diversity may, through the activity of the Holy Spirit, find themselves challenged and drawn into the story and thereby into the community. In the previous chapter I argued that tradition, properly understood, is not something static, but precisely something which furnishes the conditions for its own development and change. We may now go further and say that the task of transmission itself is one in which some degree of development and change is inevitably entailed.

Translation and Transition

That this is indeed so may be seen if we consider what happens when the church seeks to take its gospel to places and cultures where its influence is either unknown or (more likely nowadays) extremely limited. We are thinking, in other words, about what have traditionally been described as 'missionary' situations. Now, the training of missionaries is multifaceted, but entails at least two broad components. First, the missionary will be trained and given a thorough grounding in the tradition: that is to say, through a careful study of the Bible, of the history of the church and its theology, and other closely related topics, she will acquire a full and rounded knowledge of the gospel story and its interpretation within the life of the community of faith. But then second, the missionary must also be trained in the linguistic, social, practical and other skills which will enable her to engage effectively in the task of telling this same story to those who belong to a wholly different culture, the task which we may refer to as the *translation* of the story.

MacIntyre describes 'translation' as the extension of a tradition from one linguistic community to another. The task of the Christian missionary is of precisely this sort; it is the attempt to express the gospel meaningfully within a new language and a new and more or less different way of seeing things. In the majority of cases this will begin with a literal ability to translate the words of the biblical text into the language of the hearers. But in order to tell the story efficiently, of course, much more is required than this. The missionary will need also to be able to interpret, illustrate, explain, make sense of the text for her hearers, and this task demands more than a mere matching of word to word and phrase to phrase. It requires sufficient immersion within and familiarity with the shared fund of assumptions, associations, expectations and knowledge bound up with the language of the community concerned to be able to draw upon this fund creatively and play into the hands of those who listen. To be able to go beyond a mere transmission of the words of scripture and to offer an account of its meaning, in other words, the missionary must seek to become a surrogate member of the community, participating in its life over a period of time, assimilating its patterns of thought and behaviour so that in due course she will be able to interpret the gospel for the community both conceptually, and by suggesting appropriate rituals and patterns of behaviour as a response to and embodiment of it. She must 'speak the language' of her hearers in far more than a merely linguistic sense.

Only in this way, by effectively spanning two quite distinct traditions of thought and speech, will she be able to discern linguistic and conceptual equivalencies, and to discover fitting illustrations and analogies through which to communicate the story from the one to the other. Perhaps more importantly still, it is only by this painstaking acquisition of what MacIntyre refers to as a 'second first language' that the missionary will discern the 'untranslatabilities' – the words and ideas and convictions proper to the Christian tradition which find no ready equivalent within the receptor culture; the things which, without the creative adaptation of language and illustration, it is not really possible to 'say' in the language of those she is seeking to address. Failure to identify these, the borrowing and unqualified deployment of inappropriate linguistic, conceptual and symbolic material, is the most likely route to the creation of hybrid forms of the Christian story in which the vital heart of the gospel itself has in some way been betrayed, compromised, or lost along the way.

The missionary, then, like the historical critic referred to in Chapter 6, must first cultivate the 'art of hearing' in order duly to be able to speak the same language as those whose context she now inhabits. In fact, as I suggested earlier, this is merely a heightened and more apparent instance of an essentially similar translation process which takes place in every act of communication between one person and another. When two different languages or cultures are involved we are conscious of the process, but we perform it at a subconscious level many times daily. In order to ensure that what we hear is basically the same as what another person is saying to us we must attempt to align ourselves with their outlook and understanding. Transmitter and receiver must be tuned to the same wavelength. But this leads us to the essential point. For, whether it is our next-door-neighbour or a member of a wholly different race and culture that we are dealing with, we can never achieve the alignment precisely. We can only ever be partially successful. In every translation, every interpretation, there is an element of slippage, of something gained and something lost. And the communication of meaning, therefore, is never complete or absolute. What the person hears will never be precisely what we say, for all the reasons rehearsed in our discussion of this matter in Chapter 6. There will (we trust) be some considerable degree of continuity between the message sent and that received, but there will equally always be some degree of discontinuity. The task of the translator is to seek to ensure that the degree of continuity is sufficient, and that the discontinuity does not obscure the essence of the message. But whenever we attempt to say the same thing in different words (i.e. to translate) we must face the fact that we shall not actually have said precisely 'the same thing' at all, but something subtly different. The task of translation, then, always involves transition, development, change in the form and content of the tradition itself.

At first sight this may seem to be an admission of failure, and the identification of a problem for missionary strategists to overcome. But it should not be viewed in this way. The problem certainly cannot be overcome. It can only be faced up to and taken into account. With care, sufficient continuity between transmitter and receiver can be achieved for the basic message to be communicated effectively. That the result does not look and sound precisely the same as the Christianity with which we (personally or as a culturally located Christian group) are familiar ought neither to surprise nor to disappoint us. To desire that it should be so, that the form of the tradition which emerges within the new context, as the story of the gospel is told and takes root and is interpreted in word and deed there, should replicate exactly the form which it takes in our own cultural context, is to deny the legitimate particularity of both cultures, and to want to transgress way beyond the remit of the church's missionary task. We are called to make disciples of Jesus, not to clone our own particular form of Christianity. Through its translation into new cultural contexts, therefore, the tradition develops and adapts and takes on new forms. Were it not to do so, it could not take root and thrive. The fact that it does so, that it is capable of doing so – that the gospel is able to transcend the barriers of culture and to translate itself into forms of thought and life which constitute an appropriate 'interpretation' of it in a particular time and place – should be a cause for rejoicing rather than regret. To resent it, or to consider such new manifestations in some way inferior to our own is to slide into the very worst form of traditionalism.

Translation and Regeneration

But translation is not only something which must be attempted in the effort to bridge the linguistic and intellectual gaps between different traditions or cultures. Translation also goes on (and must go on) within particular traditions and cultures, as one generation seeks to communicate with the next. Thus the task of receiving the Christian story, interpreting it, and handing it on in a form which belongs not to the past but to the present, is very much a task of translation. With the passage of time, the forms of human understanding and activity which surround the church in a particular place change. The church and its gospel are not, and cannot be, a time warp, immune to such change. The call to mission is essentially a call to communication and sharing, and communication is, as we have seen, a matter of learning to speak the language of those who hear. So the church must meet the challenge of an ever-changing present by responding with new ways of expressing its message, by relating that message to the constantly revised account of the world offered by the contemporary world-view, by answering today's questions and concerns, rather than resting content with the answers which it gave to yesterday's. Unless Christians face this challenge squarely, they fail in the missionary task just as surely as if, travelling to some far-off land, they had not bothered to learn to speak the language or to understand the ways of its inhabitants. The result will be the isolation of a self-imposed irrelevance. If, rather than facing up to the task of extending God's story into the present, we seek constantly to dwell in some previous chapter of it, we should not be surprised when we are either ignored or not taken seriously by those who find our approach quaintly anachronistic. If we persist in such nostalgic inertia, we shall rapidly become a mere tourist attraction, a side stall in the fragmented freak show of contemporary pluralism, more pathetic than prophetic in the face of the needs and worries of our fellow human travellers through time.

This, then, is the heart of the theological task: the translation of the gospel into forms which are meaningful for our spatial and temporal context, that those who live alongside us in that context may hear and understand and discover the relevance and meaning of the gospel for themselves. And this task of translation involves two basic aspects. First, we must find contemporary ways of *expressing* the gospel message, of telling the story. And then, second, we must engage in the equally vital task of *interpreting* that message for a society whose understanding of the world and human existence within it is constantly moving on, giving some account of its broader meaning and significance. We must attempt to show, that is to say, how this particular story which we tell, and around which as Christians we structure our lives, relates to other elements of human understanding as offered by the various voices of authority in our context; scientific voices, technological voices, political voices, and so on. We must be concerned, in other words, with the integration of the story into some coherent and intelligible overall account of things and form of life in the world.

Transmission and Integration

As Christians we are called to give an account of the hope that is in us which is both coherent and integrated. Our Christian faith must cohere so far as is possible, that is to say, both within itself and as part of the total package of beliefs and forms of life which we affirm as intelligent beings surveying the world and seeking to make sense of our experience of it. For the truth is, of course, that the story with which the church is entrusted, the gospel which it proclaims, has a particular focus. It does not seek to answer all our questions about the world in which we live. It does not so much as touch directly on many of the important issues and aspects of reality which concern and involve us as we live our daily lives. What it does is to tell of God and his relationship with the world which he has made, and with humankind in particular; and to tell this story in such a way that in reading it people are drawn to and enabled to relate truly to him as their creator and redeemer.

That the church has sometimes forgotten or failed to recognize this fact, mistaking the contents of its story for surrogate science, history, psychology or whatever, and treating its scriptural inheritance as a sort of divinely underwritten almanac from which data on every subject under the sun might legitimately be quarried, has more often than not been to its detriment. This does not mean, of course, that the story which the church tells has no bearing on our understanding of these and other things, or that theology is to be carried on in some sort of intellectual ghetto. On the contrary, recognition of the legitimate boundaries of specifically theological concern and pronouncement forces us immediately to face up to the truth that these boundaries are shared with other human intellectual enterprises from whose contribution to knowledge the theologian may benefit, and raises the question, therefore, of what sort of relationships are to be enjoyed in the borderlands between them. Withdrawal from intellectual territories wrongfully occupied in the past opens up the delicate but vital matter of subsequent diplomatic relations with their new administrations.

This is particularly true because of the sort of story which theology tells; a story of such shape and dimensions that it has potential boundaries with every other story told in and about our world. Precisely because it is a story about God and his creation, that is to say, it lays some sort of claim to what might be called universal and ultimate status. What it offers (whether it be true or false) is a narrative framework from within which to make sense of the world and its history, parameters of meaning and purpose within which to locate human existence and experience of reality in all its rich diversity. Thus we might say that in one sense at least the gospel does claim to include within its purview those spheres of experience which are properly recognized as the legitimate domain of physics, history, the social sciences and so on. But it addresses these in its own – quite distinct – ways from the specialist disciplines involved, operating on what is sometimes called a different level of description. In other words, when it talks about the same sorts of things, it does so using very different words, and with quite distinct questions and concerns in mind.

The Quest for Coherence

What this means, however, is that the Christian who tells and lives by this story is compelled to take seriously the task of integrating other stories with it, weaving them into and around the framework which it supplies, and thereby fashioning some sort of coherent overall picture of things. Why should this be so?

First, we might mention the basic human desire for a unified and integrated existence. In our society people are living increasingly complicated lives in which they play out many different personal roles, belong to a diverse variety of human groups with their respective demands and expectations, and are subjected to a remarkable plethora of allegedly authoritative voices and traditions all competing for their attention and allegiance. Values and habits instilled into us at an early age by parental instruction and example; the fashionable views and ways of our peer group; the lightly worn and persuasively packaged learning of the TV documentary expert; the reassuring and authoritative tones of the newscaster; the smooth patter of rival political traditions – and so the list might go on: each offering some account of things which they hope will be believed and acted upon by others. And, faced with this welter of data and demands it falls to each person to make some sort of sense out of the jumble, to select and reject, to assimilate and to set aside.

The pluralist ethos of our post-modern society would have us believe that criteria for engaging in such a process in any systematic way do not exist; that in the final analysis, faced with the contemporary hypermarket of competing traditions and voices, we should choose what satisfies or titillates, since there is ultimately no way of deciding which, if any, may be deemed true or false. But in practice I doubt whether anyone could finally rest content with the sort of intellectual pot-pourri likely to result from such an attitude. The fragmentation of personal existence into an arbitrary amalgam of discrete, hermetically sealed compartments fostered by the post-modern rejection of 'grand narratives' (i.e. stories which attempt to hold everything together in a meaningful way) seems likely to result in disintegrated personalities and intellectual division of mind of a type which our being as particular human 'persons' resists at the deepest level. Deep down we want to be able to hold together our intellectual, moral, religious, political and other commitments in a meaningful manner. We do not want the sum of our beliefs and practices to resemble the contents of a vacuum-cleaner bag; a random assortment of apparently unrelated bits and pieces, united only by their all happening to have been sucked in and held together by the intellectual energies of one particular person.

I do not doubt that there are many people who manage in practice to adhere to a curious selection of conflicting beliefs or ways of thinking and behaving by effectively keeping different parts of their lives and their intellectual engagement with things sealed off from one another. Indeed, if truth be known all of us live daily with a whole host of unresolved tensions and inconsistencies in our intellectual lives at some level or another. The question is not whether this happens so much as whether it is a desirable state of affairs in which we may rest perfectly content. My suggestion is that it is not; that deep down we crave some sort of unified picture of and approach to things, some integrated account in which all the different threads of our lives are woven neatly into an identifiable pattern, furnishing us with a coherent basis for living in the world. I do not claim that anyone ever achieves this in this life; simply that it is an ideal for which, as human persons with a single intellectual identity and created in the image of the Logos of God, we strive, and we are restless till we find it. This being the case, the question naturally arises as to the basis on which we will proceed in the integrative task. If we reject the vacuum-cleaner scenario, then how do we decide which bits to pick up and use as we construct for ourselves a coherent story about the world as we experience it?

The 'Religious' Function of Tradition

We have already seen that the Enlightenment answered this question by trying to identify universal and objective standards for testing the credibility of beliefs, opinions, and stories, and allowing us to discard any which, being undemonstrable or unprovable, did not properly merit the description 'knowledge'. The end result of such a process would, presumably, be a single uniform account of things shared by all intelligent people. The failure of this quest does not invalidate the quest as such, but only its assumed starting-point. The bid to differentiate true accounts from false is respectable enough. But there is no universal set of criteria, undeniable by any rational and sane human person, in accordance with which such judgements may be made. The task of pursuing a coherent and integrated outlook on things must therefore begin elsewhere.

In practice, it begins with our commitment to and participation in an intellectual tradition; a shared way of thinking and seeing things; an agreed point of view from which to survey reality. Out of the Babel confusion of voices clamouring for our attention not all can be considered as of equal significance. Some will already have come to exercise a fundamental and formative influence upon us, furnishing us with a perspective, a set of values and assumptions, from within which we shall undertake the task of evaluating and sifting the claims of other voices. Each of us, if we dig deep enough, will find evidence that we belong to such a tradition, whether we ordinarily acknowledge it or not. We live our lives and integrate our mental world in accordance with some ultimate story which we tell about ourselves and our place within the world, the sort of place the world is, its origins and destiny, and so forth. Such a story may legitimately be dubbed 'religious'. Of course it might not include any identifiably divine or supernatural characters whatsoever. But it embraces 'a set of beliefs, experiences and practices that seek to grasp and express the ultimate nature of things, that which gives shape and meaning to life, that which claims final loyalty'.[3] In this sense Marxism and naturalistic humanism both function as 'religious' stories. So too, of course, does the Christian gospel.

The task of integration, then, is not one in which we submit the bits and pieces of life and its experiences, and the accounts of it offered to us by others, to some flawless adjudication process which leaves us holding only to what is manifestly good and true. Nor does it involve the arbitrary gathering of unrelated but attractive elements onto an intellectual smorgasbord designed to satisfy our particular appetites. Rather, we integrate our outlook by weaving it around the 'religious' story told by the intellectual tradition to which we belong. We integrate other voices with the givenness of what this voice tells us, an account which already counts for us as authoritative.

Of course, the story does not come to us naked for dress. The form of the tradition within which we stand will itself be the result of the integrative labours of others before us; those who, like us, were committed to this particular story, and deployed it in their own effort to fashion a coherent outlook from the materials available to them in their day. The intellectual product which they hand on to us, however, is already dated when we receive it. It offers yesterday's answers to yesterday's questions and concerns, and the integrative process must ever be repeated afresh to keep pace with the latest changes and developments in thinking. In addition, because our personal experience of and pilgrimage through life will be distinct even from those who inherit the same tradition, the precise form which that tradition takes will differ in every case as it is handed on, receiving the distinctive stamp of the particular person that we are, the unique set of relationships within which we exist, and the combination of voices and stories which confront us. The specific embodiment of the tradition which results will then provide the starting-point for our subsequent engagement in the intellectual task.

The tradition which we inherit is itself thereby regenerated in and through the critical and reflective activity which it facilitates. Tradition leads, through the responsible exercise of 'faith seeking understanding', to a revised and renewed version of itself. It is in this sense that theology, like all other serious intellectual activity, is, in MacIntyre's description, both tradition-constituted and tradition-constitutive. Through its activity, the Christian tradition is translated and transmitted to new and different times and places and people. The result, we should remind ourselves again, when the task is exercised responsibly and effectively, will be a continual extension and renewal of the tradition which, while it is identifiably continuous with previous forms of it, can and will never be precisely the same twice.

Coherence and Creation

For the Christian, that around which a coherent account of things will be woven will be the distinctive structure of the story told by the church: a story about God, the meaning and purpose and value of human existence, God's creative and redemptive involvement in the world in his Son and Spirit, and so forth. The first question which the Christian asks as she surveys the range of voices, claims and stories presented to her, therefore, will be about their compatibility and correspondence with this story.

This leads us to a second reason why those who engage in the theological task are compelled to seek a coherent and integrated overall account of things; namely, that certain key elements in the Christian story itself demand it. Chief among these is the fact that the God of whom Christians speak is no tribal or parochial deity, but 'the Lord who made heaven and earth'. He is not concerned only with the spiritual lives of a religious coterie therefore, but with the whole of his creation in all its aspects. Thus we cannot limit him, or keep him compartmentalized for Sunday worship and daily devotions. He will not be confined in this way, but is already to be found at work in the world which he has made, from the subatomic constituents of all physical matter to the most sophisticated of social, intellectual and spiritual activities and processes. If everything that exists has its existence only in relation to his ongoing creative and sustaining initiative, then quite clearly we must seek to understand just how he relates to different aspects of reality as we experience and know it. We must find room for him, as it were, in the story which we tell about any part of his creation, relating the God of the gospel to what we know and say about it.

Then, third, the doctrine of creation itself underpins a commitment to the view that reality is, at root, unified. The conviction that 'In the beginning ... the Lord God created heaven and earth ... and saw that it was good' leads us reasonably to expect that we indwell a physical and moral and spiritual universe, not a multiverse; that there is, indeed, an 'objective reality' out there beyond our minds to be known, and that it manifests an overall coherence and orderliness which can be explored and mapped and described. We cannot prove that this is the case, but the form of Christian faith in God as creator entails the belief that it is so.

Of course, reality is highly complex. Any one aspect of it may be approached and described in many different ways, each attaching to a distinct level of its stratified existence. But the complexity is one which, when we stand back from it, reveals an overall unity. John Polkinghorne illustrates this point very helpfully. 'Reality,' he writes, 'is a multi-layered unity. I can perceive another person as an aggregation of atoms, an open biochemical system in interaction with the environment, a specimen of *homo sapiens*, an object of beauty, someone whose needs deserve my respect and compassion, a brother for whom Christ died. All are true and all mysteriously coinhere in that one person.'[4] Thus we can see that here we need not choose between the accounts of things proffered by the authoritative voices of physics, chemistry, biology, sociology, anthropology and theology. The stories which they tell are not in this case competing with one another, but are complementary, each dealing with a distinct aspect of a common reality.

If, then, reality is indeed a unified and coherent whole, we should expect it to be possible in principle to provide a unified and coherent *account* of that whole; different disciplines and approaches providing different pieces of the overall jigsaw. To the extent that our theological, biological, sociological and other stories represent an appropriate description of things, in other words, we may legitimately expect some ultimate convergence and fitting together of the bits of the picture which each provides. The Christian conviction that it is so, therefore, compels us to pursue some such convergence, to see whether and how our particular piece of the jigsaw fits together with the most reliable and complete accounts of things offered to us by scientists, historians, artists, sociologists, and any who claim to provide some insight or avenue into the enhanced understanding of our shared human reality. It is from such materials that, through a constant process of sifting and selecting and rearranging, we gradually build up an integrated picture of reality by which to live. The precise shape and detail of our jigsaw will change from day to day as fresh influxes of data and interpretation reach us, and as we seek to incorporate them, perhaps substituting them for other (it now appears) less satisfactory pieces.

The Bid to Be Taken Seriously

A fourth reason for seeking to integrate the Christian gospel with other things which we believe and know has to do with what has traditionally been called 'apologetics'. Apologetics is the name given to the attempt to commend the gospel to those who are not Christians by persuading them that it is 'reasonable' when measured by standards or criteria of judgement which believer and unbeliever share alike, or by appealing to evidence to which both have equal access. Such an approach has always been popular in the church, and never more so than in the wake of the Enlightenment's claim that neutral and universal means of verification were available. Claims that belief in the existence of God, the incarnation, the trinity, the atonement and so forth is more 'rational' than alternatives to it abound in theological literature, as do an equal number of claims that such beliefs are wholly irrational! Once it is conceded that globally compelling standards of what is and what is not rational are lacking, this whole approach to things begins to look untenable.[5]

But this does not mean that there are no ways of commending the Christian story to others in terms of its wider coherence and correspondence with other shared elements of human understanding. There remains the possibility of what we might call a 'soft' apologetics. Such an approach would not seek to force unbelievers to concede the truth of the gospel in an intellectual arm-wrestling match, but would simply point to such convergences and correspondences as may be identified between the content of the Christian story and what other authoritative voices are currently telling us about the world. We should not have unrealistic expectations about the likely results of such an exercise. It may perhaps arouse some awareness of or interest in the Christian story as a religious option where none existed previously, but in and of itself it is unlikely to convince anyone of its truth. Nonetheless, such limitations do not make the exercise a complete apologetic waste of time. In short, the Christian story (and we as those who live it out) are much more likely to be taken notice of and our voice heard in the market-place if we are seen on the one hand to be engaging seriously with what others are saying to us, and on the other seeking to integrate our story with it as and when it is appropriate to do so. Such a task, I have suggested, is indeed possible, and it is incumbent upon Christians to pursue it at whatever level is appropriate to their personal engagement with different aspects of reality. The work of eminent scientists such as John Polkinghorne shows, for example, that such integration can be achieved at the very highest levels of understanding.

The crunch comes, however, not at those points where theological and scientific (or other) stories may be seen to converge and to complement one another, but where elements in the Christian story and the voices of contemporary understanding appear to clash and to conflict. An important part of the missionary's task, I have suggested, is the identification not only of analogies and equivalencies whereby the Christian story may be communicated to others in terms of stories more familiar to them, but also of 'untranslatabilities' and inequivalencies, aspects of the Christian story which find no parallel within and perhaps even conflict with those familiar stories. The same applies, of course, in our own modern Western context. In our attempt to integrate the Christian story with other stories belonging to this context we shall soon encounter such untranslatabilities and inequivalencies, occasions for offence, scandal and conflict. When this happens how precisely ought we to proceed? What becomes then of our apologetic concern? Where does our responsibility to integrate begin and end, and how is it related to the integrity of the Christian story itself? It is to such questions that we shall turn in our next chapter.

NOTES
1 Romans 1.16.
2 MacIntyre, A., *Whose Justice? Which Rationality?* (Duckworth 1988), p. 355.
3 Newbigin, L., *Foolishness to the Greeks* (SPCK 1986), p. 3.
4 Polkinghorne, J., *One World* (SPCK 1986), p. 97.
5 A helpful treatment of this question is provided by William Placher in his book *Unapologetic Theology* (Westminster/John Knox 1989).

— *10* —

Integration and Reformation

> However much any theology will bear the imprint of its environment, it must be remembered that, when it is really living and sensitive, Christian theology does not only submit to the cultural and conceptual framework of its time and place, but also regenerates and reforms it, sometimes very drastically.
>
> *Eric Mascall*

In the theological task as I have described it, the Christian stands Janus-faced, looking in two directions at once, addressing two distinct agendas and sets of responsibilities. First and foremost she is responsible to the Christian tradition itself, and to the story which it tells concerning human existence in relation to God. It is this story which she is called to translate and to transmit to others, 'telling' it both in the explicit proclamation of evangelistic witness and, more generally, in her daily attempts to live life on all its levels in conformity to the shape and direction of that story, to extend the story into the present within the Christian community.

But this primary responsibility already involves the Christian in another: namely, the attempt to integrate the story as she receives it with the intellectual and cultural context within which she must tell it, to show how it relates to the basic components of the 'plausibility structure' which shapes the thinking and living of the wider human community to which she belongs. Lesslie Newbigin has described this as the attempt to bring about and manage a fruitful 'missionary interaction' between the gospel and culture, a process which is sometimes referred to as the *contextualization* of the Christian story.

What contextualization really entails, then, is the extension of the task of integration along a whole series of intellectual and behavioural fronts, exploring the extent to which and the ways in which the Christian story may be woven together with the various stories told and lived out within the community and context concerned. This is a task in which the substance as well as the form of the Christian story itself is at least in principle opened up to serious scrutiny and made vulnerable to challenge and the possibility of reform. As we open ourselves up to new ways of thinking and looking at things there will inevitably be some change in our understanding and presentation of the Christian gospel; the 64-thousand-dollar question is what sort of change? What will its implications be? The task of contextualization, in other words, is one in which the identity and continuity of the Christian tradition is always at stake. It is important, therefore, that some careful questions are asked about how the responsibility of guiding the direction of change and development should be approached.

I want in this chapter to consider and respond to one approach which has enjoyed very considerable influence in the modern period at the risk, I shall suggest, of the effective disintegration of the Christian story and the loss, therefore, of its identity and integrity.

Making the Gospel Relevant?

The approach which I have in mind is that which often chooses to describe itself as 'liberal', a designation the appropriateness of which I have already questioned, but which may helpfully be borrowed in the absence of any convenient alternative. The words of van Dusen are worth citing again. 'The central intellectual motive of liberal theology,' he writes, 'is to make the Christian faith intelligible and *credible*, comprehensive and *convincing* to intelligent, informed and honest minds of each successive era.'[1] Now, what exactly does this mean? What sort of thing is involved in the task which it describes? To make the Christian story intelligible – to articulate it in ways which ensure that people can grasp what it is saying – is one thing. But what precisely is implied by the claim to be making it *credible* and *convincing* to 'intelligent, informed and honest' people? For an answer to this question we must turn at once to consider a particular example of the type. Among its most consistent and persuasive exponents is Maurice Wiles, former Regius Professor of Divinity in the University of Oxford. In a series of books Professor Wiles has explored the nature of theological activity as he sees it and attempted to articulate the shape of the Christian story as it must be told in the modern age.

Christian theology, Wiles indicates in the title of one of his books, must constantly be remade.[2] The theologian cannot simply rest content with the expressions of the faith fashioned by previous generations, oriented, as those formulations inevitably were, to yes-terday's questions and concerns. Rather, 'Our concern in doctrine is with what has to be said here and now', since 'Differing cultural and philosophical conditions require different understandings and articulations of the Christian faith.'[3] As we have put the matter, the tradition must ever afresh be translated into and integrated with the changing intellectual context. To stand still in this respect is in fact to move backwards, and the church is charged with a missionary task which makes such regression unacceptable. But the image of translation is carefully chosen, for it bears within itself the thought that what is offered to the present is in some identifiable sense con-tinuous with what was said in the past, that it is a rendering of the same signal, a transmission of the same essential message. All trans-lation entails 'saying other than' as well as 'saying the same', but my contention has been that where the task is faithfully performed the discontinuities will not obscure but will rather facilitate com-munication of the basic message which has been handed from one generation and context to the next. The problem with Wiles' own remaking of the tradition is that it does not obviously appear to be a translation of the Christian story at all, the discontinuities all but obscuring such continuities as remain. The reason for this, I would suggest, lies in the process of integration as he practises it.

The contemporary theologian, Wiles urges, must face the fact that what he produces will be essentially temporary, and 'We should be as unwilling for whatever we may decide we have to say to be binding on the future as we are ourselves unwilling to be bound by the past. Sufficient unto the day are the problems thereof.'[4] In a sense this is true enough, and is already involved in being prepared to countenance the possibility of change and devel-opment in the tradition at all. But in Wiles' hands the statement has a more fundamental significance. For here it indicates a willingness (indeed the strategic necessity) for the theologian to sit loose to the commitments of faith and the authoritative voice of the Christian tradition altogether, and to remake theology for his own specific context by bringing the critical voice of that context determinatively to bear upon the tradition. The Christian theologian, he avers, must indeed be a man or woman of faith; but too much faith can result in theological glaucoma, and what is really needed is for the tenets of faith to be tried and tested in the light cast by a critical detach-ment from the tradition itself.[5] The theologian must then rework the tradition to which he is initially committed in accordance with what he sees from his superior 'detached' vantage point, whatever the implications may be for its shape and substance.

Theology, then, on this account of things, is not practised from a place within the Christian tradition, but from a place safely outside of it from which its claims and practices may be more reliably or satisfactorily evaluated. The theologian is like a cricket fan who, while lazing in the afternoon sun and listening to radio commentary on the Test Match, feels the need nonetheless to pop into the gloom of the living room to turn the TV on occasionally, just to see for himself what is *really* happening. The assumption is that the story told by the one needs to be backed up or verified by other more full and trustworthy versions of things. Here, then, Wiles seems to embrace the Enlightenment prejudice against tradition and authority, and its supposition that critical activity cannot take place from within an intellectual or faith tradition, but is only satisfactorily accomplished in detachment from it, assumptions which I have already challenged in Chapter 9 for reasons which need no reiteration here. The result is that while the remaking of Christian doctrine which Wiles proposes is indeed continual it is not necessarily continuous. The critical task must be accomplished *de novo* by each new generation, and because this task is carried out in detachment from the tradition itself and the perspective which it offers, the story which the church tells from one age to the next is effectively determined by the outlook of the current context, and may vary quite radically in substance as well as form. Thus Wiles admits that the element of identity or continuity will be difficult to define, more akin to viewing something from a radically new angle (where what appears may look very different indeed) than to the translation of a story or message from one language and form of life into another.[6]

While Wiles does not entertain the Enlightenment's optimistic claim to have delineated an absolute or final perspective from which to adjudge the truth and falsity of our knowledge, his approach is nonetheless clearly rooted in the assumption that the angle on things provided by the contemporary outlook is the best angle available to us, and the most reliable gauge we have of the truth and viability of Christian beliefs and practices. This being so, it follows that the integration of the Christian story with this plausibility structure should be one in which the one is effectively conformed to the (more reliable offerings of the) other. Wiles lists two basic objectives for this task. The first is coherence, ensuring that 'the different affirmations that we are led to make at various times and for various purposes are consistent with one another', or, as we have put it, that we are able to tell a unified and coherent story. But, while Wiles insists that in principle the criteria for the pursuit of such coherence must not be fixed in advance, in practice the results of his own theologizing suggest, in the words of one critic, a determination 'at all costs to bring Christian theology into line with what he takes to be the intellectual outlook of the present day'.[7] Thus, the same writer continues, 'His radicalism as regards the Church's tradition goes hand in hand with a complete conformism as regards the beliefs and values of the secularised industrialised culture in which he lives.'[8]

A Different Gospel?

To be fair, the conformism is not quite complete. Wiles' second theological objective he describes as a principle of economy, by which he means being prepared to distinguish between 'What the evidence requires us to say and what the evidence does not disallow us from saying'[9] and then opting to commit ourselves only to the former. The 'evidence' in question, of course, is that admitted by and interpreted within the 'detached' outlook of modernity. Thus, Wiles' own remaking of the Christian story on this basis is one in which the possibility of some of the central themes in the tradition being seriously entertained (Jesus' identity as God incarnate, his resurrection from death as in some sense a special occurrence transcending the ordinary continuities of history, God as having wrought an objective redemptive act in the history of his Son by virtue of which things are not as they formerly were, etc.) is not ruled out absolutely. Nonetheless his own consideration of the evidence does not *require* him to include these things within the story, and its integration into a coherent package with modernity is clearly made considerably smoother by their absence. Apparently 'the evidence' does require Wiles to maintain belief in 'God' as a player in the story which he tells, and here at least a faint vestige of continuity with the Christian tradition is found; but it is torn out of its proper narrative context, and the story which is now woven around it bears little resemblance to the original.

God, we learn, undergirds his creation as the ultimate source of its being, but does not enter or act within it in particular ways. He is related to the world, but not personally present within it, or not, at least, so as we might notice. Thus there can be no personal epiphanies, no miracle, no answers to petitionary prayer – at least in the way that these things have traditionally been construed. God is, in effect, no more than a privileged spectator of the historical and natural process who 'relates to' his world and his people only in the most qualified of senses, and whose absence we should hardly notice. The game would go on undisturbed if he left the stadium. All this is clearly very far removed from the biblical story of a creator passionately concerned with the condition and fortunes of his creation, so much so that he ultimately enters into a self-sacrificial mission to redeem it by becoming related to it in the closest possible way, by himself becoming a creature and bearing the suffering and shame and guilt which is our lot in order to bear them away. But then those who first told that story and those who faithfully translated, interpreted and preserved it over the centuries (some at the cost of their lives) did not have the advantage of the perspective provided by modern secular culture as a means of checking its credibility.

Eric Mascall's final judgement on Wiles' approach and its results is harsh: 'Dr Wiles's desupernaturalized version of Christianity,' he writes, 'in which nothing ever happens that is essentially different from anything else, would seem to leave us with neither a faith by which a man could live nor one for which he might die, and to substitute for a living saviour the most shadowy, fluid, and subjective of abstractions.'[10]

The Great Decommissioning?

Of course the Christian story must be critically evaluated, as I have repeatedly affirmed in this book. But the approach commended by Wiles amounts in practice to the willing abandonment of what the Christian tradition has to offer in uncritical preference for the offerings of another – modernity. He detaches himself from the perspective of Christian confession, but willingly embraces and relies upon an alternative set of prejudices, deploying these as tools with which to handle and to reform the tradition which nurtured him. This is an approach to the integration of the Christian story, therefore, in which that same story is utterly vulnerable to reconstruction at the whim of modernity's likes and dislikes, its fashions and fads. It is, on any reckoning, a strange approach for a community called to 'go and make disciples', manifesting as it does an apparent lack of confidence or faith in the story which we supposedly confess, and a willingness to *become* rather than to make disciples at the first inkling of opposition, dissent or conflict. Several considerable problems inherent in this approach suggest themselves.

Whose Story?

First, we may mention the way in which it treats the received message or gospel as in effect a commodity at the community's own disposal. There is little sense that in pursuing a policy of 'critical detachment' from its authority we are detaching ourselves from anything more than the best that our forebears in the faith had to offer to their respective generations. Our willingness to submit the Christian story as handed on to us to the judgement of contemporay canons of rationality appears, therefore, as little more than a stated preference for one set of human convictions about the shape of reality, one tradition, over another. In such circumstances it would seem perfectly reasonable to adopt the testimony of the more reliable or enlightened group. If we assume (as Wiles appears to in practice if not in principle) that the most up-to-date picture of things furnished by our own culture is more reliable than any other known to humankind, then we should be failing in our intellectual duty if we did other than prefer its testimony over that of the 'primitive' outlook of the biblical writers, and the now dated views of reality entertained by their patristic, medieval, renaissance, and other interpreters.

What has got conveniently lost in this excited rush to embrace the fruits of enlightenment, however, is any serious reckoning with the category of revelation; the claim, in other words, that God has spoken to humankind through certain decisive personal acts and initiatives (and the – in some sense inspired – witness subsequently borne to these in scriptural form) and continues to speak to the community of faith today through the continuing inspiration of its reading and interpretation of its authoritative texts. If there is, in this sense, something which has been and is 'given' to the church from beyond, a revelation which, albeit mediated through flesh-and-blood historical realities, issues not merely from human reflection upon the world and our situation in it, but from an irruption of God's Word and Spirit which transcends and even disturbs and challenges our natural capacities to grasp and make sense of things, then we must reckon with a more than purely human authority at work in and behind the story which we handle and translate. The conviction that this is indeed so (and it is a conviction inherent in the Christian story in its traditional forms, and around which the story itself actually centres) would seem to counsel at least a rather more cautious and discriminating attitude towards the church's theological inheritance and its implicit authority for Christian faith and understanding than that exemplified in Wiles's theology.

We must beware of course, of making things appear more straightforward than they really are. Cheap appeals to divine revelation are easy enough to make, but rather harder to unpack and work with in anything other than a simplistic theological model. The conviction that God has made himself known to humankind and that the Christian story is in some way the product of this self-revealing activity certainly does not absolve us from the responsibility to reflect critically upon it or to integrate it with our wider understanding of things. It would, perhaps, be convenient if we could identify a clearly defined written or oral deposit of divinely furnished wisdom and data which we were called as a church simply to preserve at all costs. In this case, theological responsibility might amount to treating the 'revelation' like a priceless antique or art treasure, providing it with a hermetically sealed intellectual sanctuary from the destructive conditions abroad in the world with its constant developments and changes in human understanding. Far from seeking to integrate it with other sources of knowledge, we should want to isolate it and exalt it above them, convinced of its perfection in form and content, and refusing to admit or to consider the claims of any voices conflicting with what we understood it to be saying to us. Such, it seems to me, is the basic error of traditionalism and biblical fundamentalism in its various forms. Taking its talent and burying it, it fails to make the intellectual investment for the kingdom of God which is required.

But, to extend the allusion to Jesus' parable further, by contrast liberalism as we find it in Wiles could reasonably be accused of having lost what was once given to it through injudicious intellectual investments, having long since allowed itself to be swallowed up in an attractive take over bid launched by a predominantly secular culture, and having now seen its various assets stripped and broken up. Wiles does not ignore the idea of revelation altogether; but he is of the view that since what is revealed comes to us in and through the mediations of fleshly, textual and other ordinary this-wordly phenomena, the alleged truth and value of such a revelation cannot escape being subjected to the evaluative tests and judgements which we ordinarily apply to the world of our experience. The claim that revelation cannot be deconstructed without remainder into bits and pieces all of which can be accounted for adequately in historically and scientifically verifiable terms, that while God makes himself known in and through natural events and phenomena, what is revealed thereby nonetheless transcends the empirically accessible, being granted to the eye of faith but hidden to others, is one which Wiles, like Pannenberg, openly rejects.[11] What he seems to desire or require is that the content and truth of the alleged revelation should be vulnerable to publicly accepted modes of verification, that it reveals nothing which could not in principle have been discovered by human endeavour of one sort or another.

There is much that might be said in response to this; but it will suffice to observe that the church, with its identification of the wisdom and power of God supremely in a flesh-and-blood location which to the world speaks only of shame, humiliation and foolishness, has not generally agreed with him. To find God revealed in the figure of the crucified Jesus, one cannot avoid the exigencies of historical and textual and other modes of critical thinking; but something more than these must enter into the equation, something which they are unable to render, to account for, or to verify. God must speak. He must give himself to be known. The consistent witness of the biblical writers and of Christian men and women over the centuries is that he does so, and the shape of their theology has been constrained above all by an obedient response to what they believed they heard him saying. To fail to reckon adequately with or account for this divine address, to handle the created media through which it reaches us as if they were no different to any other, is to abdicate one's moral obligation in the face of reality.

The Dangers of 'Chronological Snobbery'

The second problematic aspect of the liberal approach is its susceptibility to what C. S. Lewis called 'chronological snobbery'. This is the widely held supposition that anything that is known or believed by intelligent people in our own Western culture today must by definition be better or more true or more beneficial to humankind than what was known and believed yesterday, let alone two thousand years or more ago when the Christian story received its distinctive shape and content. Therefore, it is contended, a responsible Christianity will regularly bring its articles of faith to the bar of contemporary understanding for a sort of intellectual MOT test, designed to reveal which parts are looking a bit worn and in need of replacement. This notion, that the passage of time brings with it inevitable progress in human understanding and forms of life, seems to contain a dangerous but pervasive illusion.

We cannot, of course, close our eyes to the genuine progress which has been made in human understanding of and interaction with our world, especially in recent centuries. Developments in science and technology, for example, now make it possible to travel vast distances in a matter of mere hours, and to communicate instantaneously with people on the other side of our planet. Domestic gadgets heat and light and clean our homes, giving most of us a standard of comfort and convenience which no previous generation of human beings could have expected. So too in the field of medicine it is undeniable that major advances have been made even in the last decade or so which have increased our ability to save and to prolong our lives. Diseases which formerly led rapidly to decline and death are today able to be cured or their symptoms alleviated and controlled. Those the cure for which still eludes us are the subject of constant research and investigation, and the experts assure us that it is really only a matter of time before the breakthrough comes. Who can deny that in these and many other instances the knowledge and skills now available to us are superior to those which our ancestors possessed?

But, of course, the fact that our knowledge in these areas is better than it once was has little as such to do with the fact that it is modern Western knowledge, but resides in its closer relation to the truth of the realities concerned. Modern Western people, that is to say, seem to have developed methods of engaging with the material realities of nature which actually enable us to penetrate deeper into and to handle more effectively its properties and powers and potentials than previous or alternative ways of engaging with them. We do not any longer go to the GP and expect to be prescribed leeches to suck diseases and ailments out of our bloodstream. Doctors today know more about the human body and its ways than their sixteenth-century forebears did, and are able to offer us a range of drugs and treatments more appropriate to the realities of our condition, and more likely, therefore, to do us good.

The success of the treatments which they prescribe suggests that their training and apprenticeship in the modern scientific community provides them with a more satisfactory perspective from which to approach human health, and better tools and skills with which to engage with it, than the tribal witch doctor of the Amazon jungle or the sixteenth-century leech dispenser.

Our experience, in other words, leads us to believe that modern medicine has on the whole a better grasp of the truth about the human body than various alternative ways of looking at and approaching it. But the same is not at all evidently true where other aspects of reality are concerned. The recent burgeoning and apparent success of some 'alternative therapies' in our society (many of which, we might note, far from being either modern or Western derive from the centuries-old wisdom of other societies!) would suggest, for example, that even modern western medicine has not got the whole story pinned down, and that there is more to human health and its maintenance than the story which it tells might suggest. And where technology is concerned, while we may well be able now to do more things with and in our world, it is clear enough that the results for human well-being and quality of life are far from uniformly beneficial. With every advance in understanding of the nuts and bolts of the physical world we face new dilemmas concerning how such knowledge should be handled, and the possibility of a decrease in quality of life, or even the obliteration of life itself! Even our attempts to make life more pleasurable and entertaining for ourselves could hardly be held up as genuine and unquestionable progress by comparison with the cultural and artistic and social pastimes of pre-modern societies.

The point which I am trying to make is the relatively obvious one that just because our society benefits from genuine advances in knowledge of some aspects of the reality of God's world, it does not therefore follow that there has been progress of a similar sort in every area. There is very good reason to suspect that progress and enrichment in some fields has been matched by regress and impoverishment in others: not least, perhaps, where the non-material world is concerned. Sensitivity to and awareness of the spiritual dimensions of human existence, or of questions concerning the purpose and value of human life; these are areas where modernity might reasonably be argued to have lost its bearings or grasp on things, and where the occupants of other less materially minded cultures may be better situated to offer an account of how things stand. The emergence of New Age movements within our society, with their remarkable and eclectic pot-pourri of 'spiritual' offerings from cultures spanning centuries and continents, reflects the fact that modern Western culture is leaving its children dissatisfied with the spiritually emasculated story which it tells about the world and human existence within it.

It is to the church's shame that it has mostly had little to offer in order to fill this vacuum, precisely because more often than not it has reacted to the secularism of modernity in one of two equally unfruitful ways: either by retreating into a stagnant traditionalism which refuses to engage seriously with the task of translation and integration, and which insists on telling the story in ways which pretend that human understanding has not moved on since biblical and medieval times; or else by succumbing to chronological snobbery, and fashioning a gospel fit for secular human beings, but quite frankly not much use to those seeking an encounter with reality at a level which transcends the mere spinning of atoms in the void. What such people want is an account which sets their lives in a framework of meaning and purpose and value; which furnishes a moral and not merely a mechanical description of life; which accounts for it in terms of action and the exercise of responsibility, and not merely the unfolding of physical processes; which makes sense of their implicit awareness that they are both a part of and yet in some sense apart from the natural order; which sets their personal stories within the context of some larger story and its boundaries. What they want to know is how things stand between them and God.

Christianity, when it is faithful to its calling, offers to tell just such a story. It is not the only tradition to offer to do so. But it has a story to tell. And the telling of it, the cautious claiming of truth for the perspective which it provides, is aided neither by a blinkered traditionalism nor by the effective wholesale capitulation to the intellectual trends of culture which liberalism has often been guilty of. In its infatuated attempts to make the gospel measure up to the perceived needs and demands of 'intelligent men and women today', the latter has in fact frequently done precisely the opposite.

The Gospel as Bedtime Story?

The third problem with this approach to integration, therefore, concerns the claim that it makes Christian belief more relevant to contemporary men and women. In fact, the opposite would seem to be true. Convincing the occupants of modernity that the Christian story is plausible, in the sense that it does not contradict or conflict with the things which they already believe about themselves, has served only to convince them all the more of its superfluousness, and thereby rendered Christianity worthy of being ignored or tolerated rather than listened to. The attempt, as P. T. Forsyth described it, to 'empty out the gospel in order to fill the churches' has not worked. And it is hardly surprising that it has not. For if anything is clear from the biblical story itself it is that in its fundamental elements it is always likely to provoke opposition and disquiet in the telling, and is designed not to reinforce or perfect the ways in which human beings habitually think of their circumstances under God, but precisely to challenge and to change those ways of thinking. The gospel is a call to repentance. It was in Jesus' day, and it remains so in our own. Its relevance, in other words, lies precisely at some of those points where it challenges our thinking and our behaviour most radically, and to seek systematically to eradicate or belittle this challenge can only result in making it less, rather than more, relevant.

My children, like most others, enjoy having a story read to them at bedtime. The nature of many children's books these days, however, means that this process occasionally entails some careful censorship and editing-as-we-go-along, discretely skipping over paragraphs which contain details or descriptions designed to foster nightmares rather than encourage comfortable slumber! My wife and I are now skilled at pruning away such offensive or disturbing elements, and smoothing over the resultant gaps to produce a reasonable narrative flow before anybody notices. This sometimes means, of course, that the substance and even the structure of the story which we tell is quite different from the original. Frankly, this does not weigh heavily on our consciences, it being far more important that we do not have to cope in the twilight hours with childish fears and worries induced by exposure to ideas or images designed to disturb the security of their familiar and comfortable world. Telling the Christian story, however, cannot be like this. It can never be a matter of telling people what they already know or can bear to hear but will always involve a demand for them to see their situation in the world differently, and thereby to wrestle with some uncomfortable and perhaps even disturbing claims about themselves. Any approach which is concerned above all to furnish contemporary men and women with an inoffensive account of that story, which skips a paragraph here and an unpleasant image there in order that they may rest at peace with the familiar and secure world of their prior beliefs and commitments, will fail in its responsibility to communicate this challenge. It will consequently lack the resources for the revitalizing and transformation of culture which a genuine integration of the gospel with it (a missionary encounter as Newbigin calls it) might involve.

Who is the Average Intelligent Person Today? (and What Do They Believe?)

A further problem with this liberal strategy to measure the gospel up against the canons of contemporary culture is that contemporary culture itself does not present a consistent or coherent story!

One of the distinguishing characteristics of the natural sciences in our 'post-modern' context is the fact that, where their legitimate fields of study and pronouncement are concerned at least, the story which different scientists tell and the methods by which they arrive at them are mostly remarkably consistent. The scientific guild does not treat its heretics so charitably as the Christian church in our own day is inclined to! But post-modernity in general is not like this. While science is a prominent voice in our intellectual context, it is nonetheless only one among a veritable Babel of voices clamouring for our attention and allegiance in the market-place where knowledge, beliefs and opinions are traded, and in which Christians must buy and sell in their attempt to fashion an integrated and coherent outlook upon and approach to life. And the feature most characteristic of this market-place in our society is the diversity of different brands of any one intellectual product available. In any particular field – politics, economics, ethics, history, the social sciences, religion, art, or whatever – instead of a basic consensus of method and conclusions what we find is a confusing and seemingly confused pluriformity of stories told. And from this cacophony we are invited to select, digest, appropriate and reject in our bid for a coherent picture of things.

For the thoroughgoing post-modern pluralist, this intellectual maelstrom is something to be rejoiced in, and the task of building up an overall picture of things consists not so much in a process of integration as an arbitrary pick 'n' mix of the bits and pieces which grab your attention and tickle your fancy. There are no absolutes, no truth and falsity, no right and wrong; there are only different ways of looking at and doing things, and we are invited to stop and taste each of the offerings on the smorgasbord in turn, satisfying our intellectual taste buds with a gastronomic cornucopia of contrasting flavours.

Most of us, however, are less content to embrace such a bewildering approach to things, and seek to put together a picture which holds the various aspects of our experience of the world together in a tolerable manner. But the fact remains that the pictures which we build up in this manner are very varied. There is not only one 'grand narrative' into which other stories may reasonably be woven: there are many, and the results of such weaving as practised by 'intelligent men and women today' can look very different to one another. Where this is leading us, then, is to the recognition that appeals to 'what modern men and women can reasonably be expected to believe' is in practice only a disguised appeal to 'what I (and others who happen to think like me) can reasonably be expected to believe'. To confuse these two things, and to suppose that 'no intelligent person could reasonably entertain beliefs other than those to which I hold' is to fly in the face of the realities of the case (since very many intelligent people do), and to lay tacit claim to a type of 'public' knowledge which, having considered it carefully, we rejected in earlier chapters as a will-o'-the-wisp. What counts as 'reasonable' will depend very much on who one asks.

Liberal theologians, like the rest of us, therefore, must face the fact that all our truth claims are made from the admittedly less advantageous but unavoidable standpoint of faith and personal commitment. It is here, in the intellectual market-place, that we all engage in the responsible task of buying and selling, trading what we have in order to acquire that which we lack, seeking to gather around us the intellectual wares which will enable us to engage meaningfully with reality in all its diversity, making judgements about quality and shoddy produce, commending our own goods to others in the genuine belief that we have a quality product to offer. In this conviction we shall not exchange it for some other cheaper brand, nor acquire goods which are incompatible with it in some fundamental way. Lacking this conviction we are perhaps better to pack up our stall altogether, for no one is likely to buy something which our sales patter only serves to convince them is redundant to their needs.

The Importance of Enduring Impurities

In a fruitful missionary encounter between the gospel and context, the integration between the two will be one in which there will be an element of give and take on both sides, as the genuine insights into reality which our intellectual context has to offer force the church to reconsider its understanding of God's creative and redemptive engagement with his world, and the genuine insights into reality which the gospel has to offer challenge our context to rethink and revise some of its false attitudes and assumptions. Thus, as Mascall reminds us, 'However much any theology will bear the imprint of its environment, it must be remembered that, when it is really living and sensitive, Christian theology does not only submit to the cultural and conceptual framework of its time and place, but *also regenerates and reforms it sometimes very drastically.*'[12] It is a process in which, through the critical activity of faith, both the Christian tradition and the tradition of our culture are reformed and recalibrated.

To embrace this openly bilateral approach, in which theology tolerates neither a hegemony of the Christian story in all its particulars and details nor one of contemporary culture, is to be forced to reckon with an important distinction which traditionalism and liberalism both skirt around. We cannot overlook the historically particular nature of the gospel story as we receive it in the biblical text. It comes to us, that is to say, clothed in thought forms and modes of expression which are in many respects alien to the ways of thinking and speaking of our contemporaries, even when we have attempted the task of translating them into modern English.

The average person on the street in Britain today probably has little immediate grasp, for example, of such biblical notions as messiahship, sacrifice, repentance: yet these are absolutely central to the plot of the story which scripture tells. We must not exaggerate or oversimplify the situation of course. Many elements in the Christian gospel were strange even to the ears which first heard them, since Jesus' person and his message broke into new and uncomfortable territory, refusing to fit neatly within the categories provided by the Jewish religious culture of his own day, and thereby transforming Judaism as much as fulfilling its prophetic hope. The story, in other words, has always been 'strange' in some respects. It never did fit in with what 'people in those days' mostly thought about things. But nor must we overlook the fact that the gap between our own context and that of the biblical writers is not a yawning gap which we may not cross; for it has in reality been bridged by the constant attempts of the Christian community to translate the story, to explain and unpack its meaning, across the ages. There is a place, even in our own culture, where the meanings of messianic, sacrificial and other imagery are preserved and made sense of in word and deed; and to enter this community is to be provided with a more or less direct line of interpretative contact with those whose experience and understanding is plotted in the pages of our Old and New Testaments. But the fact of their strangeness remains nonetheless, and we must grapple seriously with it.

Traditionalist biblicism in its various forms responds to this contrast between 'biblical' patterns of thinking and those which characterize our modern or post-modern situation by seeking to exalt the former at all costs and in every particular. That is a bold statement, but I do not think it fails us as a broad description of biblicist theological strategies. Where, in other words, there is an identifiable 'biblical' way of thinking (i.e. if we can identify the writer's outlook on something, or that of one of the characters in the story which he tells) then this must be preferred in all cases to alternatives which may be offered by voices in our own society. Thus (to pick what to many may seem an extreme and trivial example, but which for that precise reason serves to make the point) Paul's views on the headwear of women in church is viewed by some as possessed of equal revelatory weight and significance as his understanding of the death and resurrection of Jesus, and must be built into a Christian outlook upon and approach to life at the end of the twentieth century. Less extreme and more widely endorsed would be the assimilation of his views on the place of women within the church, or on human sexuality. Paul's thinking about these and other matters, of course, is in many ways a direct reflection of his historical and social location as a devout Jew living in first-century Asia Minor. No doubt his thought transcends that particular context in many ways, but it also reflects it. And what the biblicist strategy attempts to do in practice, therefore, is to exalt 'biblical' culture (or those elements of it reflected and revealed in scripture) over our own in its essential assumptions, practices and outlooks. It is in effect the precise reverse of liberalism's chronological snobbery, assuming that a biblical way of thinking or behaving will invariably be superior to any extra-biblical alternative.

The briefest reflection, however, suggests that this is untenable.

Quite apart from the fact that the cultural background reflected in the biblical documents is itself not uniform but quite diverse, the various documents having issued from a variety of different times and places and circumstances, it simply is not possible for us to view the world through first century Jewish or Christian eyes, ignoring or denying the learning and changes in human understanding which have overtaken us since the Bible was written. The biblical scholar Rudolf Bultmann notoriously suggested that 'It is impossible to use electric light and to avail ourselves of modern medical and surgical discoveries, and at the same time to believe in the New Testament world of demons and spirits.'[13] The fact that Bultmann's conclusion is unnecessarily negative does not invalidate his basic point; namely, that we cannot live in the modern world and avail of ourselves of its technological benefits while at the same time ignoring or arbitrarily rejecting significant chunks of what modernity offers to us simply because they apparently differ from the way in which biblical writers look at things. We must ask honestly, for example, whether that which the gospel writers attributed to the activity of evil spirits is in fact better accounted for in modern scientific terms as evidence of some psychotic disorder, or epilepsy, descriptions which were unavailable in biblical times. To admit the legitimacy of this sort of question, to face up responsibly to the task of integration, is by no means to presuppose Bultmann's answer to it. In fact there are good reasons to suppose that in this particular instance both the scientific account and the more frankly 'mythological' may be held together as addressing distinct levels of description.

Bultmann's approach, of course, is a classic example of the liberal prejudice in favour of the modern. Recognizing the historical and cultural particularity of the Christian story as told in scripture, liberalism has mostly concluded that it was historically and culturally bound and conditioned, and thus in large part irrelevant to our very different context. Paul's views about women, sexuality, the significance of Christ's death, for example, were what they were because of who and where and when Paul was, and cannot reasonably be expected to be binding or relevant for people in our very different and intellectually superior cultural environment. In order to cope with this perceived problem, liberal theologians have frequently sought to distil off from the dispensable culturally particular form of the Christian story some universally relevant ethical or religious principle which may be maintained. But the task of identifying this 'pure gospel' has proven difficult. The bid to find the 'essence of Christianity' has produced results as numerous and varied as those who have engaged in it, and most have turned out to look suspiciously like the best ideas of nineteenth- or twentieth-century theologians rather than any urgent or hope-filled communication from God to humankind.

The truth would seem to be that the essence of Christianity, the heart of the story which it has to tell, is bound up rather closely with some at least of the cultural forms in which the biblical story is couched. There is no 'pure gospel', in other words, but only the impure version polluted by the biblical culture of Moses, Isaiah, Malachi, Jesus, Paul and others. If this culture has *nothing* worthwhile to say to us about God's creative and saving purposes and achievements, but is hopelessly compromised by its historical and social particularity, then we face a difficult choice. We must either abandon the task of Christian theology altogether, or else begin it from scratch, drawing only on authorities and voices from our own particular context; and that amounts in practice to much the same thing. The alternative which I would propose (and which most Christians are forced in practice to pursue) is one which recognizes the need to make a careful and important distinction. We must distinguish within the biblical narrative between elements which we deem to be more central to its basic thrust and purpose and which may in some identifiable sense be supposed to challenge our thinking and to reveal to us God-given linguistic and conceptual tools for engaging with reality, and other more peripheral elements where the specific cultural vehicles or forms of the story may be dispensed with or acknowledged as having been supplanted by more adequate accounts and descriptions. To think in this way, to admit that something good *can* come out of Nazareth, is to take seriously the suggestion that God himself was at work in human history fashioning a historical, cultural and intellectual context (in the developing life of the nation of Israel) within which and in terms of which his final self-revealing and redemptive activity in the person of Jesus Christ would make sense and could be understood. The theological task, on this view, involves discerning in every age just which parts of the story told in scripture belong to the category of enduring or permanent elements – elements the validity or truth of which transcend the particulars of time and place and demand to be translated afresh for each new generation – and which, on the other hand, can be let go of without loss and traded in for more satisfactory ways of thinking and behaving. The retention of 'enduring impurities' in some form would seem to provide a reasonable criterion of continuity with the Christian tradition down the centuries.

If, then, the church's efforts to translate the Christian story into and integrate it with the intellectual context of modernity is one in which it must honestly face the possibility of change and development, and in the course of which its own tradition will inevitably undergo a careful critical re-evaluation and reformation, it cannot, nonetheless, be of the one-sided sort which Wiles proposes in which culture calls the tune and theology obligingly dances to it. A *genuinely* critical theology will be critical not only in respect of its own inherited assumptions and beliefs, but equally in respect of the assumptions and beliefs presented to it from elsewhere. As an identifiably Christian theology, I would suggest, it will take its initial stand quite openly and firmly on the ground provided by the Christian tradition, assimilating its basic beliefs and ways of understanding and acting as a framework from within which to adjudge the alternative, complementary, and conflicting stories told by others. As and when conflicts seem to arise, it will be open to listen to what others are saying, seeking genuinely to explore their perspective and to see things in the light of it. Once it has done this, it must make a judgement as to whether or not some element of the Christian tradition requires now to be revised or rethought, or whether in fact the perspective which this tradition provides still offers a more satisfactory account of things than any of the proposed alternatives.

But on what basis can such responsible judgements be made? If we reject a totalitarian hegemony of culture (either our own or that of the Bible); if the Enlightenment appeal to universal tests of the true and the good fails us; and if we are unwilling to embrace the arbitrariness of post-modernism with its 'flux of images and fictions' [14] contributing to a fragmented and irrational assortment of beliefs and practices, then this question remains to be answered. Each of these inadequate strategies evades the exercise of personal responsibility in knowing. How, then, may a responsible approach to integration proceed?

NOTES

1 van Dusen, H. P., *The Vindication of Liberal Theology* (Scribners 1963), p. 27. My italics.
2 Wiles, M., *The Remaking of Christian Doctrine* (SCM Press 1974).
3 Wiles, *The Remaking of Christian Doctrine*, pp. 2, 7.
4 Wiles, *The Remaking of Christian Doctrine*, p. 2.
5 See Wiles, M., *What is Theology?* (Oxford University Press 1976), pp. 7–10.
6 See Wiles, *The Remaking of Christian Doctrine*, p. 7.
7 Mascall, E. L., *Theology and the Gospel of Christ* (SPCK 1977), p. 38.
8 Mascall, *Theology and the Gospel of Christ*, p. 39.
9 Wiles, *The Remaking of Christian Doctrine*, p. 18.
10 Mascall, *Theology and the Gospel of Christ*, p. 41.
11 See Wiles, *The Remaking of Christian Doctrine*, pp. 23–4.
12 Mascall, *Theology and the Gospel of Christ*, p. 45. My italics.
13 In Bartsch, H.W., ed., *Kerygma and Myth*, vol. 1 (SPCK 1964), p. 5.
14 Cupitt, D., *Creation Out of Nothing* (SCM Press 1990), p. 77.

— *11* —

Taking the Risk of Reality

Thought without faith is empty. Faith without thought is blind.[1]

In this our final chapter I want to pick up the question which was left hanging at the end of the last. Answering it will afford an ideal opportunity to recapitulate some of the key points which have been made in the course of this book as a whole, and to tie in some remaining loose ends.

Identifying our Identity

A genuinely critical Christian theology, I have argued, will be firmly rooted in the tradition of faith, while open to the inevitable and necessary reformation of that tradition through critical reflection and interaction with new sources of knowledge, new ways of seeing things. The story must be retold for a new human audience. The message must be translated into a new intellectual and cultural language. The living Word must become incarnate again.

But a critical theology will be equally critical with respect to the offerings of these other voices, adjudging them initially in accordance with the standards and criteria furnished by the Christian story itself. It certainly will not adopt the way of the chameleon, changing its skin so as to pass unnoticed in each new environment, adapting the story which it tells in order to fit in with the prevailing outlook. The relevance of the gospel with which it is entrusted and which it is called to transmit to others lies precisely in its antiseptic sting and its prophetic challenge to many of the accepted and familiar stories which humans tell themselves about the world and their situation within it. The Christian story, we might say, is not only the object of constant reform but is itself a powerful agent of reform, an influence with the potential to transform any and every cultural and conceptual framework. The foolishness of God insists, awkwardly no doubt, on calling into question the wisdom of human beings. The incarnate Word does not blend imperceptibly into the background, but creates a scandal, proclaiming the nearness of God's kingdom, and urging us to repent. So the theologian cannot simply capitulate to the social and intellectual pressures of his day, becoming a religious 'yes-man' who only tells his political and intellectual masters what they can bear to hear. Like the prophets of old and the one whose coming they pointed to, he must often risk scorn and abuse, and proclaim an uncomfortable and unacceptable message to an obdurate people. That is a truth which theologians in the modern age have too readily forgotten.

Nonetheless, a critical theology (as opposed to a closed and self-consumed fideism or fundamentalism) will always be open to hear and to learn from what other voices are saying, and to reform the story which it tells in accordance with them *as and when it judges this to be necessary or appropriate*. This means that theologians must frequently make difficult judgements in pursuit of a coherent and integrated story to tell. When should the tradition be reformed and recast in accordance with new insights and learning; and when should it be allowed to exercise a caustic and potentially transformative role, standing out from the crowd and offering an alternative way of seeing things? When should we be flexible, bending with the winds of change? And on what issues should we stand firm, purveyors of salt and light to a society ridden with darkness and decay? The issue at stake here is that of continuity with the apostolic tradition. How much change is legitimate and necessary to the task of translating the message? and when does it mutate into another message altogether? Knowing which ditches to die in, identifying the 'enduring impurities' which must be held on to and rendered in meaningful terms for every new context, these are the judgements which face those engaged in fashioning a critical and contemporary Christian theology. On what basis can such judgements be made?

Call my Bluff

The answer to this question is both simple and highly problematic. Nonetheless, we must embrace it and suggest that what the theologian is ultimately called to do is to judge which bits of the flotsam and jetsam washed up on the intellectual shore of post-modernity offer a true account of the way things are in reality. Which voices are telling the truth that is to say, and which, by contrast, offer a false story, a perspective that must finally be adjudged unhelpful or unreliable as a standpoint from which to engage with what lies 'out there' beyond the limits of our finger-tips? Likewise, which parts of the Christian story are vital to a fruitful engagement with reality? Which are merely part of the intel-lectual furniture of another age, replaceable without loss?

In the final analysis, there is only one way to test the truth or falsity of any statement, story, or way of thinking about things, and that is to see how well it measures up to the shape of reality as we perceive it. We call its bluff, as it were, putting it to the test, laying hold of it and trying it out. We shall probably not have to eat much of the pudding before we have sufficient indication of its merits either to endorse it or set it aside. Thus, if someone tells me that there is a fire raging in the next room, I may decide to check the truth of their report before leaving the building; and I shall proba-bly do so by having a look next door for myself. If I see no fire and smell no smoke I may be content that the report was false, and return to whatever it was I was doing beforehand. We cannot always verify the claims which people make or the stories which they have to tell quite so directly as this, but in broad terms our enquiry about their truth or falsity will be tied up with their apparent consonance with the ways in which we experience the real world, and their value in opening up new and more fruitful ways of deal-ing with that world.

Theology is, in this sense, what we may properly describe as a 'realist' enterprise. It is concerned above all, that is to say, 'with ex-ploring and submitting to the way things are' in reality,[2] with giving what it believes to be a true description of circumstances pertain-ing in the world in which we live. It has a story to tell about God and his world which it believes to be true. The story concurs, that is to say, with the basic shape of Christian experience of life and the stage on which it is played out, and experience of the created and uncreated realities of which the story tells. What the theologian seeks, therefore, in his attempt to integrate the Christian story, is other 'true' accounts of things to integrate it with. He wants to iden-tify reliable and fruitful perspectives from which to approach those aspects of God's world lying beyond the remit of theology as such, and which may fruitfully be woven together with his theological story into a coherent narrative account of the way things are. He craves a coherent story which reflects faithfully the coherence of God's creation. His concern is not for the coherence of this narrative alone, therefore, but for its appropriateness as an account of things which enables us to extend ourselves into the world and to engage meaningfully with its mutifaceted reality.

Readers who have followed the argument of this book through from the beginning, however, may find themselves wondering at this point just how this blunt appeal to reality and experience as a route to it ties in with the critique of objectivism offered in earlier chapters. Our experience of things and the report which we give of that experience, I argued, can never simply be identified with 'the way things are in reality.' We can only ever describe reality as it appears or manifests itself from where we are currently standing. Things may look quite different to someone occupying a different physical or intellectual perspective. They will experience things differently, and the report which they give, the story which they tell, will differ accordingly. We can never escape from this circumstance. Wherever we choose to stand, no matter how many times we change our position, we always approach things from some perspective or another. Thus it is not given to us to be able to compare someone else's account of things with 'the ways things really are'. We can only ever compare it with the way things look from other possible points of view, including our own. The 'truth', in other words, is not available to us in any direct or immediate sense. Does this not undermine the suggestion, then, that the theologian should approach the task of integration by enquiring after the truth or falsity of the stories and voices presented to him from elsewhere? No.

Finding the Best Available View of Things

The fact that the truth is never available to us in any direct or absolute manner does not mean that we may not pursue it, or that we are unable to lay hold of it at all. The realization that our knowledge is inevitably mediated by some perspective or other does not lead automatically to the despairing conclusion that all points of view are equally useful – and therefore equally useless – in answering the question of truth. The abandonment of objectivism and its ill-fated search for certainty need not drive us into what David Tracy describes endearingly as 'a kind of Will Rogers pluralism: one where theologians never met a position they didn't like'.[3] Some positions afford a better view of things than others. Some approaches lead to a more fruitful engagement with reality than others. Believing that there is something real out there to be known, therefore, that there is a truth to be laid hold of, yet recognizing nonetheless that our particular viewpoint is precisely that, and that the 'view from nowhere' is unavailable to us no matter how hard we strive to find it, our concern will be to ensure that *we stand in the place which offers the best view available*. We shall seek out the physical, conceptual or linguistic tools and methods which furnish the greatest and most satisfying means of extending ourselves into the world and engaging with it, thereby transcending our particular perspective while yet remaining firmly located within it.

No matter what it is that we are seeking knowledge of, therefore, our constant concern will be to strive for the best possible view of it, or the most helpful tools and methods with which to engage it. To this end we may find ourselves driven to consider and compare a number of different possible alternatives; trying to see things from other points of view than our own, listening sympathetically to other reports and other stories, trying out different approaches and tools. Once we have identified the perspective which seems to afford the most advantageous standpoint, however, we shall commit ourselves to it, trusting it to facilitate an ever greater disclosure and understanding of reality for us, and commending the report which it offers as the truest account of things available to us. We shall not readily abandon or exchange it for any other viewpoint, being bound by a moral obligation in the face of the claims of reality upon us. Convinced of the genuine superiority of the perspective or approach which we have discovered we invest it with universal intent, claiming for it a truth which is not only 'for us' but for all, eagerly inviting others to come and share our outlook on the basis that 'you get a much better view of things from over here'. We cannot prove that it is so. But we passionately believe it to be so, and we invite others to put it to the test, in the hope that the truth which has, as it were, seized us from beyond ourselves, may do the same to them.

This way of thinking embraces an important distinction, failure to admit which leads objectivism and relativism respectively into their twin, equal and opposite errors. On the one hand, we affirm that there are things which are true in every time and place, and for every person and community. Reality, that is to say, is rational; it has an orderly structure which in many aspects does not change from one moment and spatial location to the next. These things are true and remain true quite apart from our knowing of them. But, on the other hand, we acknowledge that while reality may in this sense provide some fixed points of reference, our knowing of it introduces the variable of perspective and point of view. Knowledge is, as it were, in this sense the product of a transaction between the universality of the created order and the irreducible particularity of our personal standpoints, physical, intellectual and otherwise. What we know, therefore, is never simply 'the way things are' but the result of our engagement with the way things are from within a particular standpoint. And some standpoints afford a better view of the way things are than others. Failure to make this distinction leads objectivists to confuse their particular perspectives with the abiding truth of reality itself, and relativists to conclude from the obvious fluctuations of perspective that truth itself fluctuates from one time and place to the next.

The sort of truth which may legitimately be claimed for 'the best available view of things', therefore, can never be the absolute certainty or one-to-one correspondence between reality itself and our report of it which the Enlightenment craved. The most that we can ever say is that we believe that we have identified a truer or more fruitful standpoint than others currently known and available to us. We must always face the possibility that some better or more satisfactory outlook exists or may be discovered. Indeed, since our handling of the tools and skills which form an inevitable part of every act of human knowing is never perfect, we must admit the inherent corrigibility of all our results, the ever-present risk of failure, and the seeming inevitability, therefore, that some superior way of seeing things will eventually be achieved. It is this recognition, which refuses to confuse reality itself with even the best and most faithful of our reports of it and which accepts that the products of human knowing are only ever at best provisional, that characterizes the sort of 'critical realism' which I have advocated in this book.

With this one vital qualification, however, it is both possible and reasonable for the theologian to pursue the task of integration by interrogating the voices which present themselves for consideration as to their truth or falsity. While he may lack specialist knowledge and training in other disciplines, he must become sufficiently familiar with them to be able to adopt the viewpoints which they offer, listen to the stories which they have to tell, and then make some judgement based on his wider experience of life in God's world. If what he hears and sees seems to concur with that experience, or if it offers an apparently fruitful route into a deeper level of understanding some aspect of the world, then he will be sympathetic to it. To the extent that reality itself seems to seize him and to disclose itself to him through his adoption of this standpoint, that is to say, he will adjudge the account which it offers to be a true one, and one which must therefore be integrated into his overall picture of things. The judgements which he makes may always prove to be the wrong ones, and the results of his integration may be flawed to that extent. Such is the nature of realism. It invariably involves risk, and therefore a concomitant degree of personal responsibility for the outcome. By its very nature, as an activity of faith and hope rather than certainty or despair, it is always seeking to transcend even its best previous efforts, always eager and willing to revise and improve the story which it tells as reality impinges upon it.

Crisis and Conversion

Sometimes, exposure to the stories told by others may provoke what Alasdair MacIntyre calls an 'epistemological crisis' in the life of a tradition (or, we might suppose, an adherent of a tradition). In other words, something which has hitherto been accepted as a central and important intellectual component of our tradition and the story which it tells (rather than peripheral to it) may be called into question or subject to doubt because some alternative account of things seems to be more satisfying or convincing. In such circumstances, we are forced to reckon with some basic inadequacy in the tradition which we inherit, and seek to revise the version of things which it offers in accordance with what we have learned from elsewhere. Such uncomfortable adjustments form an important part of the process of development. They are the intellectual 'growth pains' which inevitably accompany progression from less to more mature ways of thinking and seeing things, and as such the tradition itself finally benefits from rather than is damaged by them. They hone and recalibrate the story which it tells, bringing it further into line with the structure of reality itself.

One important example of this is the crisis which hit the church in the mid-nineteenth century with the emergence of new hypotheses and discoveries concerning human origins and the prehistory of our planet. These eventually forced upon the church a reconsideration of its handling of certain biblical texts, and the eventual outcome, far from being the irretrievable damage to the doctrine of creation which some have suggested, was an enhanced appreciation of the legitimate remit of that doctrine and of the nature of a significant part of the church's scriptural inheritance. There was also a new appreciation of the way in which the stories of science and of faith, far from competing with one another at this point, were in fact richly complementary. But at the time the crisis was a painful one beyond which many could not see.

In some extreme circumstances, however, the nature of an epistemological crisis may be such that the outcome is far more radical than this, and the discomfort which is felt, far from constituting temporary growth pains, actually heralds the death throes of an entire tradition (or at least of our personal allegiance to it). When some genuinely irreducible aspect of a tradition, some basic thread in the plot of the story which is vital to its continuing identity, is shown to be false (i.e. is believed to be less adequate or intellectually satisfying than some alternative and incompatible account of things), then the decision may be taken to abandon the tradition altogether, and to embrace some alternative to it.

Such a radical change in our way of seeing things, exchanging one set of fundamental commitments and presuppositions for another, is what apparently happens to people when they undergo a religious 'conversion' experience. Some basic element in their outlook on things is placed in crisis, and they are compelled to let go of many of their previous commitments, and to embrace a new and radically different perspective on reality as a result. When Christians preach the gospel this, of course, is precisely what they hope will happen. Their desire (rooted not in tribal loyalties, but in their investment of the Christian story with universal intent) is that people will hear the story and find themselves drawn into the framework which it offers, committing themselves to it, as the reality to which the story testifies lays hold of them and makes itself known, placing them under a moral obligation. They are like a scientist who makes some new and exciting discovery about the natural world: once he has seen it he can neither deny it not keep his new knowledge to himself, but will be eager to share it with others that they too many benefit from it.

To put oneself in the way of the proclamation of the gospel message, to explore the story which the Christian church tells and by which it lives, therefore, is to risk a genuine encounter with the living God, an encounter which may change things quite drastically. So, at least, Christians would claim. But Christians must face the fact that a genuine willingness to engage seriously with the voices of modernity and post-modernity entails in principle the very same risk: namely, that we shall be forced into some such crisis ourselves. No tradition which is living, and which is genuinely concerned with discovering and giving an appropriate account of the truth, rather than simply preserving the forms of life and thought which it has inherited, can avoid being vulnerable in this way to the claims of reality upon it. That is the uncomfortable truth in the light of which all theological engagement must proceed. Engagement with reality by listening seriously to the accounts which others have to give of it, therefore, is potentially a risky business. We may just find ourselves forced to change our minds!

Dialoguing with the Still Small Voice of Reality

The only way to isolate ourselves from this risk is to shelter ourselves from reality in some way. Both relativism and objectivism succeed in doing this, albeit in quite different ways. Relativism refuses to admit the possibility of making genuine contact with reality, or of ever knowing that we or others have done so. It frees itself thereby to wander at will, footloose and fancy-free, from one point of view to the next without ever having to commit itself to anything; or, staying at home, it confines itself to polishing and protecting what it has inherited, untroubled by any external demands for revision, development or integration. Objectivism, meanwhile, creates its own reality. Convinced that what it sees and touches and tastes is 'the facts', it feels no need to look any further, to consider any alternative points of view. Blindly confusing its particular perspective with 'the way things actually are', it renders itself invulnerable to the claims of a reality which remains distinct from that perspective. The fact of epistemological crises pulls both these approaches up short. For here, occasionally, something intrudes into the familiar and accepted and disturbs us, something which refuses to fit into the ready-made categories furnished by our traditions, something which as yet finds no place in them. That something is reality, quietly reminding us of its presence in such a way that we can neither pretend we are ignorant of it, nor that we already have it neatly pinned down.

Alasdair MacIntyre defines a tradition as

> an argument extended through time in which certain fundamental agreements are defined and redefined in terms of two

kinds of conflict: those with critics and enemies external to the tradition who reject all or at least key parts of those fundamental agreements, and those internal, interpretative debates through which the meaning and rationale of the fundamental agreements come to be expressed and by whose progress a tradition is constituted.[4]

We might state the matter in slightly less belligerent terms by saying that a tradition is a *dialogue* extended through time: a dialogue internal to the tradition itself as its inheritance is constantly reinterpreted and transmitted; and a dialogue with those who stand in other traditions and tell other stories. Such a dialogue may well take the form of disagreement and conflict; but it can also lead to mutual enrichment and illumination as aspects of different traditions are discovered to be complementary and compatible. In terms of the thrust of this chapter so far, however, we must make the further point that the dialogue is not finally one conducted with traditions – our own or others – but with reality itself, as we seek to map its contours and to give a faithful report of what we find, indwelling the tradition (and those parts of other traditions) which best enables us to extend ourselves into the world in this way.

Theology, therefore, is and must always be an exercise in dialogue of this sort. We not only tell our own story, but are prepared to listen to and in principle to learn from the stories told by others, whether these be the stories of science, politics, philosophy, history, other religions, or whatever. We do not do this because we are uncertain of the truth of our own tradition and engaged in a wistful quest for something better. Rather, it is precisely because we are confident of its truth that we wish to share our story with others, to expose them to its truth, and to integrate it into a fruitful synthesis with whatever purchase upon truth their stories may have to offer. Once again, the point is that while we are committed to our tradition, we are more committed still to the truth, and we refuse to mistake the contents of the one for the other in any simple and arrogant sense.

When God Shows Up in Church

How, then, does the dialogue with reality take place within the Christian tradition itself? How, that is to say, is the reality of which the Christian story speaks known? In the strict sense, of course, this is the point at which we must reintroduce the theme of revelation. In the case of a mute or impersonal reality, the initiative in the knowing relation rests wholly on the shoulders of the knower; but when the object of our knowing is personal he must also be a subject in that relation. He must give himself to be known. It is the claim of the Christian tradition, and the point from which Christian theology proper must depart, that God has made himself known in this way and continues to do so. Where and how, then, is he known?

There are many parts to a full answer to this question, and we must rest content with brief mention of some of the more obvious. God is known in and through our attending to and experience of certain historical and created phenomena within the community of faith. The reading and interpretation of scripture is perhaps chief among these, and we have already granted it considerable attention. But other features in the life and experience of the community of faith ('interpretations' of scripture in the broader sense) must also be mentioned. There is prayer, in which we invoke God's presence and revealing activity among us. If God may only be known as and when he chooses to reveal himself, then clearly this invocation, indicating as it does an earnest and humble attempt to under-stand God, i.e. to submit our minds, wills and forms of expression to the shape which his self-revealing in our midst takes, will be of vital importance. P. T. Forsyth sums the matter up nicely. Prayer, he informs us, is to the theologian what original research is to the scientist. It is that whereby we put ourselves in touch with the reality to be known. Without it, or without the divine activity which it craves, the various media of the Christian's knowing of God remain opaque. Our knowing terminates on the textual, verbal, fleshly and other created realities of church life. But when God is active in making himself known these same media assume a transparent aspect, serving as tools through which it is granted us to extend ourselves into the world, and to lay hold of (or more properly to be laid hold of by) the reality of God himself, Father, Son and Holy Spirit.

Rather than listing these media individually, we may simply indicate that in an important sense the entire Christian community – in its worship, its ministry and witness to the wider human community, its attempts to interpret the Christian story, to write the next chapter of that story in its own life in the world – furnishes the context, the framework, the tools and methods through which the reality of God may most adequately be known. God, that is to say, makes himself known here. He has done so in the past, he does so in the present, and we trust that he will continue to do so in the future. It is on this basis and this basis alone that we commend the Christian story and the church as the place where that story is (we hope) faithfully interpreted and transmitted, to others who would seek to know God and to understand the world in its relationship to him. We invite them to come and view things from within this community, to indwell its assumptions and ways of thinking, to join in its rituals and practices, to live life in accordance with the plot of the story which it tells, and to see whether the perspective which all this furnishes does not grant them genuine contact with the reality to which that story refers. We cannot guarantee that they will find it so. That responsibility does not rest with us, but with the one whose story we tell, whose activity we can crave but never coerce, whose grace we can trust in but never presume upon. All we can do is bear obedient witness to what he has done in the past, to tell his story, and to direct others to the place where he is known still to act and make himself known today. Whether the media of this knowledge will become transparent or remain opaque, whether faith will or will not be granted, eyes opened and ears unstopped or not, is not and never has been something which is in the church's gift to decide.

Faith Without Thought is Blind

The model of theological engagement which I have proposed in this book is one which seeks above all to take seriously the inevitabilities of our situation as thinking beings. Theology, I have suggested, is an activity of faith seeking understanding; but in this it is differentiated from other rational activity only by its specific object. The knowledge which it seeks is knowledge of God in and through his Son, Jesus Christ. But 'faith thinking' is an equally apt description of what goes on whenever human beings are engaged in the responsible pursuit of knowledge of any sort. Those who pretend otherwise are fooling only themselves. Thought without faith – that is, reflection which, because it believes in nothing, can have nothing to reflect upon – must inevitably be empty. But faith without thought is blind, and sometimes dangerously so.

Christian theology is faith thinking in community – the critical reflection which takes place within the community of the church.

We begin with the tradition, that part of our present which we inherit from our forebears in the faith, a view of the world and pattern of life worked out within their particular situation, integrating the Christian story as found in the scriptures with the cultural and intellectual context of their day. They hand the baton on to us in the great relay race which spans the period between Christ's resurrection and the end of the age. And we are called not to cling to the past, but to repeat the complex task of translation and integration and discovery afresh for our own generation, responding to the new intellectual, moral and practical challenges with which the world presents us, and in due course handing the baton on to those who will bear it beyond us into the future. Standing firmly within this living tradition we are caught up in an endless dialogue with reality: the reality of the living God and the world which he has made. This dialogue is conducted through the skilful handling of tools and resources which enable us to extend ourselves into the world: the textual resources of scripture, which must be carefully interpreted; the interpretative heritage of the Christian community itself which has sought through the centuries to make sense of scripture in intellectual, moral and practical ways in its forms of life; and the resources of our wider context with its bewildering Babel of competing voices demanding to be heard and made sense of.

Theology thus defined is not an optional activity for Christians. Whether they engage with it at the most technical and sophisticated or the most basic and down-to-earth of levels it is a task to which they must address themselves. The attempt to relate the story of faith to the wider context in which we live and our experience of life in general is in some sense the very problem of our own identity and existence as Christians in God's world, and a vital part of our witness to Christ's Lordship in that world. We cannot shirk our responsibility to face up to it. In the strictest sense we cannot really avoid being involved in it. Wherever there is genuine faith there will be theology of some sort being carried on, for theology is no more and no less than the activity of faith thinking. My hope is that our journey through this book will have contributed to the general cause of its being done more appropriately more often.

NOTES

1 Adapted from Immanuel Kant – with apologies.

2 Polkinghorne, J., *One World* (SPCK 1986), p. 97.

3 'Defending the Public Character of Theology' in *The Christian Century* 98 (1981), p. 355, cited in Placher, W., *Unapologetic Theology* (Westminster/John Knox 1989), p. 17.

4 MacIntyre, A., *Whose Justice? Which Rationality?* (Duckworth 1988), p. 12.

—— Bibliography ——

Achtemeier, P. (1980), *The Inspiration of Scripture* (Philadelphia: Westminster Press)

Arendt, H. (1958), *The Human Condition* (University of Chicago Press)

Bartsch, H. W., ed. (1964), *Kerygma and Myth*, vol. 1 (London: SPCK)

Barton, J. (1988), *People of the Book?* (London: SPCK)

Berger, P. (1971), *A Rumour of Angels: Modern Society and the Rediscovery of the Supernatural* (Harmondsworth: Penguin Books)

Church of England Doctrine Commission (1976), *Christian Believing* (London: SPCK)

Cupitt, D. (1990), *Creation Out of Nothing* (London: SCM Press)

Dampier, W. (1946), *A History of Science and its Relations with Philosophy and Religion* 3rd edn (Cambridge University Press)

Dulles, A. (1992), *The Craft of Theology* (Dublin: Gill and Macmillan)

Eagleton, T. (1983), *Literary Theory: An Introduction* (Oxford: Basil Blackwell)

Fish, S. (1980), *Is There a Text in This Class? The Authority of Interpretive Communities* (Cambridge, MA: Harvard University Press)

Frei, H. (1974), *The Eclipse of Biblical Narrative* (New Haven: Yale University Press)

Green, G. (1987), *Scriptural Authority and Narrative Interpretation* (Philadelphia: Fortress Press)

Hebblethwaite, B. (1980), *The Problems of Theology* (Cambridge University Press)

Hirsch, E. D. (1976), *Validity in Interpretation* (New Haven: Yale University Press)

Joad, C. E. M. (1936), *Guide to Philosophy* (London: Victor Gollancz)

Klein, W., Blomberg, C., and Hubbard, R. (1993), *Introduction to Biblical Interpretation* (Dallas: Word Books)

Lindbeck, G. (1984), *The Nature of Doctrine* (London: SPCK)

MacIntyre, A. (1988), *Whose Justice? Which Rationality?* (London: Duckworth)

Macquarrie, J. (1977), *Principles of Christian Theology* revised edn (London: SCM Press)

Mascall, E. L. (1977), *Theology and the Gospel of Christ* (London: SPCK)

Migliore, D. (1992), *Faith Seeking Understanding* (Carlisle: Paternoster Press)

Mitchell, B. (1990), *How to Play Theological Ping-Pong* (London: Hodder & Stoughton)

idem (1980), 'Faith and Reason: A False Antithesis?', *Religious Studies* 16

Nagel, T. (1986), *The View From Nowhere* (Oxford University Press)

Newbigin, L. (1986), *Foolishness to the Greeks* (London: SPCK)

idem (1989), *The Gospel in a Pluralist Society* (London: SPCK)

idem (1991), *Truth to Tell: The Gospel as Public Truth* (London: SPCK)

Pannenberg, W. (1969), *Revelation as History* (London: Sheed and Ward)

idem (1970), *Basic Questions in Theology* vol. 1 (London: SCM Press)

idem (1971), *Basic Questions in Theology* vol. 2 (London: SCM Press)

Placher, W. (1989), *Unapologetic Theology* (Louisville: Westminster/John Knox)

Polanyi, M. (1958), *Personal Knowledge* (London: Routledge & Kegan Paul)

Polkinghorne, J. (1986), *One World* (London: SPCK)

Saxbee, J. (1994), *Liberal Evangelism* (London: SPCK)

Steiner, G. (1992), *After Babel* 2nd edn (Oxford University Press)

Thiemann, R. F. (1991), *Constructing a Public Theology: The Church in a Pluralistic Culture* (Louisville: Westminster/John Knox)

Thompson, J. B., ed (1981), *Hermeneutics and the Human Sciences* (Cambridge University Press)

Tracy, D. (1981), *The Analogical Imagination* (London: SCM Press)

van Dusen, H. P. (1963), *The Vindication of Liberal Theology* (New York: Scribners)

Watson, F. (1994), *Text, Church and World* (Edinburgh: T. & T. Clark)

Wiles, M. (1974), *The Remaking of Christian Doctrine* (London: SCM Press)

idem (1976), *What is Theology?* (Oxford University Press)

—— Index ——